THE GOLDEN BOOK
OF MELCHIZEDEK

The Golden Book of Melchizedek:

How to Become an Integrated Christ/Buddha in This Lifetime
Volume 2

Dr. Joshua David Stone

Writers Club Press
San Jose New York Lincoln Shanghai

The Golden Book of Melchizedek:
How to Become an Integrated Christ/Buddha in This Lifetime
Volume 2

Writers Club Press
an imprint of iUniverse.com, Inc.

For information address:
iUniverse.com, Inc.
5220 S 16th, Ste. 200
Lincoln, NE 68512
www.iuniverse.com

ISBN: 0-595-17095-1

Printed in the United States of America

Contents

1

Revelation of GOD Ascension Activation Meditation

Let us begin by closing our eyes.

We now call forth GOD, Christ, and the Holy Spirit as well as the entire Cosmic and Planetary Hierarchy to help with this Meditation.

We begin by calling forth a Cosmic Pillar of Light from the Beloved Presence of GOD.

We call forth the Divine Mother and the Divine Father to Balance the Energies in the auditorium and all in attendance.

We call forth Melchizedek, the Mahatma, and Archangel Metatron to bring forth the Platinum Net through all in attendance.

We call forth Archangels Michael and Faith to place around this auditorium and all in attendance a Golden Dome of Light of Protection.

We formally begin this Meditation by Grounding Ourselves into the Physical Body of GOD.

We do this by Calling Forth the Cosmic Mother of GOD's Infinite Physical Universe and our Planetary Earth Mother.

We also call forth Archangel Sandalphon, Pan, and the Mountain of Mount Shasta, to help us now Collectively Establish a Grounding Cord down through our Spine into the Center of the Earth.

Feel this Grounding Cord of GOD moving down into the very Granite Core of the Earth, and establish itself there, Unshakably like the Sword of Excalibur.

Feel now, with the help of these Beloved Masters, Roots Growing out of your Feet into the Earth.

Feel these Roots, with the help of the Cosmic and Planetary Earth Mother, Grow at a Rapid Rate like a Gigantic Cosmic Tree of Life that is Firmly and Unshakably Planted into the Earth.

Breathe now your Love, through your Grounding Cord and Roots, into your feet, and into the Very Center of Mother Earth.

Now feel Mother Earth Breathe her Love back through your Grounding Cord and Roots into your feet, up through your Physical Body, Igniting the Three-Fold Flame in your Heart Chakra.

Firmly now Connected and Attuned to GOD's Physical Body, we now begin our Ascension and Climb up through the "Seven Chakra's of GOD."

This Process Begins with the Beloved Presence of GOD, Christ and the Holy Spirit sending down through GOD's Pillar of Light what can only be described as "The Merkabah of GOD."

This Merkabah is made of such a Fine and Sublime Sacred Geometry, that words do not suffice to describe It.

Feel GOD's Merkabah also known as the "Merkabah of the Trinity of GOD," descend now Collectively upon this Esteemed Group Gathered Here.

Feel the Merkabah begin to Rise and Lift us into the First Chakra of GOD, while simultaneously still keeping our Connection to the Physical Body of GOD.

Feel GOD's First Chakra, which is like an enormous "Cathedral of Light, Love, and Power" stretching through Infinity.

In GOD's First Chakra there is a faint Reddish, Pink Color, and Light pervading this entire infinite Cathedral.

In the Background can be Seen and Heard "Choirs of Angels" Singing the Glory of GOD to the "Music of the Spheres."

Here we are met by all the Archangels, Angels, Elohim, Elementals, Devas, Plant Spirits, Nature Spirits, Earth Spirits, Gnomes, Sylphs, Salamanders, and Undines Connected with the Material Universe of GOD.

This Cathedral is so Magnificent it defies description. It is filled with the Crystals of the "12 Rays of GOD" and of the "10 Lost Cosmic Rays of GOD."

Every Color can be Seen, Ordaining the actual Cathedral which is Infinite in size.

It is here that GOD, Christ, and the Holy Spirit now Merge their First Chakra with our First Chakra on a Permanent Basis, so they are forevermore, one in Consciousness.

If you would like to Receive this Blessing, Be still, and Receive this Blessing Now!

As this Occurs, GOD's Merkabah now Lifts us into His Second Chakra and Cathedral.

This Cathedral is even more Beautiful and Spectacular than the Previous One, and is Pervaded by an Orange Glow that Spreads Out Infinitely.

Again, the Cathedral is made of Crystals and Gemstones of all the Colors of GOD.

Here the Divine Mother, all the Lady Archangels, Lady Elohim and Lady Masters Step Forward Led by Mother Mary, Quan Yin and Isis, to name a few.

The Divine Mother and these Beloved Masters step forward as Representatives of GOD to help now in the Process of Merging and Integrating GOD's Second Chakra, perfectly into our Own on a Permanent Basis.

If you would like to Receive this Blessing, Be Still and Receive This Blessing Now!

As this Great Blessing Occurs GOD's Merkabah Lifts us into His Third Chakra and Cathedral of Light, Love and Power.

This Great Crystal Cathedral spanning Infinitely through Time and Space is Colored with a Tinge of Beautiful Yellow, like the Sun.

Here we are Met by Lord Buddha, Lord Maitreya, Saint Germain, Allah Gobi, The Seven Chohans, Djwhal Khul, Helios and Vesta, and all the Planetary and Solar Masters of the Planetary and Cosmic Hierarchy.

With all the Archangels, Angels, and Elohim Masters looking on, these Beloved Masters help this Group and Each Person Individually, Merge your Third Chakra with the Third Chakra of GOD.

If you would like to Receive this Blessing, Be Still and Receive this Blessing Now!

As this Great Blessing occurs, we now move in GOD's Merkabah into GOD's Fourth Chakra, also known as GOD's Heart Chakra.

In this Incredibly Magnificent Crystal Cathedral there is a tinge of Emerald Green Light pervading this Infinite Holy Sanctuary.

The Light and Love here is so Sublime and Beautiful, it is almost Intoxicating.

The Holy Spirit asks us now to be completely Silent and Still, so we may Listen and Attune to "The Heartbeat of GOD…"

By doing this in this moment, we are Attuning to the Actual Heart Beat of the Infinite Multi-dimensional Omniverse of GOD.

Stepping forward now as Representatives for GOD's Heart Chakra are the Divine Mother, His Holiness the Lord Sai Baba, Lord Maitreya, Sananda, Paul the Venetian, Mother Mary, Quan Yin and Isis.

These Beloved Masters step forward to help us now Merge, Blend and Integrate our Heart Chakra and Heartbeat with GOD's Heart Chakra and Heartbeat.

If you would like to Receive this Blessing, Be Still and Receive This Blessing Now!

As we Receive this Blessing, GOD, Christ and the Holy Spirit's Merkabah, Lifts us even Higher into GOD's Fifth Chakra and Cathedral.

This Infinite Crystal Cathedral is pervaded by the Color Light Blue, like the Sky on a Beautiful, Clear Summer Day.

This Magnificent Crystal Cathedral with all the Colors of the Rainbow, Shimmers with this Beautiful Blue Color in its Reflection.

In this Wondrous Cathedral and Fifth Chakra of GOD, we are Met by Melchior, Vywamus, The Lord of Sirius, The Lord and Lady of Arcturus and the Arcturians, Sanat Kumara, Lenduce, Commander Ashtar and the Ashtar Command, and all the Galactic Masters of the Cosmic Hierarchy.

These Beloved Masters as Representatives of GOD, now step forward to Help Us Completely Merge and Integrate our Fifth Chakra with the Fifth Chakra of GOD.

If you would like to Receive this Blessing, Be Still and Receive this Blessing Now!

As this Great Blessing takes place, we are now Lifted by GOD's Merkabah into GOD's Sixth Chakra and Crystal Cathedral of Light, Love and Power.

This Crystal Cathedral of Light and Sixth Chakra of GOD, also known as the Third Eye of GOD, is Tinged with the Color Indigo.

The most Exquisite Colored Indigo Crystals and Clouds, Color the Infinite Panorama of this Cathedral.

Stepping Forward as Representatives of GOD in this Cathedral are His Holiness Lord Melchizedek, all the Archangels connected with the Earth's Evolution, and all the Elohim Councils connected with Earth's Evolution.

These Beloved Masters offer their Assistance in Helping us to now Merge our Sixth Chakra with the Sixth Chakra of GOD.

If you would like to Receive this Blessing, Be Still and Receive This Blessing Now!

GOD's Merkabah now Lifts us Even Higher Still into GOD's Crown Chakra and Crystal Cathedral of Light, Love and Power.

Here we are Bathed in the Most Beautiful Violet Light you have ever Seen or Experienced.

The Cathedral is made of Beautiful Amethyst Crystal, Interspersed with Gemstones of all the Colors of the Rays.

In the Violet Clouds and Sun can be seen the Angels, Seraphim, and Cherubim, Dancing and Singing to the "Music of the Spheres."

Stepping Forward here are the 24 Elders of Light, and the 12 Cosmic Logoi, and/or Cosmic Ray Masters, the Mahatma, Archangel Metatron, Archangels Michael and Faith, all the Archangels, Elohim Councils and the Entire Cosmic and Planetary Hierarchy.

They Collectively Offer their Assistance now in Helping us to Merge our Seventh or Crown Chakra, with the Seventh or Crown Chakra of GOD.

If you would like to Receive this Blessing, Be Still and Receive this Blessing Now!

Beloved Brothers and Sisters, we have now by the Grace of GOD, Christ and the Holy Spirit, and the Cosmic and Planetary Hierarchy Merged, Integrated and Perfectly Aligned on a Permanent Basis our Seven Basic Chakras, with the 7 Cosmic Chakras of GOD, Christ and the Holy Spirit!

Praise be to GOD, Christ, the Holy Spirit, the Cosmic and Planetary Hierarchy and Ourselves, for All is One!

We now, for this last step in our journey, are taken by GOD, Christ, and the Holy Spirit to a Place Never Visited by Earthlings Before.

By the Grace of GOD, Christ and the Holy Spirit in Honor of this "Golden Wesak 2000 Millennium Event," we are now being Taken in GOD's Merkabah, up through the "Ain," the "Ain Soph," and the "Ain Soph Or," also known as the "Limitless Love and Light," to "GOD's

Secret Crystal Chamber" where the Three-Fold Flame of GOD's Own Heart Resides.

We find ourselves now in the "Cathedral of all Cathedrals"!

This Cathedral is Filled with the Most Exquisite Clear Light you could Possibly Imagine.

The Angels in the Background are Singing Hymns of Praise to the "Most High GOD."

The Beautiful Smell of Roses of all Colors Pervades this Magnificent Cathedral.

Standing Before us on the "Altar of GOD" is the "Three-Fold Flame of GOD's Own Heart," Burning Eternally as it has from the Beginning of Time!

It is in this Sanctified and Holy Cathedral that GOD, Christ, and the Holy Spirit give to us; His Beloved Sons and Daughters of GOD, the Gifts and Activations of All Creation this Evening!

If you would like to receive these "72 GOD Activations of all GOD Activations," Be Still and Receive these Gifts of all Gifts Now!

GOD, Christ, and the Holy Spirit now Fully Anchor and Activate into Each Person's Chakra System, and 12-Body System, the following Activations:

GOD, Christ, and the Holy Spirit now Request that we all be like a Sponge, and Sit back now in "GOD's Ascension Seat," which He is now placing around us, and Soak in this first GOD Activation He is now giving us.

For Our Second GOD Activation, we now call forth from GOD, Christ and the Holy Spirit, "The Light Rod of GOD," to ignite our Entire Chakra System and 12-Body System.

We now call forth "The Love Rod of GOD," to completely ignite the Anchoring and Activation of Our "Zohar Body of Light," "Anointed Christ Overself Body," "Higher Adam Kadmon Body," and "The Lord's Mystical Body."

We now call forth "The Power Rod of GOD," to fully Anchor and Activate the "330 Chakras of GOD" and the "48 Dimensional Bodies of GOD."

We now call forth "The Cosmic Fire of GOD," and the perfect amount for each person to completely cleanse and purify each person's Auric Fields.

We now call forth the Complete Anchoring and Activation of "The Cosmic Tree of Life of GOD!"

We now call forth an Anchoring and Activation of "The 12 Sephiroth of GOD," and "The Hidden Sephiroth of Daath"!

We now call forth the Complete Anchoring and Activation of "The Sacred Ember of GOD" from "The "Sacred Fire of GOD"!

We now call forth an Anchoring and Activation of the "The Divine Scriptures of GOD"!

We now call forth an Anchoring, Activation, and Divine Merger with "The Divine Blueprint of GOD"!

We call forth an Anchoring and Activation of "The Divine Seed of GOD"!

We call forth an Anchoring and Activation of "The Holy Scrolls of the Living Light of GOD"!

We call forth an Anchoring, Activation, and Opening of "The Seven Seals of GOD"!

We call forth an Anchoring and Activation of "The Tetragrammaton of GOD," as described in the *Keys of Enoch*!

We call forth a Reawakening on a Conscious and Subconscious Level of each person's "Original Covenant of GOD"!

We call forth a total downpouring of "The Language of Light of GOD," to activate full God Realization on all levels to each persons Highest Potential in this Moment!

We call forth from GOD, Christ, and the Holy Spirit for the complete Anchoring, Activation and Opening of the "Gifts of the Holy Spirit," to each person's highest potential in attendance!

We call forth the Anchoring, Activation, and Merger into each person in attendance to their Highest Potential of the 72 Sacred Universes of GOD as described in the *Keys of Enoch*!

We call forth in this "Holy Instant," for a "Divine Revelation of GOD," to each person's Highest Potential, and in the way that is best suited for each person in attendance!

We now call forth the Complete Anchoring and Activation of "GOD's Transmitting System" into our Chakras and 12-Body System!

We now call forth the Complete Anchoring and Activation of "GOD's Divine Plan, Mission, and Puzzle Piece" for your Life on Earth!

We now call forth "GOD's Complete Cleansing all the way Back to Source"!

We now call forth the Complete Anchoring and Activation of "GOD's 72 Names," to Eternally Run Through our Chakra System and 12-Body System!

We now call forth the Complete Anchoring and Activation of "GOD's Fire Letters, Key Codes and Sacred Geometries"!

We now call forth a "Baptism of GOD, Christ, and the Holy Spirit"!

We now call forth an Anchoring and Activation of the "Cosmic Antakarana of GOD"!

We now call forth a Complete Merger with "The Clear Light of GOD."

We now call forth a Permanent Anchoring of The "72 Virtues and Attributes of GOD"!

We now call forth a Complete Anchoring, Activation and Brain Illumination of "The 72 Areas of the Mind of GOD," into our Brain and Mind Now!

We now call forth an Anchoring and Activation of "The Electron of GOD"!

We now call forth a Complete Anchoring and Activation of all Levels of "The Cosmic Christ of GOD"!

We now call forth and ask to Completely Merge with "The Cosmic Pulse of GOD"!

We now call forth and ask to fully Merge with "The Cosmic Aum of GOD"!

We now call forth and ask to Merge and Integrate with "The Cosmic Monad of GOD"!

We now call forth and ask to merge and Integrate with all "352 Levels of GOD"!

We now call forth and ask to Completely Merge and Integrate with "The 10 Lost Cosmic Rays of GOD and the Yod Spectrum of GOD."

We now call forth and ask to Merge and Completely Integrate with "The "Divine Template of GOD"!

We now call forth and ask to Merge and fully Integrate with "The Ray of GOD"!

We now call forth an Anointing given through the Vehicle of "The Direct Shaktipat of GOD"!

We now call forth an Anchoring and Activation of "The Light Packets from the Treasury of Light of GOD"!

We now call forth an Anchoring and Activation of "The Love Packets from the Treasury of Love of GOD"!

We now call forth an Anchoring and Activation of "The Power Packets from the Treasury of Power of GOD"!

We now call forth an Anchoring and Activation of "The Crystals and Diamonds of GOD"!

We now call forth an Anchoring and Activation from "The Gemstones of GOD"!

We now call forth an Anchoring and Activation of "The Book of Life of GOD"!

We now call forth an Anchoring and Activation of "The Seed Atom of GOD"!

We now call forth a Complete Integration Merger with "The Burning Bush of GOD," that Purifies but does not Consume!

We now call forth from GOD, Christ, and the Holy Spirit, an Anchoring and Activation of "The Holy Breath of GOD"!

We now call forth from GOD, "The Keys to the Kingdom of GOD," to be given to each person's Highest Potential!

We now call forth an Anchoring and Activation of "GOD's Cosmic Book of Knowledge"!

We now call forth "The Full Spectrum Seeing and Vision of GOD," to Merge and Integrate with our Vision.

We now call forth a Complete Merger and Integration with "GOD Consciousness"!

We now call forth to Merge and fully Integrate with "The Joy and Bliss of GOD"!

We now call forth to Merge and fully Integrate with "The Heart of GOD"!

We now call forth a Complete Merger and Integration with All "The Infinite Universes of GOD"!

We call forth an Anchoring and Activation of "The Cosmic Pyramid of GOD."

We now call forth a Complete Anchoring and Activation of "The Waterfall of GOD"!

We now call forth a Complete Merger and Integration with "The Light Body of GOD"!

We now call forth a Complete Merger and Integration with "The Love Body of GOD"!

We now call forth a Complete Merger and Integration with "The Power Body of GOD"!

We now call forth a Complete Integration with "The Combined Love, Light and Power Bodies of GOD"!

We now call forth an Anchoring and Activation of "The Love Shower of GOD, and the Entire Cosmic and Planetary Hierarchy"!

We now call forth an Anchoring and Activation of "The Light Shower of GOD, and the Entire Cosmic and Planetary Hierarchy"!

We now call forth an Anchoring and Activation of "The Power Shower of GOD, and the Entire Cosmic and Planetary Hierarchy"!

We now call forth an Anchoring and Activation of "The Combined Love, Light and Power Shower of GOD, and the Entire Cosmic and Planetary Hierarchy"!

We now call forth a Complete Merger and Integration on All Levels with "GOD, Christ and the Holy Spirit"!

We now call forth a Complete Merger and Integration with "The Consciousness of GOD on All Levels Known and Unknown"!

We now call forth a Divine Anchoring of a Revelation of God for Each Person in the way that is the best for Each Person to receive.

We now call forth a Complete Merger and Integration with the "Unfathomableness of GOD"!

We call forth an "Ordination by GOD, Christ and the Holy Spirit," for Each Person in attendance, to be "A Messenger of Light and Love, with the Authority to Teach and Demonstrate as a Basic Pillar and Witness to the Kingdom of GOD"!

We now call forth to GOD, Christ, and the Holy Spirit in this Holy Instant, for all who choose to receive this, for a Divine Marriage with the God/Goddess within.

Now, my Beloved Brothers and Sisters, GOD, Christ, and the Holy Spirit's final Activation and Gift for this "Golden Wesak 2000 Millennium Event" is to Now Receive from GOD a Complete Merger and Integration with His "Three-Fold Flame" into your Personal Three-Fold Flame, which is Now Burning Eternally on "The Altar of GOD" before you.

If you Choose to Receive this Blessing, Be Still, and Receive This Blessing of all Blessings Now!

In the Sanctuary of your own Heart, take a moment now to Thank GOD, Christ and the Holy Spirit for their Most Sublime and Sanctified Gifts you have Received this Evening!

Also, take a Moment to Thank the "Entire Cosmic and Planetary Hierarchy," for Their Bountiful Gifts and Blessings as Well!

GOD, Christ, and the Holy Spirit have now One Final Request that they would like to make to us all.

They collectively request in "One Voice," that "we take the Bountiful Blessings given forth to us this Evening, and Dedicate Our Lives from this Moment Forward, to our Highest Potential, and Share Them in Unconditional Love, with our Brothers and Sisters on Earth and to All Sentient Beings."

Our Brothers and Sisters, and all Sentient Beings on Earth, regardless of their Level of Consciousness, are All Incarnations of GOD.

For there is only one Being in the Infinite Universe, and that is GOD, and We All Share in that One Identity!

Let us all Dedicate our Lives to Sharing GOD's Love and Blessings, as GOD, Christ, and the Holy Spirit have so Freely and Generously Shared their Love, Blessings and Gifts with Us this Evening!

Let us All Make this Dedication Now in the "Silent Sanctuary of Our Own Heart," in the Way and Manner that is Comfortable and Right for Each of Us!

As we Conclude this Process, "GOD's Merkabah" now appears, and we begin to be Lifted out of the "Secret Cathedral and Chamber of GOD."

We begin moving down through "the Ain Soph, the Ain Soph Or, the Ain, and/or Limitless Love and Light."

We begin Descending Down now into "GOD's Crown Chakra and Cathedral," being Bathed in "Violet Light, Sound and Color"!

We Continue Descending Down into "GOD's Sixth Chakra and Cathedral," being Bathed in "Indigo Light, Sound and Color!"

We Continue Descending Down into "GOD's Fifth Chakra and Cathedral," being Bathed in "Light Blue Light, Sound and Color"!

We Continue Descending Down into "GOD's Fourth Chakra and Cathedral," being Bathed in "Emerald Green Light, Sound, and Color"!

We Continue Descending Down into "GOD's Third Chakra and Cathedral," being Bathed in "Yellow Light, Sound, and Color"!

We continue Descending Down into "GOD's Second Chakra and Cathedral," being Bathed in "Orange Light, Sound, and Color"!

We Continue Descending Down into "GOD's First Chakra and Cathedral," being Bathed in "Pinkish/Red Light, Sound, and Color"!

Now Feel GOD's Merkabah Fully Anchored back into your Physical Body, onto GOD's Physical Body, The Material Universe, and Mother Earth.

Here we are Greeted Again by the Earth Mother, the Mountain of Mount Shasta, Pan, and Archangel Sandalphon.

Feel yourself now back in the Auditorium of Mount Shasta, and Feel Yourself now Fully grounded back onto the Earth, and into the Earth.

Feel your "Grounding Cord" still Fully Established into the "Center of the Earth."

Feel your Feet Again Growing Roots, Filling the Entire Earth with these Roots.

Breathe Now Again all the Love, Light and Power you have Received from GOD, Christ and the Holy Spirit, and the Cosmic and Planetary Hierarchy, into the Earth Mother, through your Grounding Cord and your Feet like the "Cosmic Tree of Life"!

Feel Yourself as Fully Connected to Your Physical Body and the Earth Mother, as you feel to "GOD, Christ, the Holy Spirit, and the Cosmic and Planetary Hierarchy."

Fully now Realizing that Ascension is not Leaving the World but rather is Fully Anchoring the Presence of GOD into your Physical Body on Earth, and Manifesting Heaven on Earth!

Feel how Good it Feels to Feel So Connected to GOD, Christ and the Holy Spirit and the Godforce, as well as your Physical Body and the Earth Mother, Simultaneously!

In Final Conclusion, take one last moment to share the Love and Light that you have received from Heaven and Earth, and now Inwardly Fully Open Your Heart as Wide as it has ever been ever Before, and Inwardly Share this Unconditional Love that you Feel with your Brothers and Sisters in this Auditorium!

When you are ready you can open your eyes and we will now take a 30-minute break!

2

GOD and The Godforce Golden Chamber of Melchizedek Ascension Activation Meditation

Let us begin this Meditation by having everyone close their eyes.

We call all the Masters of the Cosmic and Planetary Hierarchy to help in this Meditation.

We call forth from GOD, Melchizedek, the Mahatma, and Metatron for the anchoring of a Gigantic Pillar of Light and Ascension Column from Source!

We call forth Melchizedek, the Mahatma, Archangel Metatron, and Archangel Michael, to bring forth a Platinum Net, to remove any and all imbalanced energies.

We call forth Archangels Michael and Faith for a "Gigantic Platinum Dome of Protection" for this entire Meditation.

We begin this Meditation by calling forth the Earth Mother, Pan and Archangel Sandalphon to help us now firmly establish a Grounding Cord down our spine, legs and feet into the Earth.

Feel this Grounding Cord now move into the very Center of the Earth and securely fasten itself.

Take a deep breath now and breathe your Love and Energy down your Grounding Cord into the very Heart of the Earth Mother.

Feel yourself now connecting with not only the Earth Mother, but with all her Kingdoms: Mineral, Plant, and Animal.

Breathe your Love to those Kingdoms, and feel their Love now returning through the Earth, and coming back to you through your Grounding Cord and Feet Chakra.

With your sense of Grounding to the Earth firmly in place, we now move to the next step in our journey this evening.

We now call forth to His Holiness Lord Melchizedek, the Seven Chohans, Djwhal Khul, Lord Maitreya, and Lord Buddha, to provide a "Gigantic Golden Crystalline Merkabah," for all in attendance in this auditorium.

We ask now to be taken Spiritually to the "Golden Chamber of Melchizedek in the Universal Core."

We again call forth from Melchizedek each person's 144 Soul Extensions, from their Monad, and or Mighty I Am Presence, to join us if they choose to for this Meditation.

For our First Ascension Activation in the Golden Chamber, we call forth the Earth Mother, Pan, Archangel Sandalphon, and the Mountain of Mt. Shasta.

These Wonderful Beings now combine together for a Special Ascension Attunement and Alignment to the Vortex of Mt. Shasta.

They do this so that all in attendance may be similar Vortexes for the Light and Love of GOD, in our daily lives.

We call to the Seven Chohans for the Opening of all our Chakras, our Ascension Chakra, and all Petals, Chambers, and Facets of all Chakras.

We call forth the Divine Mother, Quan Yin, Isis, and Mother Mary for the permanent anchoring of each person's Higher Self and Mighty I Am Presence.

We call to the Seven Chohans, Djwhal Khul, and Helios and Vesta, for an anchoring of an "Ember of the Nine Sacred Flames" of each of the Seven Rays, plus the "Ray of Synthesis," and the "Ray and Flame from the Solar Core," into each person's Heart Chakra.

Be Still and Receive this Blessing now, if you would like to receive this Ascension and Activation.

We call to the Lord of Sirius for the Anchoring and Activation of the "Scrolls of Wisdom and Knowledge," from the Great White Lodge on Sirius.

We call forth Sananda and Djhwal Khul to fully anchor and activate our Zohar Body of Light, also known as the "Coat of Many Colors"!

We call forth the Lord of Arcturus, Commander Ashtar and the Ashtar Command, for the Complete Illumination of each person's Etheric Nadis and Acupuncture Meridians for full Planetary and Cosmic Ascension Realization.

We call forth Lord Maitreya to fully Anchor and Activate each person's "Anointed Christ Overself Body."

We call to Lord Buddha to Anchor and Activate each person's "Higher Adam Kadmon Body."

We call forth Vywamus, Sanat Kumara, and Lenduce to fully Anchor and Activate our "Electromagnetic Body, Gematrian Body, and Epikenetic Body."

We call to the Archangels for the full Anchoring and Activation of our 50 Chakras, which takes us through Planetary Ascension.

We also request from the Archangels, the Anchoring and Activation of our 330 Chakras, helping us to move in the direction of "Fully realizing Cosmic Ascension on Earth."

We call forth the Elohim Councils to now Anchor and Activate our "Elohistic Lord's Body."

We call to Melchior, Horus, Isis, Serapis Bey, Osiris, and Vywamus for the Permanent Anchoring and Activation of our Twelve Bodies, including the Solar, Galactic, and Universal Bodies.

We call forth Archangel Metatron to fully Anchor and Activate each person's "Garmet of Shadai" or "Light Body of Archangel Metatron."

We call forth the Permanent Anchoring and Activation of "The Full Living Light Garment of the Christ."

We call forth the Permanent Anchoring and Activation of "The Full Garment of Perfection."

We call forth the Permanent Anchoring and Activation of "The Jeweled Vehicle of Ascension," at each person's Highest Potential.

We call forth to the 14 Mighty Elohim, for the Anchoring and Activation of the "Yod Spectrum and the 10 Lost Cosmic Rays."

We call forth to the Holy Spirit for a Divine Baptism of the Light of GOD.

We call forth to the Mahatma, for the Anchoring and Activation of the "Deca Delta Light Encodements and Emanations from the Ten Superscripts of the Divine Mind."

We call forth to Melchizedek, Mahatma, Metatron, and the Divine Father, for the Highest Possible Building of our Light Quotient at this time.

We call forth to the Divine Mother, Sai Baba, Mother Mary, Quan Yin, Isis, Lord Maitreya, and Sananda, for the Highest Possible Building of our Love Quotient at this time.

We call forth to Helios, Vesta, Allah Gobi and Sai Baba for the Highest Possible Integration and Cleansing of our Soul Extensions from our Monad, and our Higher Group Monadic Consciousness, that is available to us at this time.

We call forth to Melchizedek, for the Anchoring and Activation of the "Star Codes of Melchizedek."

We call forth the Anchoring and Activation of the "Light Encodements of the Mahatma."

We call forth His Holiness the Lord Sai Baba, for an Anchoring into the Core of our Being, the "Love Seat of Sai Baba."

We call forth the Lord of Arcturus and the Arcturians for an Anchoring now of the "Arcturian Joy Machine."

We call forth the Anchoring and Activation of "Melchizedek's Transmitting System" into our Chakras, and ask that it be Tuned-up to each person's Highest Potential.

We now call forth the "Seven Planetary Logoi, and the Six Buddhas of Activity," for a Special Wesak Ascension Acceleration, for all that are gathered here in the Golden Chamber.

We now call forth the "Great Divine Director and the Lords of Karma," for a Special Dispensation of Cleansing and Clearing of as much of our karma as possible.

We now call forth Commander Ashtar and the Ashtar Command for a Cleansing and Clearing of our Monad, and Mighty I Am Presence.

We call forth to Melchizedek for the full Anchoring and Activation of his Light, Love and Power Body as a Special Gift of this first Wesak of the New Millennium, to each person's Highest Potential.

We ask Lord Buddha, Lord Maitreya, Allah Gobi, and St. Germain to now step forward and Balance each person's Chakra System, entire 12-Body System, and Remove now: all negative implants, elementals, and any and all negative energy.

We now call forth Melchizedek, the Mahatma, Metatron, and Archangel Michael, for a "Cleansing and Clearing back to Our Original Covenant with GOD."

We call forth the Mahatma to now fully Anchor and Activate to our Highest Potential all 352 levels of its Holy and Divine nature.

We call to Lord Buddha, Lord Maitreya, St. Germain, Allah Gobi and the Seven Chohans, for the Permanent Anchoring and Activation of the Great Central Sun, into the Core of our Being.

We call forth from GOD, Christ, The Holy Spirit, Melchizedek, The Mahatma, Archangel Michael, The Divine Mother to now bring forth the Full Positive Spiritual Force of the Grand Planetary Alignment for the purpose of Spiritually accelerating the Ascension Process for Planet Earth, Ourselves, and all Sentient Beings on Earth!

We call forth Melchizedek, the Mahatma, Metatron, and Archangel Michael for the Anchoring and Activation of "The 43 Christed Universes."

We call forth GOD, Christ, and the Holy Spirit for a Divine Anchoring and Activation of the Lord's Mystical Body of each person's Highest Potential.

His Holiness Lord Melchizedek now takes the Entire Group into a "Secret Chamber, within the Heart of the Universal Core," where no large gathering of Initiates and Masters from Earth has ever entered before.

As we now collectively step into this "Secret Chamber," we see before us the "Sacred Fire of the Universal Core" burning Brilliantly on a Golden Altar.

This is the "Sacred Fire" which is the Core and Very Center of the "Melchizedek Universe" we all live in.

Melchizedek with a wave of his "Sacred Rod," Gifts all in Attendance with an "Ember of his Sacred Fire," and places it very Gently and Delicately in each person's Third Eye.

This most Blessed and Sanctified Gift of Melchizedek is now being given, He says, for the Purpose of Solidifying each Person in attendance, in Eternal Connection with Him.

Receive this Most Sacred Blessing now from Melchizedek Himself, if you would like to receive it...

Melchizedek now has a Seven Part Final Surprise and Gift for all in attendance here.

This surprise might be called the "Seven Part Revelation From GOD," as GOD and Melchizedek's final Gift and Blessing for this "Golden Wesak 2000 Millennium Event" to begin the New Millennium.

To begin this "Seven Part Revelatory Surprise," His Holiness Lord Melchizedek, gathers us all up now in His "Golden Crystalline Merkabah," and takes us as a Group, with the help of the Mahatma, Metatron, and Archangel Michael, back to the "Throne of Grace" at the 352nd Level of Creation.

As we arrive again, we are Greeted by the "Cosmic Council of 12, the 24 Elders that surround the Throne of Grace," as well as the Divine Mother, the Divine Father, the Elohim Councils, all the Archangels and the Holy Spirit.

We also call the Entire Planetary and Cosmic Hierarchy, as well as the over One Million inner plane Ascended Masters and Beings attending this Wesak Celebration to join us.

The First Revelatory Surprise that GOD, Melchizedek, the Mahatma, Metatron, and Archangel Michael have in store for us, as an Initial Purification directly from GOD, is the Anchoring of a "Matchstick amount of Cosmic Fire directly from GOD," around each Person in attendance and the Entire Group.

The purpose of this "Cosmic Fire" is to Burn away any last remnants of Astral, Mental, Etheric and/or Physical Dross, that is not 100% of the Melchizedek/Christ/Buddha Consciousness.

Be Still and Receive this "Ray of Cosmic Fire" directly from GOD now, if you would like to receive this Purification…

The Second Revelatory Surprise and Gift from GOD and the Godforce, is an Anchoring and Activation from the "Cosmic Treasury of Light."

GOD and the Godforce now Anchor and Activate the "Light Packets of Information from The Tablets of Creation," the "Elohim Scriptures," "The Archangelic Scriptures," the "Torah Or," the "Cosmic Book of Life," and the "Cosmic Ten Commandments."

Be Still and Receive these "Cosmic Light Packets" now, to each person's Highest Spiritual Potential, if you would like to receive this Gift from GOD and the Godforce.

The Third Revelatory Surprise and Gift from GOD and the Godforce, is to now call forward the Entire Cosmic and Planetary Hierarchy, and the over One Million Masters in attendance on the inner plane.

We now ask from GOD and the Entire Godforce, for the merging of the "Light Bodies of this Entire Celestial Cosmic Group," with the individual and Group Body of all Earthly Wesak Participants in attendance, for the purpose of Greater Planetary World Service.

If you choose to receive this "Supreme Cosmic Merger," then Be Still and Receive this Blessing now....

The Fourth Revelatory Surprise and Gift now comes Directly and Singularly from GOD Himself.

GOD's Gift here is to give each Person in attendance at this "Golden Wesak 2000 Millennium Event," for the First Time in the History of the Earth, the Anchoring and Activation of the "Light, Love and Power Body of GOD" for each Person in attendance.

If you would like to receive this Gift of all Gifts, and Blessing of all Blessings, Be Still, and Receive this Blessing now...

We now ask that this Gift be also given to the Earth Mother, to help Her in Her Physical and Spiritual Evolution and Ascension Process...

The Fifth Revelatory Gift and Blessing for this "Golden Wesak 2000 Millennium Event," comes directly from GOD, The Divine Father, The Divine Mother, Melchizedek, the Mahatma, Metatron, Archangel Michael, the 24 Elders, the Cosmic Council of 12, the Cosmic Christ Essence, the Holy Spirit and the Godforce.

These Great and Noble Beings led directly now by GOD, Raise their "Combined Light Rods" into the Air, and bring them forward in a Sweeping Fashion.

This Sweeping Motion of the "Light Rods" Clears the Spiritual and Energetic Way for Planet Earth and all Sentient Beings to move with Godspeed into the New Millennium and Seventh Golden Age with Grace and Comfort.

We also request at this time for a Second Sweeping from GOD and the Godforce of their "Combined Light Rods," so that Earth and all Her Inhabitants may avoid all Thoughtforms and Energy Related to "Armageddon Type Predictions or Prophesy," so we may move into the Seventh Golden Age in a Harmonious and Balanced fashion.

We ask that all these Predictions and Prophecies of an Illusionary and/or True Prophetic Nature, be Completely Cleared, Cleansed, and Undone now, by the Grace of GOD and the Godforce, if this be in Harmony with GOD's Will.

Let us be Still and Receive this Blessing now, so we may now move fully into this next 2000 year cycle in Ease and Grace rather than Karma.

We now Invoke one last time the "Light Rods of GOD and the Godforce," to now Sweep their "Light Rods" forward again, to help the Earth Mother bring in the New Millennium, with as little or few Major Earth Changes and Catastrophic Disturbances as possible.

Let us Be Still now, and Receive this Blessing along with Planet Earth and all her Inhabitants, to officially now bring in the "New Millennium and the Seventh Golden Age."

GOD now steps forward for GOD's last Individual and Singular Gift and Blessing, which is the Sixth Revelatory Surprise and Blessing that GOD will be Giving this evening.

This gift contains a series of seven most profound and sublime GOD Activations as another Special Gift and Blessing this evening!

GOD now steps forward to Anchor and Activate that which has never been Anchored and Activated to Earthly Disciples, Initiates, and Masters in the History of the Earth.

We call forth to GOD to now Anchor and Fully Activate from the "GOD Core of Creation" to all in attendance, that which is Esoterically been spoken of as "The Light/Love/and Power Packets of GOD."

If you would like to Receive this Gift of all Gifts, and Blessing of all Blessings, Be Still, and Receive this Ultimate Cosmic Ascension Activation now.

We call forth to GOD for the Permanent Anchoring and Activation of "The Full Garment of the Father."

We call forth to GOD for the Permanent Anchoring and Activation of "The Infinite Garment of YHWH."

We call forth to GOD for the Permanent Anchoring and Activation of "The Holy Scrolls of the Living Light of GOD."

We call forth to GOD for the Permanent Anchoring and Activation of "The Torah Or" also known as "The Cosmic Divine Scriptures of GOD," in its Splendor and Glory!

I ask you now to all become like a "Chalice of Light," as we now call forth from GOD for the Permanent Anchoring and Activation of "the Infinite Garment of GOD, Christ and the Holy Spirit."

We also call forth in this Divine and Sacred Moment from GOD for the Anchoring and Activation into ourselves and our world in this New Millennium of The Heavenly Jerusalem!"

GOD and the Godforce, the Entire Cosmic and Planetary Hierarchy, and the over One Million Masters, now have one Final Gift for all in attendance and for the Earth.

This Final and Seventh Gift from GOD, and the Entire Godforce, is One Final Light and Love Shower, infused by the Full Power and Will of GOD, and the Entire Godforce.

Let us receive this "Love and Light Shower" of all "Love and Light Showers" now...

GOD and the Entire Godforce, now has One Final Loving and Humble Request to make of all Light/Love/ and Power workers in attendance, who have Received these Blessings and Activations.

GOD and the Godforce hereby officially and Lovingly Request that each Person Receiving these Gifts make the Firm Commitment on your return to Earth to act as "Transmitters and Resolute Masters," to give forth to your Brothers and Sisters in an Unceasing Fashion the Unconditional Love and Light you have Received so Generously and Graciously from GOD and the Entire Godforce this Weekend.

Let us all now take a few Moments of Silence, to answer this Request from GOD and the Godforce, in the Silence and Sanctuary of your own Heart, as you personally feel comfortable doing.

In this "Poignant Period of Silence," where we have the "Rapt Attention of GOD and the Godforce," is now also a Perfect Time to say any "Personal Prayers for Yourself, your Spiritual Mission, for Family, Friends, Students, Pets, and for the Entire Planet."

We will now take one minute of silence to do this...

We now call forth our inner plane Spiritual Hosts this weekend and Request to now re-enter "Lord Melchizedek's Golden Crystalline Merkabah."

Let us feel ourselves now very slowly and gently, begin to leave the "Throne of Grace," and begin moving from this Cosmic Level of GOD, to the Multiuniversal Level of Divinity.

Feel the Merkabah continue to Descend now, back through the Universal Core and Level of Melchizedek's Ashram and Sanctuary.

Continuing to Descend now through the Galactic Core level of Melchior.

Descending further now through the Solar Core and Solar Regions of Helios and Vesta.

Descending further still now, through the Planetary Core and Planetary Levels of Lord Buddha and Sanat Kumara.

Gliding now back towards Mt. Shasta, where the Mountain of Mt. Shasta, Pan, and the Earth Mother welcome us with a Loving Embrace.

Let us now take one last moment to inwardly Thank GOD and the Godforce, and His Holiness Lord Melchizedek, for being our Celestial Guides and Caretakers on our Journey back to Source this evening.

Feel yourselves now Easily and Comfortably enter your Physical Body, bringing with you Total Recall and Complete Integration of all the Light and Love received from GOD and the Godforce this evening!

Feel yourself now completely reconnect with your Grounding Cord, and feel it still firmly connected to the Center of the Earth!

Feel your Feet Chakras also firmly connected, like the "Roots of a Tree" going deep into the Earth.

Feel these roots growing from your feet fill the entire Earth.

Take one more moment now to Breathe all the Light and Love you have just received form GOD, Melchizedek and the Godforce into the very center of the Earth, and again to all the Kingdoms of the Earth Mother.

Feel all the roots that have grown from your feet filling the Earth with the Light and Love from GOD, the Godforce, and yourself.

See and Feel your Feet Chakras, the Root System you have grown, and the entire Earth, completely filling-up and lighting up from this process.

Again now feel the Earth Mother and all Kingdoms: Mineral, Plant, and Animal, respond to your Love and Light, and now send you their Love and Light in a Glorious Exchange of Unconditional Love.

With this wonderful Earthly exchange now complete, take one last moment to share your Unconditional Love with all your Brothers and Sisters in the auditorium.

When you are ready, you can open your eyes and we will take a 20-minute break!

3

GOD and the Mahatma Ascension
Activation Meditation

We will begin by closing our eyes.

We now call forth the Mahatma to Overlight and Infuse us with His Divine Presence of Synthesis, Love, and Light.

Let us now take a deep "Breath of Oneness," as we prepare now to be carried up the 352 Levels of Existence, to the "Throne of Creation."

The "Throne of Creation" I speak of here, is at the Level of the Godhead Itself.

To begin this Meditation, the Mahatma now Etherically Manifests a "Mahatma Merkabah," composed of an Aspect of all 352 Levels of His Being.

Magically find yourself within this Group Merkabah, and become aware of your Physical Body.

Feel yourself in touch with Mother Earth, as you Sit and Feel your Feet Upon Her.

Now also feel the Embrace of the Wings of Archangel Sandalphon, who helps to Anchor the Mahatma at this 3rd Dimensional Level.

Feel the Incredible Love Infusion, from both the Mahatma and Archangel Sandalphon, and know at this moment, the Essence of the Mahatma Interpenetrates and Blesses your Physical Embodiment, Totally and Completely.

Feel the Profundity of this Union, as the Mahatma Installs and Fully Activates and Actualizes, the "Matrix of Synthesis" of His Very Self, within Every Cell, Atom, Electron, and Subatomic Particle of your Physical Vehicle.

As you drink in this Joy of Unity, let yourselves now begin to be Carried Upwards within the 352 Levels of the Mahatma.

Feel the Equanimity of Grace and Love, as you move Smoothly and Calmly up through the Seven Subplanes of the Emotional Dimension of Reality.

It is here now that the Mahatma, Quan Yin and Mother Mary, connect the "Spark of the Heart of GOD," directly with Each Individual Person's Heart in attendance.

Feel now the Bliss and Joy, as Unconditional Love and Compassion Fill your Entire Being.

Feel, See and Visualize Beloved Archangel Michael, Encircle you in a "Ring of Blue Fire," with His All Powerful "Blue Flame Sword of Protection."

Archangel Michael comes forth, Creating a "Platinum Gold Blue Bubble of Light," at the request of the Mahatma, in order that you feel 100% Empowered and Protected throughout this Meditation.

The Mahatma wishes you to know in this moment, that each and every Level of Existence, is the Manifestation of the Godhead.

In the Reality of the Mahatma, also known as the "Avatar of Synthesis," all 352 Levels of His Group Consciousness are Equally Valued, Honored, and Sanctified.

Feel now through your God and Goddess Selves, the Feeling of Love and Unity which is Truly what You Are.

Feel the "Magnificent Radiance of Pink Love," Expand and Enlarge, as you are now Drawn Upward, to Embody all Seven Subplanes of the Mental Realm.

In a "Burst of Golden White Light," comes forth Lord Maitreya, who is the Essence and Embodiment of Love and Wisdom.

Lord Maitreya and the Mahatma now fill your Entire Mental Sphere, with Divine Wisdom and Brain Illumination.

The Mahatma now Comes forward and Connects the "Spark of the Mind of GOD," directly with the Mind of Each of Us.

Bask in this "Radiant Glow of Synthesis," as the Mind of GOD and your Mind Merge as Never Before.

Receive this Blessing of the Mahatma, that from this Moment Forward, your Thoughts shall be Blessed by the Intent of the Universal Mind of the Mahatma.

We now move upwards into the Buddhic or Causal Plane.

Here Lord Buddha and the Mahatma, Download into your Higher Mind the "Encoded Wisdom" of all the Causes that have set your Individual Lifestream in Motion.

Know this Wisdom is now being Installed into the "Causal or Higher Mind" of Each One of You, along with the Encodements that will Activate you to Fulfill your Divine Blueprint and Destiny.

Feel yourselves moving now into the Atmic Plane.

Know it is, in truth, the Mahatma who is now carrying you Up the Many Levels of His Being.

Feel yourself now Expanding into your "Monad and Mighty I Am Presence," as you move through the Monadic Plane and into the Logoic Dimension of Reality.

The Mahatma now takes you into "Full Integration and Oneness Consciousness" with your Solar Selves.

In a "Blaze of Copper Gold," Helios and Vesta, and the Mahatma, Merge your Body with Theirs.

They Permanently Install within the Heart and Crown Chakras of each and every one of you, a Portion of the "Flame that Burns But Does Not Consume."

By the Grace of the Mahatma you are now merged 100% with the Solar Logos, and are now being Gifted with an "Aspect of Solar Fire" that shall ever Radiate within you; by Helios and Vesta, and the Mahatma.

As the Warmth, Unity, Love, and Light of this Fire Glows within, Lord Melchior Surrounds you with His Galactic Embrace.

The Mahatma and Melchior move you now Further Within the Vastness of the 352 Levels of the Mahatma, into the Deepest Expanse of the Galactic Core, over which Melchior presides as the Galactic Logos.

Beyond what the Mind can possibly conceive at this Level, you are now Suddenly Aware that an Incredible Downloading of Galactic Light and Information is Pouring into your Crown Chakra and 12 Body System.

This Downloading is a Spiritual Current that moves from the Galactic Spheres down into and through your 12-Body System, and through your first 150 Chakras.

This includes Grounding into your Seven Primary Third Dimensional Chakras.

Both the Mahatma and Lord Melchior now state that this Galactic Downloading manifests as a Great Increase of Love and Light upon the Physical Plane, in your Physical/Etheric Vehicle.

His Holiness Lord Melchizedek, our Universal Logos, now stands before you.

His Body is Composed of the Very Essence of this Entire Universe.

His Expanse carries you far up the 352 Levels of Divinity.

Lord Melchizedek now takes on "Robes of Gossamer Golden White Light," and the form of His "Higher Adam Kadmon Body."

He does this in order to Personally Connect with You at this High Point upon the Spiraling Ladder, within the Mahatma's Vastness.

He touches each and everyone of you with the Essence of His Light, and Caresses each of you, with the Essence of His Love.

He places now a "Crystal of His Universal Golden Light," into each of your 200 Chakras.

This Light Permeates your Being from the Universal Level, through all the Intermediary Levels, including your Physical Body.

He now Awakens at each of these Levels, the Most Sacred Universal Fire Letters, Key Codes, and Sacred Geometries, into the Core of Your Being.

As a Special Blessing and Grace, the Mahatma and Melchizedek now Install to each Person's Highest Potential, their "Zohar Body of Light" and "Anointed Christ Overself Body."

As a Second Special Universal Blessing, the Seven Lady Archangels: Faith, Christine, Charity, Hope, Mother Mary, Aurora, and Amethyst, now step forward and Anchor and Activate the "Universal Archetypal Imprint" of Perfect God/Goddess Balance, within Each Person in attendance, both Male and Female.

This Activation of the Universal God/Goddess within each of you, will in turn allow you to Activate the God/Goddess Ideal within all whom you Meet and Interact with.

Now See, Feel, and/or Visualize the "Platinum Light of Archangel Metatron," carrying you upward ever so gently, towards the "Throne of Creation."

To the left of Archangel Metatron, Archangel Michael appears.

To His right, Archangel Gabriel "Sounds Forth His Trumpet."

As the Luminous Tones and Colors of Gabriel's Trumpet move through the Universe and your Being, you begin to Hear and/or Feel the "Music of the Spheres," Bathing You in Exquisite Tones and Colors of Cosmic Sound and Radiance.

Even as this is occurring, Feel now the Full Totality of the Mahatma.

Know that He is about to bring you into the Very Heart of the Godhead.

Before this is done, He does what is called simply, the "Mahatma Activation of Synthesis."

This He now does by Placing His "Cosmic Hand" over your Highest Body or Vehicle of Light, which is the "Lord's Mystical Body," which He now Fully Activates within Each of You.

He now moves His Hand down through all 352 Levels of your Being and Activates all of your 352 Bodies.

He simultaneously Integrates an Aspect of His Infinite Cosmic Body into all 352 Levels of Each Person in attendance.

Any Illusion of Separation between the Godhead and your Third Dimensional Existence are now Healed by the Mighty Hand of the "Mahatma Himself."

From within this Place of Absolute Oneness, we now call forth the Holy Spirit, for a "Cosmic Baptism of Light and Love"...

If you would like to receive this Baptism of the Holy Spirit, be Still and Receive this Blessing now...

The Holy Spirit also brings forth a Second Baptism for all in attendance.

This Second Baptism Activates and Cleanses the Four Elements that make up the Manifested Worlds.

The Holy Spirit now Baptizes, Activates, and Cleanses all in attendance through Fire...Air...Water...and Earth.

If you would like to receive this Second Baptism, Be Still and Receive this Blessing now...

In doing so, the Holy Spirit is now "undoing" all remnants of negative ego, separative consciousness, imbalanced consciousness, and physical lack of health, in each person's 12-Body System.

We now call forth all the Male and Female Archangels connected with Earth's Evolution.

We now ask for a Divine Dispensation, as a Special Grace and Gift for this 1999 Wesak to Bring in the New Millennium, for the Anchoring and Activation for Each Son and Daughter of God in attendance, of all 330 Chakras back to the Godhead.

Be still, and receive this Enormous Cosmic Blessing now...

We now call forth the Mighty Elohim and all Elohim Councils connected with Earth's Evolution.

We call forth now for a Second Divine Dispensation for this 1999 Wesak Celebration congregation of Lightworkers; for the Highest Potential Anchoring and Activation of our Elohistic Lord's Body, of our Higher Adam Kadmon Body, our Electromagnetic Body, of our Paradise Son's Body, of our Overself Body, of our Order of Sonship Body, of our Gematrian Body, of our Epi-kenetic Body, of our Aka Body, of our Monadic Blueprint Body, and our Mayavarupa Body, as described in the book *The Keys of Enoch*.

We ask for these things in the Name of the Melchizedek, the Christ, and in the Name of the Buddha, so we may be of Greater Service.

If you would like to receive this Blessing and Activation, be Still and Receive this anchoring and activation now...

We now find ourselves Ascending even Higher by the Grace of the Mahatma, and find ourselves in the Presence of the Divine Mother, at the Left Side of the "Throne of Creation."

The Divine Mother Lovingly and Sweetly Brings Forth Her Cosmic Hand, and Gently Touches Each Person in attendance on the Third eye.

As She does so, She Activates and Actualizes the Twelve Strand of "DNA/RNA God Matrix," both on the Etheric and Physical Level, as Her Special Gift and Blessing for this 1999 Wesak Celebration to help bring in the New Millennium.

Receive the Full Impact and Spiritual Penetration of this Gift and Blessing now…

As this Activation is Complete, the Mahatma Magically transfers the Entire Group to the Right Side of the "Throne of God," to be in the Presence of the Divine Father.

The Light here is so Brilliant, as was the case with the Divine Mother, that it takes a few moments for our Spiritual Eyes to adjust.

The Divine Father is Very Pleased to Welcome Us here in this fashion.

The Divine Father also has a Very Special Gift and Blessing for this Sanctified Group, which is a Special Dispensation of Unimaginable Magnitude.

The Divine Father now brings forth His Luminous Right Hand, and touches Each Person on the Crown Chakra, which causes an Instantaneous Merger and Integration at Each Person's Highest Potential with the 48 Dimensions of Reality, that Compose the 352 Levels of Divinity.

My Beloved Brothers and Sisters, be Still and Receive this Sublime and Profoundly Gracious Gift of the Divine Father now…

As this Activation is Complete, the Beloved Mahatma now brings us directly in front of the "Throne of Creation" Itself!

There Standing before the "Throne of Creation," Stands the "Cosmic Council of Twelve," also known as the "Twelve Cosmic Logoi."

Seated behind them, in a semi-circle, are the "Twenty-four Cosmic Elders of Light," who surround the "Throne of Grace."

It is by the Grace of the Mahatma, as His Special Gift to this Group for this 1999 Wesak to bring in the New Millennium, that we are Graced with this Experience.

"The Cosmic Council of Twelve" and the "Twenty-four Elders" that Surround the "Throne of Grace," are very Joyous and Pleased to Receive this Gathering of Lightworkers, and Servants of GOD.

They too wish to now join in the Festivities and Blessings that are being given forth at this Turn of the New Millennium on Earth, and for Lord Buddha's Birthday.

The "Twenty-four Elders" and the "Cosmic Council of Twelve," all Raise their Right Hand with an Open Palm, and Send Forth a "Beam of Unfathomable Cosmic Light."

This collective Cosmic Beam of Light and Love now causes an Anchoring and Activation for the First Time in Earth's History, of the "Cosmic Monad" at Each Person's Highest Potential, and for the Beloved Earth Mother Herself.

My Beloved Brothers and Sisters, the "Cosmic Monad" I speak of here is not the Individualized Monad merged with to achieve Planetary Ascension, but rather the Cosmic Equivalent at the 352nd Level of the Godhead to achieve Full "Cosmic Ascension."

The Profundity and Significance of this Activation is Beyond Words and Comprehension.

My Beloved Brothers and Sisters, if you wish to Receive this Anchoring and Activation, be Still and Receive the Full Impact and Spiritual Penetration of this Enormous Gift of the "Cosmic Council of Twelve," and the "Twenty-four Elders" now…

As this Activation Concludes, the "Cosmic Council of Twelve" and the "Twenty-four Elders" disappear, and by the Grace of the Mahatma we stand before the "Throne of God!"

The Light is so Brilliant that it is almost blinding.

The "Love and Peace so Profound," that even a word such as "Bliss" does not come close to describing the feeling.

We stand in the Presence of "Sat Chit Ananda."

"Pure Existence, Pure Consciousness and Pure Bliss"!

Out of this "Unfathomable Cosmic Light, Love and Power," GOD steps forward with a Final Gift and Blessing, on this Momentous Occasion in Earth's History and Evolution!

Appearing now, out of this Glorious Light, emerges the "Cosmic Burning Bush."

GOD now takes an "Infinitesimal Spark of the Burning Bush," and places it as GOD's Special Gift, into each Person's Heart Chakra.

This Spark of GOD serves as a "Light of Remembrance," that each of the 352 Levels in GOD's Body is Sanctified and Holy Ground.

It is GOD's Wish that Each Person Receiving this "Gift of Gifts," take it Back to the Earth, and Share it through the "Vehicle of Loving all your Brothers and Sisters."

Also sharing it with all Animals, Plants, Minerals, all Sentient Beings, the Very Earth, and the Material Universe itself.

GOD now asks each person under "Complete Divine Protection of GOD and the Mahatma," to now consider stepping forward as an individual and as a group, and Bathe Yourself in the "Cosmic Burning Bush" to completely purify your entire Auric Field and 12-body system.

This Unbelievably Profound Blessing, Gift, and Grace of GOD, will serve to "Completely Purify and Cleanse" any last remnant of Thought, Word or Deed that is not Completely in Harmony with the Will of GOD.

GOD now invites you to Step Forward Individually and as a Group, and receive this Blessing of all Blessings, and in doing so, Dedicate your Life to Serving the GOD In All.

If you Choose in this Moment to Receive this Gift of all Gifts, and make this your Intent, then be Still in your Consciousness and Step Forward in your Light Body and Receive this Purification and Anointing of "The Cosmic Burning Bush of GOD."

We will now take a Minute of Silence to Fully Receive this Gift of Gifts and Blessing of Blessings...

Now fully Bathed and Purified in GOD'S "Cosmic Burning Bush," find yourself Conscious of being in the Loving, Cool Embrace, of the Mahatma's Merkabah.

Feel the Mahatma's Merkabah begin to move the group out of the area of The "Burning Bush," and Prepare for Descent back to Earth.

Take one last moment to Face GOD, and to Give Thanks for this Profound Blessing and the Grace we all Enjoy in our Daily Lives under GOD's Care...

Feel the Mahatma's Merkabah begin to Descend now; first moving down through the "Cosmic Logoic Plane."

Now descending through the "Cosmic Monadic Plane."

Descending through the "Cosmic Atmic Plane."

Descending through the "Cosmic Buddhic Plane."

Descending further now, through the "Cosmic Mental Plane."

Descending further still, through the "Cosmic Emotional Plane."

Now entering the "Cosmic Physical Plane."

Feel yourselves moving now down through the Seven Subplanes of the "Cosmic Physical Plane."

Feel yourselves now Seeing and Enjoying the Panoramic View of the City and Sacred Mountain of Mt. Shasta.

Finally now Feel yourselves entering this Auditorium, and now Slowly and Comfortably Anchor Yourself Fully into Your Physical Body, Bringing all that You have Just Experienced Fully Back with You, into Your Physical Vehicle and this Present Moment.

Take one last moment to Inwardly Thank the Mahatma for the Grace He has Bestowed upon Each and Every One of Us, to allow Us to travel through the 352 Levels of His Sublime Infinite Body.

On this note, when you are ready, you may open your eyes and see the Manifestation of GOD and the Mahatma all around you, in the Beloved Hearts, Minds and Souls of your Beloved Brothers and Sisters who sit with you in this auditorium.

We will now take a 20-minute break.

Namaste!

4

GOD and Archangel Metatron's Cosmic Tree of Life Ascension Activation Meditation

This meditation was first channeled for the 1999 Wesak Celebration.

We will begin by closing our eyes.

We call forth now Beloved Archangel Metatron and the entire Planetary and Cosmic Hierarchy to help in this Meditation.

We ask for a Balancing of the Energies

We call forth a Platinum Net from Metatron, the Mahatma, and Melchizedek to Cleanse any and all Unwanted Energies.

We call forth to Archangel Michael, for a "Platinum Gold Dome of Protection," throughout this entire Meditation and Experience.

We officially begin this Meditation by calling to Each Person's "144 Soul Extensions from their Monad," to join us for this meditation, if it is their free choice to do so.

We call forth now the Full Anchoring of the "Garment of Shaddai," also known as the "Light Body of Metatron," to serve as our Merkabah for this Meditation, both Individually and Collectively.

We now call forth from Metatron, the Mahatma, and Melchizedek, for the Full Anchoring and Activation into each person in attendance, and for the entire group, the "Cosmic Tree of Life."

We begin this Cosmic Tree of Life Ascension Activation, by calling forth a "Cosmic Ascension Column" and "Pillar of Light," back to Source.

Within this "Cosmic Pillar of Light," we request from Archangel Metatron, the Mahatma and Melchizedek, for the Establishment of Each Person's Antakarana, back to the Godhead.

We call forth from Beloved Ascended Master Djwhal Khul, for the full Anchoring and Activation of each person's Mighty I AM Presence and/or Monad, at the 100% Light and Love Quotient Level.

We call forth for the Anchoring and Activation from El Morya, Kuthumi, Serapis Bey, Paul the Venetian, Hilarion, Sananda, and St. Germain, of each Person's 12 Higher Bodies.

We call forth from Metatron, the Mahatma, Melchizedek, and Archangel Michael, for the Anchoring and Activation of each person's "330 Chakras."

We call forth from the Divine Mother and the Divine Father, for the Full Anchoring and Activation of each person's "48 Dimensional Bodies," providing Complete Connection and Attunement, back to the Godhead.

We call forth to His Holiness the Lord Sai Baba, for the Highest Potential Cleansing of Karma that is permitted by Divine Grace, for each person in attendance.

We call to Metatron for the Permanent Anchoring and Activation of the GOD Electron, into each person in attendance.

We call to the Divine Mother and all the Lady Masters, for a Cosmic Downpouring and Divine Increase of each person's Love Quotient.

We call to Sanat Kumara, Vywamus, and Lenduce, for the Integration and Cleansing of each Person's "144 Soul Extensions from their Monad".

We call to Melchizedek to now Anchor and Activate all the Fire Letters, Key Codes, and Sacred Geometries, to Fully Ignite the "Cosmic Tree of Life," and "Seven Sacred Seals."

My Beloved Brothers and Sisters, now that we are officially warmed up and Cosmically Activated, we are ready now to begin our Climb Up the "Cosmic Tree of Life," back to Source.

We call forth Archangel Metatron and Archangel Sandalphon, to officially Ignite, Anchor and Activate the First Sephiroth of the "Cosmic Tree of Life," known as "Malkuth, or the Kingdom."

As this Sephiroth is Ignited, we are given from Sandalphon, a Divine Vision and Experience of the "Infinite Physical Universe."

We now call forth Archangel Gabriel, to officially Ignite, Anchor, and Activate the Second Sephiroth of "Yesod, or Foundation."

As Archangel Gabriel ignites this Sephiroth, we are given a "Vision of the Subconscious Mind of GOD."

We now call forth Archangel Raphael, to Fully Ignite, Anchor, and Activate the Third Sephiroth, known as "Hod, or Splendor."

As Raphael Ignites this Sephiroth, we Fully Receive the Experience of the "Splendor of the Divine Mind of GOD."

We now call forth Archangel Auriel to fully Ignite, Anchor, and Activate the Sephiroth know as "Netzach, or Victory."

As Archangel Auriel does this now, we receive the Vision and Experience, of the "Perfect Divine Feeling of GOD throughout the Cosmos."

We call forth Archangel Michael, to Fully Ignite, Anchor, and Activate the Sephiroth known as "Tiphareth, or Beauty."

As Archangel Michael does this now, we receive the "Vision and Experience of the Perfect Harmony of GOD throughout Creation."

We now call forth Archangel Khamael, to Fully Ignite, Anchor, and Activate the Sephiroth known as "Gebrurah, or Severity."

As Archangel Khamael does this, we now receive the "Vision and Experience of the Power of GOD throughout Creation."

We now call forth Archangel Tzadkiel, to Fully Ignite, Anchor, and Activate the Sephiroth known as "Chesed, or Mercy."

As Archangel Tzadkiel does this, we receive the "Vision and Experience of the Divine Cosmic Mother, Face to Face."

We now call forth Archangel Ratziel, to Ignite, Anchor, and Activate the Sephiroth known as "Chokmah, or Wisdom."

As Archangel Ratziel does this, we receive the "Vision and Experience of the Divine Cosmic Father, Face to Face."

We call forth Archangel Metatron, to Ignite, Anchor, and Activate the Sephiroth at the Top of the Tree of Life, known as "Kether, or the Crown."

As Archangel Metatron does this, we receive the "Vision and Experience of Union with the Cosmic Light of GOD."

We now call forth His Holiness Lord Melchizedek, to Fully Ignite, Anchor and Activate the "Cosmic Hidden Sephiroth of Daath, or Hidden Wisdom."

As Beloved Melchizedek does this, we receive the "Vision and Experience of the Wisdom of the Universe Unfold before Us."

We now call forth the Mahatma, to now Ignite, Anchor, and Activate, the Never Before Revealed "Twelfth Sephiroth in the Cosmic Tree of Life, known as Synthesis!"

As the Mahatma does this, we receive the Vision and Experience of all Twelve Sephiroth working together in "Perfect Integration, Balance, Synergy and Synthesis."

Be Still and Receive this Blessing and Activation now if you would like to receive this now…

We now call forth Metatron, the Mahatma, and Melchizedek, to now fully Anchor and Activate the "Three Pillars of the Cosmic Tree of Life," known as the "Pillar of Severity," "the Pillar of Equilibrium," and the "Pillar of Mercy."

As Metatron, the Mahatma, and Melchizedek do this, feel the Incredible Sense of Balance now within Yourself, of Firmness and Compassion, as these Pillars are Installed.

We now call forth all the Archangels of the Cosmic Hierarchy, to Fully Anchor and Activate into the "Cosmic Tree of Life," for each person, the "Twelve Signs of the Zodiac," in perfect Balance and Integration.

We now call forth the Elohim Councils, to Fully Anchor and Activate the Major Archetypes of the Tarot Deck, into the "Cosmic Tree of Life," in Perfect Balance and Integration, for each person in attendance as GOD would have it Be.

We now call forth the Holy Spirit, who appears as the "Sap" Breathing throughout the Entire Cosmic Tree of Life.

The Holy Spirit now requests that we deeply Feel and Experience Its energies, as we Breath the "Holy Breath" of the Holy Spirit together, through the Entire Cosmic Tree of Life that is now installed within each of us.

We now continue climbing into even Higher Dimensions of Reality by the Grace of His Holiness Archangel Metatron, and His Light Body Merkabah.

We now move from the Crown, or Top of the "Cosmic Tree of Life," into the Sphere above the Cosmic Tree, known as the "Ain Soph Or," or "Limitless Universal Light."

Here the Light is so Bright, one can hardly see.

Metatron now continues to take us Even Higher Still, into the "Ain Soph," or "Undifferentiated Source."

Here the Light is so Refined that it has become Colorless, and can only be described, as the "Clear Light of GOD."

Archangel Metatron takes us Even Higher Still now, into the region of GOD's Kingdom, known as "Ain," or "Utter and Complete GOD Essence."

The Peace and Love at this 352nd Level of Divinity is a Grace beyond Words and Description.

It is here we find ourselves standing before the 12 Cosmic Logoi, and the 24 Elders that Surround the "Throne of Grace."

The 12 Cosmic Logoi, also known as the 12 Cosmic Ray Masters, lift up their "Individual Light Rods," and one by one Ignite the "12 Cosmic Rays" within each person in attendance, that are the Foundation and Source of GOD's Infinite Creation.

Be aware that this Activation is not of the 12 Planetary Rays we are all familiar with, but rather an Activation of their 12 Cosmic Equivalents at the 352nd Level of the Godhead.

Receive this Extraordinary Blessing now, as a Gift of the Creator, and of the Cosmic Ray Masters, for this 1999 Wesak, to bring in the New Millennium.

We also ask at this time that this Gift be Given to the Earth Mother Herself, to Accelerate Her Spiritual and Material Evolution as Well.

Let us all Receive this Blessing and Gift as well now, from each of the Individual Cosmic Ray Masters…

The 24 Elders of Light that Surround the "Throne of Grace" now step forward.

Through a Process that can only be described as the "Language of Light," the 24 Elders now Transfer Telepathically to each person in attendance, a "Light Revelation into each person's Crown Chakra."

The 24 Elders give the Gift of the "Cosmic Wisdom of the Ages," which will Unfold as an Acorn grows into an Oak Tree, throughout each Lightworkers Cosmic Journey Back to Source.

Be still and receive this Tremendous Blessing now…

As this Enormous Blessing is Fully Received, we find Ourselves Raised even Higher by Metatron, and the 24 Elders, and we find ourselves in the "Ashram of GOD," at the "Throne of Creation."

We have moved Beyond the Beyond, by the Grace of Metatron.

Here GOD now steps forward with "GOD's Light Rod," and as a Special Dispensation for this 1999 Wesak Celebration to bring in the New Millennium, GOD brings forth this "Light Rod" upon each person's Crown Chakra.

GOD does this for the Specific Purpose of "Bestowing Full Sonship and Daughtership at the Highest Possible Level, for all in attendance."

Be still and receive this Blessing of all Blessings, and Activation of all Activations, now if you would like to receive it...

As this is Complete, GOD now Bestows a Second Blessing of "Unfathomable Magnitude."

GOD now brings forth what is esoterically known as the "Cosmic Waterfall of GOD," from the "Throne of Creation."

Experience this Cosmic Cleansing and Purification of this "Cosmic Waterfall of GOD" now...

Adding to and Joining the Experience now, is the entire Cosmic and Planetary Hierarchy, and the over One Million inner plane Masters in attendance, at this year's Wesak Celebration.

Let yourself now Experience the "Light and Love Shower of all Light and Love Showers" from GOD and the Entire Godforce...

We Humbly now Request that this Shower be given to the Earth Mother, and all Sentient Beings on Earth, to help bring in the New Millennium...

Now as a final Cosmic Gift and Blessing from GOD...

GOD requests now that we Collectively all Focus our Attention on "GOD's Cosmic Inbreath and Outbreath."

GOD requests now that we listen to GOD's "Cosmic Pulse," or even more exactly, to the "Stillpoint Between GOD's Cosmic Inbreath and Cosmic Outbreath."

It is in this Stillpoint, between the "Inbreath and Outbreath of GOD," that GOD can Truly be Experienced.

Let us be Silent Now, and Experience this "Final Revelation of GOD."

As we Conclude this Process now, take a moment to Thank GOD for this Experience, and to also Thank GOD for all the Blessings you have received this night.

As you Conclude this Process, you find yourself Floating before the "Throne of Creation," in "Metatron's Light Body Merkabah," with all your Brothers and Sisters.

Metatron's Group Merkabah begins to Descend back down through the Cosmic Dimensions of Reality, to the Multiuniversal Level.

Find yourself now, sitting upon the "Top of the Tree of Life, at the Multiuniversal Level."

Feel Metatron's Merkabah, Descending down the "Cosmic Antakarana," like an Elevator, to the Universal Level!

Here again you find yourself sitting on Top of the "Cosmic Tree of Life of Melchizedek at the Universal Level."

As Metatron's Group Merkabah continues to Descend, we find ourselves now sitting on Top of the "Cosmic Tree of Life at the Galactic Level" with Melchior, our Galactic Logos.

Descending further still, we find ourselves now, at the Top of the "Cosmic Tree of Life at the Solar Level" with Helios and Vesta.

Descending again within Metatron's Merkabah, we find ourselves sitting at the "Top of the Cosmic Tree of Life at the Planetary Level" with Lord Buddha in Shamballa.

Lord Buddha gives us another "Special Wesak Blessing and Ascension Activation," as we begin to Travel Downwards through His "Planetary Cosmic Tree of Life" to Ground Ourselves once again to Planet Earth.

As we begin Grounding Ourselves now back to Mount Shasta and back into our Physical Bodies, simultaneously feel and know that all of the "Cosmic Trees at all the Different Levels of Divinity of Life" remain connected within you through the "Cosmic Antakarana," which is now Fully Established between Yourself and the Godhead.

Now feel yourself Fully Connecting with your Physical Body and the Earth Mother, with the help of Archangel Sandalphon, Pan and the Earth Mother Herself.

It is only by the Grace of "Archangel Metatron's Protective Light Body and Merkabah," that we have been allowed to make this sojourn to GOD, as a Special Gift and Blessing from Him for this 1999 Wesak Celebration, to help bring in the New Millennium.

Take one last moment now to Thank Beloved Archangel Metatron for His "Supreme Grace" in allowing each and every one of us to make this Journey to Source and Back Again...

When you are ready, you may open your eyes, feeling the entire "Cosmic Tree of Life Fully Anchored and Activated within you by the Grace of GOD and the Godforce"!

As your eyes fully open now, share this Profound New Sense of Love, Wisdom, and Power in Perfect Balance, with your Brothers and Sisters in a Moment of Heart Expanding Love for them.

Namaste!

5

The Lord of Arcturus and the Arcturian Ascension Activation Meditation

Please close your eyes!

We now call forth The Cosmic and Planetary Hierarchy and most specifically The Lord of Arcturus and the Arcturians!

We call to Archangel Michael and Faith to place a Golden Dome of Protection around all involved in this Meditation!

We call forth Melchizedek, the Mahatma, and Metatron to bring forth a Platinum Net to remove any and all imbalanced energies.

We call forth to the Lord of Arcturus and the Arcturians, to now take us in our Etheric Bodies to your Ascension Seat on the Arcturian Mother Craft…

We call forth to the Lord of Arcturus to bring down the "Prana Wind Clearing Device" to cleanse and clear all our Nadis and Acupuncture Meridians…

We call forth to the Lord of Arcturus to now install the Arcturian Plating System to each person's highest potential…

We now call forth the Lord of Arcturus and the Arcturians for a Light and Love Quotient Building, to each person's highest potential.

We now call forth to the Arcturians for the tightening of each person's grids to each person's perfect balance, as GOD would have it be…

We now call forth the Lord of Arcturus to anchor the Arcturian Liquid Crystals into each person's four-body system, to deactivate any and all negative energies

We call forth to the Lord of Arcturus, for the anchoring and activation of the Golden Cylinder, to remove any and all negative energies 100% completely, including all negative implants and negative elementals.

We call forth to the Lord of Arcturus to now be taken to the Arcturian Light Chamber.

We now call forth to be taken on the Arcturian Mothership to the Arcturian Healing Chamber, for the specific healing of any and all etheric and/or physical health lessons!

We now call forth from the Lord of Arcturus and the Arcturian Temple Workers, for the "Arcturian Revitalization Program."

Lastly, we call forth the "Arcturian Joy Machine." I tell you now my friends, there is not a person on planet Earth who I have found who could not stop smiling or laughing once this Arcturian Joy Machine was turned on…

We now call to the Lord of Arcturus to connect each person officially up to your computers on your Mothership, so if they ever want to call on you again they are Online!

Take one last moment to thank the Lord of Arcturus and the Arcturians for their most gracious and generous help!

We ask the Lord of Arcturus now to help gently guide us in our Etheric Bodies, back to Earth, and safely back into our Physical Bodies bringing with us in total recall all the Light and Love we have just experienced!

Namaste!

6

The Cosmic and Planetary Hierarchy Protection Meditation

Close your eyes.

We begin this meditation by calling forth Archangels Michael and Faith and Their Legions of First Ray Angels.

We also call forth Melchizedek, the Mahatma, and Archangel Metatron, as well as each person's Higher Self and Mighty I Am Presence.

We begin by calling forth from Melchizedek, the Mahatma, and Metatron for a Platinum Net to be anchored, and to remove all negative and imbalanced energies.

We also request at this time that all negative implants and elementals be immediately cleared from the field.

We call forth to all the Cosmic and Planetary Masters gathered, for a permanent Pillar of Cosmic and Planetary Light, Love, and Power to be placed around all who are participating in this meditation.

We call forth from Melchizedek, for an additional permanent Golden Dome of Protection to be placed around each person.

We call forth to Melchizedek, the Mahatma, and Metatron, to place around each individual a permanent Wall of Light Protection.

We call to Archangel Michael to place around each individual His permanent Blue Shield Armor of Protection.

We call to Archangel Faith to place around each individual a permanent ever-rejuvenating Ring of Red Roses that will absorb all negative energy before it enters the field.

We call to the Mahatma to place a permanent Rainbow Bubble of Light around each person's auric field as an additional Protection.

We call to Archangel Metatron to place a permanent Platinum Tube of Light around each person as still another added Protection.

We call forth His Holiness the Lord Sai Baba to place around each individual your permanent Protective Robe of Love, Wisdom, and Power to prevent any unwanted energies from entering your auric field without your permission.

We call forward to Lord Buddha and the Karmic Board for a "Ban of Non-Interference" against all energies of psychic attack from within and without!

We call forth to Helios and Vesta, to place around each individual a Copper Golden Sun of Protection, that is so bright and so filled with GOD's Love that all misqualified or negative energy is immediately burned up and transmuted into the Pure Radiant Light of GOD.

We now call forth Melchior to bring forth a matchstick worth of the Cosmic Fire from the Great Central Sun, to burn away in a completely safe manner any negative energy that remains in the field.

We call forth the Lord of Arcturus to anchor the Arcturian Liquid Crystals to de-activate and re-balance all negative energy in the field.

We call forth Dr Lorphan and the Galactic Healers to tighten the Grids and strengthen the Spiritual, Psychological, and Physical Immune Systems of all listening to this meditation.

We call forth the Healing Angels to now balance the chakra's and four-body system.

We call forth the Lord of Arcturus and Djwhal Khul to now anchor and activate the Prana Wind Clearing Device, to blow Pranic Energy through all the Meridians and Nadis, to clear them and strengthen them and completely clear the 12-body system.

We call forth to the Divine Mother and the Lady Masters to bring forward a Platinum Net through each persons house to clear it of all etheric, astral, and mental energies that are not completely of the Christ/Buddha Energy.

We call forward to Beloved Saint Germain and Lady Portia for the anchoring and activation of a permanent Pillar of the Violet Flame that will transmute any and all misqualified energy from entering the auric field from within and without.

We call forth the Legions of First Ray Angels and each persons Guardian Angels, to stand as Sentries around each individual doing this meditation, to protect them on all sides, 24 hours a day, 7 days a week, 365 days a year, during waking and sleeping hours.

We call forward the 14 Mighty male and female Elohim to anchor and activate a special Elohim Shield of Protection against all negative thoughtforms from within and without.

We call forth Melchizedek, the Mahatma, and Metatron to bring down a Platinum Net around each individual every morning, afternoon and night before bed for one years time as a special Dispensation of Protection.

We call forth the Divine Mother to place a permanent Platinum Net of Protection around each person's house, and in every doorway, window and opening of their home or apartment.

We call forth the Divine Mother and Lady Masters, to place around each individual a protective field of Pink Love Light, that is so filled with Divine Love that no misqualified energy can penetrate its radiance.

We call forward the Holy Spirit to undo all negative energy and conflict, that has been set in motion in the past, so as to erase the need, as much as possible, for any karmic return of negative energy. We ask that this transmuted energy be used to increase unconditional Love and Service of the Planet.

We call forward the Lord of Arcturus and the Arcturians to bring forward their advanced Arcturian Technology to protect the energy fields of this Son and/or Daughter of GOD.

We call forward Commander Ashtar and the Ashtar Command to overlight this individual with one of your UFO crafts from your Motherships, to protect this individual at night while they sleep and during the day while they demonstrate GOD on Earth.

We call forward Lord Maitreya and Lord Buddha to place around each person a Pillar of Wisdom and Light, which causes all negative energy from within and without to bounce off this Pillar of Wisdom like a rubber pillow.

We call forth to the Seven Chohans to create a "Ring-Pass-Not" around each individual, that serves to create an invulnerable Protective Shield of Protection, that is invincible to negative energy from within and without.

We call forth to Quan Yin to place each person in a Lotus Blossom of Pink Blue Light of Protection.

We call forth to Vywamus and Djwhal Khul to tighten the etheric, emotional, mental, and spiritual webbing of the four-body system, to provide greater Protection as would be GOD's Will.

We call forth Mother Mary to now place around each individual an etheric Rosary filled with the full Protective Powers of Mother Mary Herself in all Her glory.

We call forward the 14 male and female Archangels to place around this individual a special Archangelic Light of Protection, that we request be reinforced every morning and every night as a Divine Dispensation of Protection for this individual.

We call forward the Lord of Sirius and the Lady Master of Sirius, to now fully anchor and activate within each individual their "Anointed Christ Overself Body" and their "Zohar Body of Light" for the purpose of Spiritual Advancement and Greater Protective Light.

We call forth to Lenduce and Sanat Kumara to place around each individual an "Ascension Column of Light" for greater Spiritual Advancement and Protection.

We call forth Isis and Serapis Bey to place around each individual a permanent Pyramid of Golden White Light, that will serve as a Mystical Shield of Protection the rest of this incarnation.

We ask that this enormous Protective Field that has been established be completely cleansed from within, so only Energies of GOD and Christ/Buddha Consciousness live now within this Protective Force Field.

We call forth the entire Planetary and Cosmic Hierarchy from the Three-fold Flame of GOD and the Twelve Cosmic Rays of GOD, and request for a Divine Dispensation of merging your Lightbodies with all doing this meditation, to serve as an invulnerable Shield of Love, Wisdom, and Power the rest of this incarnation so this individual may be free to dedicate their lives to serve GOD and their Brothers and Sisters.

We call forward the Beloved Presence of the Godhead to now permanently anchor and fully activate the Lord's Mystical Body, for the supreme purpose of Protection by your Divine Grace.

I ask each person doing this meditation to now fully claim and own their Personal Power, which will be visualized as holding in their right hand the Blue Flaming Sword of Archangel Michael.

I now ask each person doing this meditation to place around themselves a Golden Bubble of Light to keep out others people's negative energy and any negative energy from your subconscious mind in the form of negative thoughts or negative feelings.

I ask now for each person to fully claim their Unconditional Love and Self-worth, which appears as a Golden/Platinum/Pink Rose in your heart.

I ask each person now to fully claim their attunement to GOD, their own Mighty I Am Presence, and their own Higher Self; which can be visualized as a Tube of Platinum/Gold Light coming down directly from GOD through each person's Mighty I Am Presence, Higher Self, and into each person's Crown Chakra and entire chakra column.

See this Platinum/Golden Light filling your entire 12-body system on a permanent basis.

See this Bubble of Protection keeping out all negative energy, but allowing in all thoughts and feelings of Love, Positivity, and Kindness.

All negative ego fear-based energy and/or separative energy is denied entrance.

I ask each person doing this meditation to now make a commitment to GOD and to yourself, to every moment of your day and night, to never allow a negative thought or negative feeling to enter your consciousness.

Every time a negative thought tries to enter, make a solemn oath to GOD and yourself that you will remain vigilant to push those negative thoughts and feelings out of your mind and you will replace them with only Christ/Buddha Positive Thoughts and Feelings.

Make a firm commitment to GOD and yourself to now never allow yourself to lose your Personal Power again.

Make a firm commitment to GOD and Self in this moment to never give your Power to any person, to your mind, your emotions, your physical body, to fatigue, to your subconscious mind, to your inner child, to lower-self desire, and most of all to the negative ego thought system.

Make a firm commitment in this moment to GOD and to Self to be decisive at all times and to never allow yourself to be indecisive and sit on the fence.

Make a firm commitment in this moment to be vigilant at all times to deny any thought that is not of GOD to enter your mind.

Make a firm commitment in this moment to never allow yourself to have any attachments to anything, only preferences, which hence allows you to be happy if they are taken away.

Make a firm commitment in this moment to look at everything that happens in life as a Teaching, Lesson, Challenge, and most of all a Spiritual Test.

In this moment, make a firm commitment that you will pass every test to the best of your abilities and if you don't you will forgive yourself, learn the lesson, gain the Golden Nugget of Wisdom and do better the next time.

Make up your mind in this moment that you will fully claim your Personal Power in an Unconditionally Loving Manner even in relationship to the inner plane Ascended Masters and in relationship to GOD, who wants you to own your Power and your True Identity as the Eternal Self.

Make a 100% commitment now to GOD and Self that you will be a Spiritual Warrior on Earth for GOD and Unconditional Love and no matter what happens in life and no matter how you are tested you will not give up, even for an instant.

As you make this commitment, Archangel Michael, Faith, Melchizedek, the Mahatma, Archangel Metatron, His Holiness the Lord Sai Baba, Your Guardian Angels, the Legions of Angels of Archangel Michael and Faith, and all the Masters helping in this meditation, all step forward in front of you and bow to you in respect as the Spiritual Master you are in truth.

Lord Melchizedek, the Mahatma, Metatron, and Archangel Michael now anoint you with Their "Light Rods" on the top of your head.

They also wave Their collective "Light Rods" around your auric field to permanently seal all the work that has been done in this meditation.

They bid you now to go forward, handing you one last Gift which They place in your left hand which is the "Rod of Love, Wisdom, and Power."

They bid you to go forth in absolute knowingness that you are now completely protected, for the Ascended Hosts are protecting you and even more importantly, you are protecting yourself as well.

The inner plane Ascended Hosts make one final request of you which is to every morning, when first arising, re-attune to this meditation for at least 30 seconds.

They say that it will be there 100% even if you don't; however, it is important for the conscious mind to re-attune each morning even if just for a second, to resolidify it for the conscious mind to keep the GOD Flame of Self-Mastery ever-present in your conscious mind.

They also request in extreme situations when testing may be occurring that this meditation be done every day, and even twice a day if necessary, until 100% Self-Mastery and Protection is fully established again, which is your Natural God-state!

So let it be Written! So let it be Done!

Namaste!

To reactivate this Meditation anytime you need a boost of Protection; call to GOD and the GOD Force and say, "I now request to reactivate the full Love, Wisdom, and Power of Protection of my Protection Meditation!"

7

Planetary World Service Meditations for the Earth

We now call forth the entire Planetary and Cosmic Hierarchy, and all the Archangels and Elohim, to help in this meditation.

We silently and within ourselves, begin this meditation by blessing and sending love to the rain forests.

We ask that the Masters and overlighting Devas of the rain forests carry our personal prayers into the collective consciousness of those who execute their power, to render decisions upon the fate of the rain forests.

We now join with each other to form a group conscious prayer that links us with the group body of those who share the same concern, over the preservation of the rain forests.

We call upon the Earth Mother to support us in this prayer.

We call once again upon the Masters and the overlighting Deva of the rain forests, and ask to be assisted in building a group thoughtform that is strong enough to affect the thoughtforms of those who wish to destroy these sacred woodlands.

We ask that truth be revealed, and that all alike may see and intuit the preciousness of these hallowed grounds, and know that it is in Divine Order that the rain forests be left to thrive.

We now visualize these forests thriving healthily, and functioning in wonderful harmony with humanity and all the various kingdoms of evolution upon this planet.

We give thanks to all the various Devas and Elementals, who help to maintain the growth of the rainforests, and to the forests themselves.

We now allow ourselves to smell the forest, and to feel the gentle breezes of the woodland as they caress us in Love, and we caress them with the same Love.

We meditate now for a few moments upon the harmony of all nature.

(*Allow time for silence*)

For the Second stage of this meditation, we now invoke the presence of beloved Commander Ashtar and the entire Ashtar Command, as well as the beloved Lord of Arcturus, and the Arcturians who serve with him.

We now ask that they use their combined energies to sweep across the entire planet, and to vacuum up all pollution that has lodged itself within Earth's atmosphere, on a physical, etheric, astral, and mental level.

We now watch as all the pollutants that humanity has let loose within the physical and psychic atmosphere of our world, are lifted up upon this energy stream, to be rendered neutral and harmless, aboard their ships.

Feel a wonderful sense of purity and cleanliness pervade the entire planet.

While watching this cleansing process take place, we also ask them to use their advanced technologies to help repair the ozone layer all around the globe, as well as balancing out the greenhouse effect.

Feel the joy within at the making of these requests, for we are helping to create our world, as GOD would have it be.

(*Allow a moment of silence*)

We now give thanks to the Lord of Arcturus, and Commander Ashtar, and all those who work beside them, for their help in this meditation.

For our last segment of this meditation, we now call forth the entire Planetary and Cosmic Hierarchy.

We ask them to send their combined healing radiance and touch, in order that any auric holes, leakages, spots, and irritations in the aura of the Earth be healed.

Sit and bathe in this most Divine Radiance, as we now feel this enormous healing and cleansing taking place by the Grace of these noble Planetary and Cosmic Masters.

Feel health and vitality returning to the Earth, and all that dwell thereon.

(*Allow time for silence*)

We now call forth from the Planetary and Cosmic Hierarchy for another Cosmic Love and Light Shower to bathe the Earth the Earth Mother and all Her inhabitants, both physical and etheric in nature.

Allow this Love and Light Shower to now fully penetrate the Earth, and fill her with this Divine downpouring of energies.

Silently and deeply, thank all of the Planetary and Cosmic Masters who have aided the Earth in this healing.

We now call forth to our inner plane Spiritual Hosts this weekend, for our group Merkabah to take us back from Shamballa to Earth, since we have been bi-located there all day.

Let us now glide gently and comfortably back into our physical vehicles.

Core Fear Matrix Removal Program for the Earth Mother Herself And for All of the People of the Earth

We begin by calling forth the inner plane Cosmic and Planetary Ascended Masters, and the One Million Masters in attendance for this year's Wesak Celebration.

We ask that the "Core Fear Matrix Removal Program" be brought into effect for the Collective Body for all People of the Earth, and the Earth Mother as well.

We request that any and all fear within the Four Lower Bodies of Earth Mother and the Collective Body of the People of the Earth, be Lifted, Vacuumed Up, and Completely Removed at this time.

We watch with our Inner Eye, as these black and gray weeds are pulled from the Energy Fields of the Earth Mother and Ourselves, and are lifted directly out of our Collective Subconscious Minds and Twelve-Body System.

All that is of a fearful and negative ego nature within the Bodies of the Earth Mother and the Collective People of the Earth, are now being Transmuted into Energy that shall be used only for a Positive Christed Purpose.

In place of the fear that has been removed, we now ask the Cosmic and Planetary Hierarchy to replace it with Unconditional Divine Pure Love.

As part of the Earth Mother and the Collective People of the Earth, we feel this Love filling our Physical, Etheric, Emotional, Mental, and Spiritual Bodies now.

We give Thanks to the Glorious Beings who have Assisted the Earth and Ourselves in this Planetary World Service Work.

Bridging the Extraterrestrials with the Consciousness of Humanity to Prepare for more Open Dialogue

For the next Segment of our Meditation: We call forth the Entire Cosmic and Planetary Hierarchy, as well as all the Christed Extraterrestrial Races currently working with the Earth.

We also open ourselves up to The Arcturians, The Ashtar Command, and The Confederation of Planets that have come from other worlds in order to assist the Earth in its Evolution.

We now Pray and Visualize for the most Spiritually Attuned Political Leaders being Elected into Office.

We ask the Hierarchy and Christed Extraterrestrial Races to Intercede in whatever manner that they are able, in order to place Lightworkers in these Key Political Positions.

We also ask for the Mass Consciousness of the World itself to begin to open to Greater and Greater awareness and acceptance of these Wonderful Extraterrestrials Beings who have come to Aid us in our Evolution

We also Pray and Visualize for all the Lightworkers of the world to become clearer in their Attunements to the Work of our Extraterrestrial Brothers and Sisters.

We see with our Inner Vision, the Governments of the Planet Openly Communicating with our Space Brethren, for the Purpose of the Betterment of Earth, and the Cooperation of our Planet with Divine Intent.

We Pray and Visualize that the People of the Earth become more aware and educated, through the Intervention of Governmental Leaders taking a stand for "Truth," as to the Reality and Purpose of our Space Brothers and Sisters.

We also see with our Inner Vision how the Lightworkers of the Planet are able to work Openly and Collectively upon their Particular Mission, in Mutual Cooperation with this Confederation of Planets.

We can feel the Joy of all of the people of the Earth, as well as that of our Space Brothers and Sisters, as together we participate in Manifesting the Plan of GOD and bringing the Earth forward into Even Higher Frequencies of Light, Love, Power and the Will-to-Good.

We take a few moments to connect ourselves with Incoming Transmissions from the Lord of Arcturus, the Arcturians, and from Commander Ashtar and The Ashtar Command. We are now receiving it through the "Universal Language of Light."

We Bathe in this Wonderful Outpouring of Grace and Connectedness.

We make one final prayer to all the "Christed Extraterrestrial Races gathered here," not just the Arcturians and Ashtar Command, but all Christed Extraterrestrial Races, that you make yourself openly physically known to the people of the Earth as soon as possible. We ask for this so we may accelerate the Divine Plan for Earth and the Full Realization of the Seventh Golden Age.

As one of the Main Collective Groups of Spiritual Leaders on this Earth, we invoke this Divine Dispensation for the Earth now, if this Prayer be in Harmony with GOD's Will.

We thank the Cosmic and Planetary Hierarchy, and all the Christed Extraterrestrial Races, for all Past, Present, and Future Help you have Brought and Will Bring.

As one of the Main Earthly Spiritual Leadership Groups of this Planet, we Hold Out our Hands in Friendship to You, and are officially requesting your Full Help and Support on all Levels of Earth's Evolution as soon as it is possible to help bring in the New Millennium in Full Realization of the Divine Plan, as GOD would have it be!

Amen!

Mass Implant and Negative Elemental Removal for the Entire Planet

For our final Planetary World Service Meditation we call upon the Cosmic and Planetary Hierarchy to assist now in Neutralizing and Eliminating all Negative Implants and Negative Elementals within each of our Four Lower Bodies...

We ask the Cosmic and Planetary Hierarchy to now Remove all Negative Implants and Elementals within all of the people of the Earth, as well as from all the Animals of the Earth, and from the Earth Herself...

Feel a Lightness come over your Entire Being and let this Lightness Flow across the Globe as you Visualize, See and Feel all Implants and Elementals of a Negative Nature now Being Removed Altogether.

We ask Beloved Archangels Michael and Faith for Extra Protection against any further Negative Implants being Installed in the Future, for Ourselves, our Pets and the Earth.

We now call forth from the Cosmic and Planetary Hierarchy for a Final Platinum Net of Cleansing for Ourselves and all of Planet Earth.

We also now call forth a Downpouring from the Presence of GOD and the Cosmic and Planetary Hierarchy, of Platinum Gold Light to Fill our Own 12-Body System and to Fill the 12-Body System and Aura of the Entire Earth and All Her Inhabitants...

Let us Be Still and Receive this final Blessing now, from GOD and The Cosmic and Planetary Hierarchy.

We thank all the Beloved Beings of the Cosmic and Planetary Realms who have been of Assistance during this Meditation.

We now call forth our Inner Plane Spiritual Host this weekend, to again bring forth our Group Merkabah, to take us back from Shamballa to Earth, as we have been bi-located there all day.

Let us all Gently, Comfortably, and Easily Glide Back into our Physical Vehicles.

When you are ready, you can open your eyes!

Invocation of Liberation for All Souls who are Earthbound and/or Are Trapped in the Astral Plane

We now call forth a Semi-permeable Bubble of Golden/White Light of protection.

We invoke the inner plane Planetary and Cosmic Ascended Masters, the Archangels and Elohim for help in this Meditation.

In whatever way we each are personally bound to the Earth or trapped within the lower caverns of our own nature, we now ask for the Divine Assistance of the Masters to help to set us Free!

On behalf of any of our Brothers and Sisters who are specifically trapped within the lower astral realms, and are tied or held to the Earth in any unhealthy manner, may immediately be assisted to make their full transition to the inner planes, in order to continue their Evolution.

We ask and invoke the Masters and Angels aid to help awaken these Earthbound Souls to their situation, that they may willingly and joyfully let go of all attachments that no longer serve them and seek their rightful place within the Many Mansions of GOD.

We Pray that they accept the help being offered them in this moment, and joyfully find their Higher Purpose within the Light.

We ask that any negativity or astral residue that we may have unknowingly taken in be immediately removed by the Masters.

Amen!

Healing any Auric Holes, Spots, Irritations, and Leakages in the Physical, Etheric, Astral, and Mental Body of Planet Earth

We call upon the entire Planetary and Cosmic Hierarchy, all Archangels and all Elohim, for help in this Meditation.

We ask you to all send your Healing Radiance in order that any personal auric holes, leakage's, spots and irritations within the four lower bodies of all Gathered here in this esteemed group, now Be 100% completely healed.

We now Request that you collectively radiate your Cosmic Healing Energies in order to plug up any leakage's, auric holes, and to clear up all spots and irritations in the physical, etheric, astral and mental bodies of the Planet as a Whole.

Feel the Divine Aura Surrounding and Penetrating the Entire Planet as we make this Invocation. Feel, See, and Visualize Health and Vitality returning to the Earth and all that Dwell Thereon.

Sit and Bathe in this most Divine Radiance and Benediction, as you feel this enormous Healing and Cleansing taking place as millions of Masters and Angels are on the job!

Drink in the Aura of Divinity within all your Four Lower Bodies and all your Spiritual Bodies as well.

Let us Sit and Meditate upon the Divine Healing that is now occurring for the Earth, and Each One of Us, who have Prayed on Her Behalf.

(*Allow time for silence*)

Anchor your Grounding Cord and Feet Chakra with their Roots, into the Core of the Earth, and Radiate your own Love and Light into Her.

Accept back the Earth Mother's all encompassing love, as it is radiated to you through the Stream of Light moving through your Grounding Cord.

Silently and deeply thank all of the Planetary, and Cosmic Masters and the Earth Mother herself, who have aided the Earth and ourselves in this healing.

Endangered Species and The Tender Handling of the Animal Kingdom

We call forth all the Planetary and Cosmic Masters, Archangels, and the Elohim.

We now officially call forth to all the Masters gathered for help for the Endangered Species of our World, to help put a Stop to Animal Abuse in Any and Every Kind, and to help in its place promote the Tender Handling of the Animal Kingdom.

Visualize the Animals of the Wild Roving Freely about, following their Natural Instincts without interference by unconscious people. See the Forests and Jungles free and clear of any Traps that could Potentially Harm these Animals.

Allow your Visualization to expand to include Tenderness to all Animals. See Alternatives being Imprinted upon the mind of all people, which will allow the knowledge that is currently sought through animal experimentation to Utterly Cease Being, replaced instead by Loving and

Harmless forms of study and experimentation. Hear within the Joy, as all Animals know that they are free to follow their own destiny without any harmful interference by man.

Now let your thoughts and feelings drift to Divine Harmony between all people and our Animal Brothers and Sisters. See the loved and cared for animal, living, learning, loving and evolving along with the people of the Earth.

Go deep within to that place where Love alone Abides, and that time where the Lion shall indeed lay down with the Lamb!

Feel the Utter Joy that exists between the Kingdom of the people of the Earth and the Kingdom of Animals.

Meditate, See, Feel, and Visualize upon this harmony.

(*Allow time for silence*)

When you are complete, you can very slowly and gently open your eyes bringing all this Love and Joy with you!

We now call forth His Holiness Lord Buddha, to serve as the High Priest for all inner plane Masters gathered here, and we ask you Lord Buddha for your last Silent Blessing and Benediction upon this Esteemed Group of Masters, who have all come in service of the One. We ask to receive your final Silent Blessing and Benediction now…

Thank you Beloved Lord Buddha

Let us all hold hands!

My Musical friends, Let the Songs of God begin!

Integration and Harmony between the Human, Elemental, and Angelic Kingdoms

We begin this Planetary World Service Meditation by calling forth GOD, Christ, The Holy Spirit, the entire Planetary and Cosmic Hierarchy and the One Million Inner Plane Masters in attendance at this Platinum Wesak celebration!

We call forth a Platinum Net from Melchizedek, The Mahatma and Archangel Metatron to remove any imbalanced energies!

We now call forth Lord Buddha, Lord Maitreya, The Seven Chohans and Djwhal Khul to perfectly Balance the energies in this bi-location experience that is still going on to prepare us for Meditation and Planetary World Service Work!

We call forth Archangels Michael and Faith, to place a Platinum/Golden Dome of Protection around this Entire Meditation Experience!

We now pray to all the Overlighting Masters, and we ask that all the people of the Earth Individually set their Intention to work in Harmony with the Nature Spirits, Devas, Elementals and all of the Angels and Lesser Builders, as well as the Archangels and Elohim!

Within our Inner Vision and Imagination, we can see the Elementals and Nature Spirits at Work within the Grasslands, Meadows, Gardens, Forests, Oceans, Lakes, Rivers, within the Currents and Streams of Air, Wind and the Movement of the Seasons.

We see these Beings, Dancing within the Flames that Heat the Earth and Warm our Bodies, within the Great Fire of the Sun.

We ask and pray that all the People of the Earth be Attuned to this Harmony and Synergy between the Three Lines of Evolution: Angelic, Human and Elohim or Elemental!

We now call forth a Light and Love Shower from GOD, Christ, the Holy Spirit, and all the Masters in Attendance!

We now Breathe this Love Outward to these other Streams and Lines of Evolution, who share the Work and the Glory of Establishing the Seventh Golden Age upon our World!

We seek them to know us as Beings of Light and Love, and we likewise Acknowledge them as such Beings!

We Ask and Pray to GOD and the Godforce that this cooperation may be manifested for all on Earth!

We Call upon the Masters to help Guide Us, that all the People of the Earth may Walk Gently upon the Soil, and that all Actions are in Harmony with the Purpose of the Whole, which includes the Divine Purpose of the Nature Spirits and Elementals!

We Ask and Pray that all the People of the Earth are Guided and Shown how to Properly Respect and Honor them, and request the same from them, that we may all work in Closer Cooperation!

We especially invoke the Guidance and Direction of the Great Archangels and Elohim!

We Pray for a "Special Divine Dispensation" that this entire Prayer/Meditation and Light Service continue unceasingly until this Prayer is made fully manifest on the Earth!

We now Visualize and Meditate upon the Love, Joy and Peace of this Divine Cooperation and Integration of the People of the Earth and the Angelic and Elohim or Elemental Lines of Evolution!

We give thanks for the work of the Nature Spirits and Elementals, for the Lesser Builders, the Angels, the Grace of the Archangels and the Elohim, and the Service Work of the Noble Lightworkers on Earth!

We establish our Grounding Cord within the Earth and in so doing make a Deeper Connection from Spirit to Earth!

Amen!

Core Fear Matrix Removal Program For The Earth Mother Herself and For All of Humanity

We now move to our second World Service Meditation!

We again call forth GOD, Christ, the Holy Spirit, and the Planetary and Cosmic Hierarchy!

We ask that the "Core Fear Matrix Removal Program" be Brought into Effect for the "Collective Body of Humanity," and include Ourselves in this, and for the "Earth Mother"!

We request that Any and All fear within the Four Lower Bodies of the Earth Mother, and the Collective Body of Humanity, be Lifted, Drawn out, and Completely Removed!

We Watch with our Inner Eye as these black weeds are taken from the Inner Field of the Earth Mother and Lifted Directly into the "Pure Light of GOD and the Godforce"!

All that is of a fearful and negative nature within the Bodies of the Earth Mother and the Collective of Humanity are now being Transmuted into Energy that shall be used only for Positive Purposes!

In place of the fear that has been Removed, we now ask Spirit and all the Masters gathered to fill all the Empty Spaces with Unconditional Divine Love!

As Part of the Earth Mother and the Collective of Humanity, we Feel this Love Filling our Physical, Etheric, Emotional/Astral and Mental Bodies!

We give thanks to Spirit and the Glorious Masters, who have and who are Assisting us in this Planetary World Service Work!

We also make a special Prayer to the Holy Spirit to undo all Negative Ego within the Earth and all the People of the Earth and bring it back to the "Atonement or At-one-ment"!

Extend your Grounding Cord deep Within the Earth's Core!

Send or Channel Love through that Cord and Feel the Nectar of this Divine Love Bathe You in its Sanctified Light!

We call forth a second "Divine Dispensation" that this Service Prayer of the "Core Fear Matrix Removal Process" and this Prayer of undoing by the Holy Spirit now continue unceasingly until all remnants of the negative ego have been removed from the people of the Earth and the Earth Mother and all Her Kingdoms!

We request that this World Service Prayer and Work will not be stopped by Spirit and the Masters until all negative ego, fear, separation, selfishness, suffering, and faulty thinking has been 100% cleared from the Earth!

We thank Thee and accept this done, as is GOD's Will!

Ashtar Command and Lord of Arcturus:
To Help Vacuum Up Physical Pollution in the Atmosphere
and Help Repair the Ozone Layer

We call forth the Lord of Arcturus, the Lady of Arcturus, the Arcturians, Commander Ashtar and the Ashtar Command!

We also call forth all the Christed Extraterrestrial Races!

We ask and pray that GOD, Christ, the Holy Spirit, the Planetary and Cosmic Hierarchy and you the Christed Extraterrestrials, use your

Advanced Technology to Vacuum Up all negative energies which form the personal pollutants in our own Four-Body System!

We ask for this, so our own bodies may be in a state of increased purity in order that we can serve as a better Vessel for the Service Work that we are Now Engaging in!

We allow for a Moment of Silence as you Visualize any and all imbalanced energies within your Aura being Vacuumed up by these Wonderful Beings.

See these Energies Lift from your Four-Body System, upon a Stream of Light that Serves as a Highly Developed Etheric Vacuum!

This Vacuum will be taken from you and transmuted and neutralized into harmless, neutral energy upon their Great Ships, and by the Masters in their own Mystical Ways!

Trust in their Advanced Technologies to do this work, and enjoy the Feeling of Lightness coming into your Four-Body System now!

We now ask and pray for this exact same prayer for all the people of the Earth, for the Earth Herself, and for the Atmosphere, Air, Rivers, Lakes, and Oceans!

We ask that all pollution, in every sense of the term, now be removed from this Planet and all her Inhabitants, on a Physical, Etheric, Astral, Mental, and Spiritual Level!

Visualize their Combined Technologies Creating a Vacuum that Spans the Globe, and Watch as all the Pollutants that we have let loose within the Four-Body System of the Globe on every Level, are lifted up upon this Light Stream!

See, Feel, and Visualize a Wonderful Sense of Purity and Cleanliness Pervade the Entire Planet.

While still Holding to this Visualization, we also pray to our Christed Extraterrestrial friends and the Masters that you use your Advanced Technologies to help Repair the Ozone Layer all around the Globe!

Continue to sit in Meditation for awhile; Seeing, Feeling and Visualizing a Lightness, Purity and Healing taking place both within your own Four-Body System and within the Four-Body System of all the people of the Earth and the Earth Herself!

Visualize all the Pollutants being Vacuumed out of Earth's Atmosphere, and Feel the Incredible Love and Compassion of these Wonderful Beings who are helping us according to our Prayer Request.

We now call forth this day a Third Divine Dispensation "By the Grace of GOD, Christ, the Holy Spirit, the Planetary and Cosmic Hierarchy, and Christed Extraterrestrial Races"!

We hereby pray, as one of the Leading Spiritual Leadership Groups of this Planet, for a Special "Divine Dispensation" that this prayer request and this Planetary World Service Work continue unceasingly seven days a week, 365 days a year, until all "Pollution on every level" is removed from this Planet and all her Inhabitants on every Level!

We ask for this, as is our Divine Right as Sons and Daughters of GOD, Spiritual Leaders, and Members of the Spiritual Hierarchy in Good Standing!

We ask that this "Divine Dispensation" and the two others requested previously, all now be "Officially Granted" by the Grace of GOD and the Godforce, to help this Planet fully realize the Seventh Golden Age and become a Shining Star in the Melchizedek Universe!

We ask that these "Divine Dispensations" that are now being requested continue unceasingly until this is achieved, if this Prayer be in Harmony with GOD's Will!

We Thank Thee and accept this done, as is GOD's Will!

Amen!

Give thanks to the Lord of Arcturus, the Arcturians, and Commander Ashtar and the Ashtar Command, the gathered Masters, Celestial Hosts, and all those who work beside them.

When you have done this, Anchor your Grounding Cord, feel yourself fully in the Body and upon the Earth, and open your eyes, feeling Totally Cleansed and Refreshed!

Amen!

8

GOD and the New Millennium Wesak Ceremony Meditation

Let us begin by closing our eyes.

We begin by calling forth the Entire Planetary and Cosmic Hierarchy, including all the Archangels, Angels, and Elohim, to help in this Meditation.

We call forth a Gigantic Pillar of Light and Ascension Column from Source.

We call forth a Platinum Net from Melchizedek, the Mahatma, and Archangel Metatron to clear any imbalanced energies.

We call forth an Anchoring and Activation of all our Higher Light Bodies called forth in our opening night.

We also now call forth all the Activations that we received in the opening night meditation in the Golden Chamber of Melchizedek!

We call forth all 72 Activations of GOD we experienced in last night's "Revelation of GOD Ascension Activation Meditation."

We now call forth all those Energies of this Entire Wesak Celebration to pour in at this time.

We call forth all the Energies from the Past Five Wesak Celebrations held in Mt. Shasta, to fully open the window for "Mass Ascension" on Planet Earth.

We also call forth at this time all the Energies of the New Millennium, the Grand Alignment, and the Seventh Golden Age to pour into us now!

We call forth the "Core Fear Matrix Removal Program" to remove all core fear and negative ego programming from each person's field individually and collectively, so we are each "Crystal Clear Diamonds of GOD," to begin this Actual Wesak Ceremony Meditation.

We call forth the Holy Spirit to add to this cleansing process by undoing in this "Holy Instant," all negative ego energies of all in attendance from the beginning of time.

We call forth Archangels Michael and Faith to now cut all imbalanced and negative ego cords from the beginning of time, for all in attendance, for all that choose to receive this gift and blessing!

We call forth GOD, Christ and the Holy Spirit for a final "Cleansing and Baptism" in the "Holy Baptismal Water of GOD"!

We call forth all these Energies from all the Wesak Ceremonies being celebrated on Earth from around the world to join with us now.

We call forth all the Energies from the Wesak Ceremony in the Wesak Valley this year and in all Past Years from the beginning of time!

We call forth all the Wesak Energies from all the Wesak Ceremonies going on in the Infinite Universe, and similar ceremonies of a like nature that are Celebrating Unity and Oneness with GOD!

We also call forth a Special Anchoring and Activation of our Twelve Higher Bodies, including the "Zohar Body of Light," the "Anointed Christ Overself Body," "The Higher Adam Kadmon Body," Our "Solar Galactic and Universal Bodies," "The Lord's Mystical Body," and "The Love, Light, and Power Body of GOD."

We call forth the full opening now of all our Chakras, all the Petals in all the Chakras, and all the facets of each Individual Chakra, so we are completely open and receptive to begin this Meditation.

We are now literally going to "Soul Travel" together, to the Wesak Valley in the Himalayas.

There we will experience the "Actual Wesak Ceremony," conducted by the inner plane Ascended Masters.

This Ceremony has been going on every year at the Taurus Full Moon, for eons of time.

Let us now prepare ourselves for this Holy and Sanctified experience, with a "Moment of Silence."

We now call forward our inner plane Spiritual Hosts and ask for the Creation of a "Group Merkabah," in the shape of a "Gigantic Holographic Crystalline Sphere of Light."

We ask now to be taken to the Wesak Valley, in the Himalayas, to experience the Actual Wesak Ceremony.

As we travel now through time and space, feel your energies blending with all the other groups that are participating in the Wesak Ceremony around the Globe this Night.

Let us feel ourselves now descending into the Actual Wesak Valley, joining all the other Ascended Masters, Initiates and Disciples.

See and/or feel the Presence of Lord Maitreya, St. Germain, and Allah Gobi.

See these three Masters standing in a Triangular Formation, around a "Bowl of Water," that sits upon a Very Large Crystal.

See, feel, and/or visualize, all the rest of the Masters of the Spiritual Hierarchy, standing in a Circular Fashion around these Three Masters.

Just prior to the precise moment of the Rising of the Full Moon, which is now upon us on the inner plane, the Expectancy and Excitement begins to build!

As a Special Dispensation, for this Wesak of the year 2000, Melchizedek, Melchior, Helios & Vesta, and Lord Buddha, have Special Attunements and Activations, to accelerate our Personal and Planetary Movement into the New Millennium.

We now begin by calling forth a Permanent Anchoring and Activation of our Higher Self and Mighty I AM Presence.

We watch in profound joy as Helios and Vesta, our Beloved Solar Logos, make their Descent toward the Wesak Valley.

Helios and Vesta now take their place as one, just above the Sacred Spot, where Lord Buddha will soon Descend.

All in attendance hold Silent Reverence as Helios and Vesta now Anchor and Activate, a "Golden Halo of Light" around each person's Third Eye and Crown Chakra.

This Divine Dispensation will serve as a "Baptism of Light" for this entire incarnation and beyond, to connect you permanently with your Solar Source.

Now Descending from the Galactic Core is our Beloved Galactic Logos, Melchior.

He comes with the Specific Mission of Assisting us to fully Anchor and Utilize our Light Bodies upon the Physical Plane.

Melchior does this now by bringing forth a "Special Spiritual Current and Electrical Charge of Energy" into our Chakra Column and 12-Body System.

This Divine Dispensation is now being fully Anchored and Activated as well, into the Etheric/Physical Vehicle.

The Blessing Melchior brings is vital to each and every one of us in order to help bring forth the Full Actualization of the New Millennium upon the Earth.

Melchior now takes his place next to Helios and Vesta.

Now from the Universal Realm comes His Holiness Lord Melchizedek.

Melchizedek forms the Third Part of the "Cosmic Trinity," which floats just above the Sacred Place where Lord Buddha will Momentarily Appear.

Melchizedek comes not only to Honor Lord Buddha and the Sacred Ceremony of Wesak, but also to Honor and Assist those, who have come forth from His Sacred Heart, to Assist in Earth's Evolution.

He comes also to Honor and Bless all the Cosmic and Planetary Masters in attendance, as well as the Planet Earth Herself.

As a Special Activation for the Wesak Ceremony to institute this purpose, Melchizedek brings forth now his "Rod of Light," and touches each person's Crown Chakra.

This causes an instantaneous "Ring of Fire," in the form of a "Figure Eight," to appear in each person's Chakra Column and entire Auric Field.

This "Ring of Fire," in the form of an Infinity Sign, serves to Activate on a Permanent Basis each person's Entire Chakra System, and Enormously Enhances each person's Auric Field and Light Body, on all Planes of Existence.

This Melchizedek Infusion Fills and Bonds each person Eternally, with an Impenetrable Field of Melchizedek Light, Love, and Power...

Feel now the added energies of the "Silent Watchers," on a Solar, Galactic, and Universal Level, come pouring in to add to this Sanctified Moment.

Take a few moments now to Bathe in these Glorious Blessings given forth by our Universal Logos, and the "Silent Watchers," this night.

Sacred Ritualistic Movements and Mantras now Sound Forth, under the Guidance of the Seven Chohans of the Seven Rays.

As the moment of the Rising Moon now takes place, a Supreme and Unparalleled Stillness settles down upon all in attendance.

All Cosmic and Planetary Masters, Initiates, and Disciples, turn with Great Expectation towards the Northeast.

In the Far Distant Northeast, a Tiny Speck can be seen in the Sky.

This Speck gradually grows larger and larger, and the form of the Buddha, seated in a Cross Legged Position, appears.

He is Clad in a "Saffron Colored Robe," and Bathed in Light and Color, with his Hands Extended in Blessing.

While Hovering above the "Bowl of Water," a Great Mantra is sounded forth by Lord Maitreya that is only used once a year at Wesak.

This Invocation sets up an Enormous Vibration of Spiritual Current.

It marks the "Supreme Moment of Intensive Spiritual Effort," of all Initiates and Masters in attendance, for the entire Year.

In this moment let us watch now, Lord Buddha Hovering over this "Bowl of Water," Transmitting his Divine and Cosmic Energies into this Water.

As a Special Dispensation for this Wesak 2000, Lord Buddha, our Planetary Logos, brings forth His "Rod of Initiation."

He now Anchors into each Person in attendance, the Divine Attributes of "Peace and Tranquillity."

Lord Buddha now states that these Divine Attributes that are now being Anchored, are two of the Most Powerful Christ/Buddha Qualities in the Universe.

Feel the "Peace and Tranquillity" now begin to Permeate every Atomic Particle of your Being.

These two qualities, Lord Buddha now states, will serve as a type of Spiritual Anchoring and Activation for all in attendance, on the Inner and Outer Planes.

This Blessing is given forth to help move the Entire Planet into the New Millennium, with Ease and Grace.

Helios and Vesta, Melchior, His Holiness Lord Melchizedek, and the Silent Watchers, now add their Combined Outpouring of Energy, into this already Sanctified Bowl of Water.

This Water now takes on an Intensity of Cosmic Vibrational Frequency Never Before Given Forth.

The Frequency of Grace itself keeps Building and Building, flowing both into the Water, and through Lord Maitreya.

The Energy is then sent forth by Lord Maitreya to the Entire Spiritual Hierarchy, and into all of us who form a part of this Hierarchy on Earth.

Feel this Massive Downpouring of Cosmic Energies, from the Cosmic and Planetary Hierarchy, now flow through Us.

As these Energies move through us, we feel ourselves being transformed into Pure Vessels of Divinity.

We now allow these most Rarefied and Holy Frequencies of Divinity to flow out into the World, and into the Very Core of the Earth Herself.

As these Energies continue to pour in, see the "Bowl of Water," which sits on the "Large Crystal," being passed around the "Gathered Crowd."

See and feel yourself taking a Sip of this Most Holy, Blessed, and Sanctified Water.

Take the "Essence of Light and Love from this Water," and allow it to Integrate into every Cell, Molecule, Atom, and Electron of your Being.

See yourself now walking towards Lord Buddha, Lord Maitreya, and Sanat Kumara.

Feel the Radiance of Pure Love flowing to you from them, as well as The Cosmic Trinity of Helios and Vesta, Melchior, and His Holiness Lord Melchizedek.

Stand now before these Glorious Masters, and share with them on the Inner Plane as to what you feel your Service Work, Mission, and Puzzle Piece is, in God's Divine Plan on Earth.

Take this time also to make any Prayer Requests to GOD and These Masters, for help in Manifesting your Mission.

Also, make any Personal Prayer Request, on Behalf of Yourself or Others.

Let us now take 30 Seconds of Silence, to allow you to make these Prayer Requests.

Feel and Visualize these Prayers being Answered.

Know that you have the Full Love and Support of GOD, and These Most Beloved Cosmic and Planetary Masters.

You now move away from the Crowd, almost Gliding rather than Walking.

You find yourself by a Small Lake surrounded by Magnificent Flowers of Every Color.

Appearing above you now are the 14 Mighty Archangels and the 14 Mighty Elohim.

Feel now these Archangels and Elohim Surround and Caress your Auric Field, with the Touch of their Gentle Wings and Arms.

Immediately feel a Downpouring of Cosmic Current directly from the Archangelic and Elohim Realms.

Feel your Entire 12-Body System, now become Illuminated with Unconditional Love and Translucent Light.

This Divine Dispensation will have an Enormous Accelerating Effect on Each Person's Path of Initiation and Ascension, as a Special Gift from the Archangels and the Elohim.

Bathe and Completely Soak in these Blessings given forth by the 14 Mighty Archangels and the 14 Mighty Elohim, for this Wesak 2000 Ceremony in the New Millennium.

As a Final Divine Dispensation for this actual Wesak Ceremony to help bring in the Seventh Golden Age; the Beloved Presence of GOD now steps forth and Anchors and Activates within each Person's Heart a Divine and Cosmic Increase of the Radiance of each Person's

"Three-Fold Flame," to each Person's Highest Potential, as GOD's Gift on this Most Holy and Sanctified Occasion.

Be still and feel a Most Rarefied "Divine Shaft of Light" now enter your Crown Chakra, and move down your Chakra Column to Ignite your own Personal "Three-Fold Flame," with this Most Sublime and Sanctified Blessing from the Beloved Presence of GOD.

Now allow yourself to Integrate into the Core of your Being, the Full Totality of all the Wesak Energies, set in motion by GOD, Lord Buddha, and this Sanctified Gathering of Planetary and Cosmic Beings this Evening!

Find yourself again Magically Standing within the Ceremonial Circle and Gathering, where the Large Crystal and Bowl stand.

See, Feel, and Visualize, Lord Buddha, begin to Rise and make his Ascent in the Lotus Posture, and begin to now Float Back to the Northeast, to the Realm from whence He came.

As Lord Buddha leaves, He raises his Right Hand, Palm Face Up in Blessing and Love to all who are Gathered Here, on this Most Joyous and Sanctified Occasion.

As Lord Buddha again becomes a Small Speck in the Distance, watch now as Helios and Vesta, Melchior, and His Holiness Lord Melchizedek, also make their Ascent.

Feel again the Depth of the Blessings given forth, as these Glorious Beings return to the Vast Cosmic Realms wherein they Dwell.

See and Feel the Arrival of our inner plane Spiritual Hosts, with their "Gigantic Holographic Crystalline Sphere of Light Merkabah."

Feel yourself now entering this Merkabah, in Total Oneness, Joy, and Love.

Feel again the Tremendous Illumination of Energies in your Auric Field, which has been Vastly Expanded by your Participation in this Experience.

Also feel an Enormous Expansion of Love and Unity for all your Brothers and Sisters, who have Shared this Experience with You.

Feel now the Group Merkabah begin to Rise into the Air above the Wesak Valley.

See and Feel the Merkabah floating now High above the Himalayan Mountains and Begin its Journey back to the United States.

Feel the Merkabah Traveling, through Time and Space, and Magically now beginning to Descend Towards the Mountain of Mt. Shasta.

The Mountain of Mt. Shasta now welcomes us back with Open Arms and an Open Heart to Her Sacred Vortex, and into this Auditorium.

Feel yourself now Gently Entering your Physical Body, bringing all the Light and Love you have just Experienced, Fully and Permanently with You.

Feel yourself now fully connecting with your grounding cord, which is fully anchored to the Core of the Earth.

Feel your feet chakras totally open and feel them again growing roots filling the entire Earth.

Now allow all the Wesak energies from this Meditation and from the entire Weekend Celebration that you have received and are continuing to receive this moment, to flow through you and into the Earth through your feet chakra and root system.

Feel the Earth Mother being now filled with the Light and Love of GOD through each person's channel here in attendance.

Feel the Earth Mother now in total Unconditional Love and Joy, send Her Love and Light back through your feet root system, back to you.

Feel now within yourself both the exquisite mix of receiving the energies from GOD and the Godforce pouring in, as well as from the Earth Mother and the Nature Kingdoms.

Enjoy this final Light and Love Shower from both Heaven and Earth Simultaneously.

Feel the exquisite mixing of these energies within your 12-Body System, completely filling your Auric fields with the perfect mix and Balance of GOD/Goddess Energies.

Feel how good it feels to be fully integrated and balanced on all these levels.

Let us take one last moment now to inwardly thank GOD, all the Masters in attendance, the Earth Mother, and the Nature Kingdoms, for all their Blessings and Gifts in this meditation and for the entire Weekend!

On this note, when you are ready you can open your eyes bringing all the Light and Love you have experienced with you!

As you open your eyes, fully open your Heart Chakra as Wide and Open as it has ever been in your entire life and share your Unconditional Love with your Brothers and Sisters inwardly in this Auditorium for one last moment!

9

The 25 Spiritual Wisdom Pillars of the World's Religions

My Beloved Readers, even though I am not an exact follower of each and every one of the religions I mention in this chapter in terms of the spiritual wisdom principles that each one ascribes to; I think it would be very interesting for you, my readers, to get a quick synthesis overview of the major religions and the teachings and principles they teach. Although here and there a few notions may be just slightly off the mark, overall, I think much can be gained from the study of the world's religions and their teachings. There are many paths back to GOD, and they all lead to the same place. My mission and work is that of "Synthesis"; to show that all paths are really teaching the same thing but using slightly different words, and maybe looking at things from a slightly different lens. This is why the study of the principles of the different world's religions can be interesting, for it just might spark a thought or new spiritual practice that might be useful and can add to your "Full Spectrum" understanding of GOD in all His Glory!

The Four Noble Truths

The first Noble Truth states that suffering and frustration are the result of the difficulty of facing the basic fact of life that everything is impermanent and transitory; "All things arise and pass away."

The second Noble Truth is that the cause of suffering is the clinging to wrong points of view. Out of ignorance people divide the perceived world into individual and separate things, attempting to confine the fluid forms of reality into fixed categories created by the mind.

The third Noble Truth states that suffering and frustration can be ended. It is possible to be free from bondage and to reach the state of total liberation.

The fourth Noble Truth states that it is possible to end all suffering through self-development, which leads to enlightenment; enlightenment is achieved through right seeing, right knowing, right action, right awareness and right meditation.

The Eight-Fold Noble Path

Right Perspective and Understanding

Right Thought

Right Speech

Right Action

Right Livelihood

Right Effort

Right Mindfulness

Right Concentration

The Three Refuges

I take my refuge in the Buddha

I take my refuge in the Dharma (Teachings)

I take my refuge in the Sangha (Spiritual community)

The Six Perfections

Giving

Ethics

Patience

Effort

Concentration

Wisdom

The Four Ripening Factors in Tibetan Buddhism

Giving material aid

Speaking eloquently

Always giving the right counsel

Setting an example by living the principle taught

The Six Vassals of the Zoroastrian Religion

Good Thought

Right Law

Noble Government

Holy Character

Health

Immortality

The Five Duties of the Islamic Faith

Shahadah: to profess belief ("I witness that there is no GOD but Allah,

and the Mohammed is the prophet of Allah.")

Salat: to pray five times a day

Zakat: to give alms to the needy

Saum: to fast in the month of Ramadan

Haj: to make the pilgrimage to Mecca

Jainism

The Five Great Vows

To injure no creature

To speak the truth

To abstain from stealing

To renounce all worldly goods

To practice sexual self-control

The Nine Vows

Not to take human or animal life

Not to be unfaithful to their spouses

Not to lie, steal, or cheat

To give alms

To practice self-denial

To guard against evil

To meditate regularly

To avoid needless travel

Not to be greedy

The Seven Great Egyptian Hermetic Principles

The Principle of Mentalism—"The all is mind: the universe is mental."

The Principle of Correspondence—"As above, so below; As below, so above."

The Principle of Vibration—"Nothing rests; everything moves; everything vibrates."

The Principle of Polarity—"Everything is dual; everything has poles; everything has its pair of opposites; like and unlike are the same; opposites are identical in nature, but different in degree; extremes meet; all truths are but half-truths; all paradoxes may be reconciled."

The Principle of Rhythm—"Everything flows, out and in; everything has its tides; all things rise and fall; the pendulum swing manifests in everything; the measure of the swing to the right is the measure of the swing to the left; rhythm compensates."

The Principle of Cause and Effect—"Every cause has its effect; every effect has its cause; everything happens according to the law; chance is but a name for law not recognized; there are many planes of causation, but nothing escapes the law."

The Principle of Gender—"Gender is in everything; everything has its masculine and feminine principles; gender manifests on all planes."

Judaism

The Ten Commandments of Judaism

And the Angel of the Lord appeared unto Moses in a flame of fire out of the midst of a bush: and he looked, and behold, the bush burned with fire, and the bush was not consumed. GOD called unto him out of the midst of the bush and said, "Moses, Moses." And he said, "Here am I." And he said, "Draw not nigh hither; Put off thy shoes from off thy feet, for the place whereon thou standest is Holy Ground. I am the GOD of thy father, the GOD of Abraham, the GOD of Issac, and the GOD of Jacob."

Moses asked, "What is thy name?" The answer came: "I AM THAT I AM. Thus shalt thou say unto the children of Israel, I AM hath sent me unto you."

"I am the Lord thy GOD, which have brought thee out of the land of Egypt, out of the house of bondage. Thou shalt have no other gods before me. Thou shalt not make unto thee any graven image, or any likeness of any thing that is in Heaven above, or that is in the earth beneath, or that is in the water under the earth. Thou shalt not bow down thyself to them, nor serve them, for I the Lord thy GOD am a GOD that demands obedience, visiting the iniquity of the fathers upon the children unto the third and fourth generation of them that hate me; and showing mercy unto thousands of them that love me, and keep my commandments. Thou shalt not take the name of the Lord thy GOD in vain; for the Lord will not hold him guiltless that taketh his Name in vain. Remember the Sabbath day, to keep it holy. Six days shalt thou labor, and do all thy work, but the seventh day is the Sabbath of the Lord thy GOD; in it thou shalt not do any work, thou, nor thy son, nor thy daughter, nor thy manservant, nor thy maid servant, nor thy cattle, nor thy stranger that is within thy gates; For in six days the Lord made Heaven and Earth, the sea and all this in them, and rested the seventh day; Wherefore the Lord blessed the Sabbath day, and hallowed it."

"Honor thy father and thy mother; that thy days may be long upon the land which the Lord thy GOD giveth thee.

Thou shalt not murder.

Thou shalt not commit adultery.

Thou shalt not steal.

Thou shalt not bear false witness against thy neighbor.

Thou shalt not covet thy neighbor's house; thou shalt not covet thy neighbor's wife, nor his manservant, nor his maidservant, nor his ox, nor his donkey, nor anything that is thy neighbors."

The Thirteen Articles of Faith of Judaism

Faith in GOD, the Creator

His Unity

His Incorporeality

His Eternity

To Him alone worship is due

Belief in the words of the prophets

Moses as the greatest Jewish Prophet

The Revelation of the laws of Moses

The law as unchanging

Belief in GOD's All-Knowledge

His rewards and punishments

The coming of the Messiah

The resurrection of the dead

The Nine Precepts of Shintoism

Do not transgress the will of the Gods

Do not forget your obligation to your Ancestors

Do not offend by violating the decrees of the state

Do not forget the profound goodness of the Gods, through which calamity and misfortunes are averted and sickness is healed

Do not forget that the world is one Great Family

Do not forget the limitation of your own person

Do not become angry, even though others become angry

Do not be sluggish in your work

Do not bring blame to the teachings

The Great Invocation

From the point of Light within the Mind of GOD

Let Light stream forth into the minds of men.

Let Light descend on Earth.

From the point of Love within the Heart of GOD

Let Love stream forth into the hearts of men.

May Christ return to Earth.

From the center where the Will of GOD is known

Let the Purpose guide the little wills of men –

The Purpose which the Masters know and serve.

From the Center which we call the race of men

Let the plan of Love and Light work out

And may it seal the door where evil dwells,

Let Light and Love and Power restore the Plan on Earth.

Hatha Yoga

Abstinence

Observance

Sitting postures

Breath control

Nonattachment to possessions

Bhakti Yoga

Listening

Singing of praise

Meditation

Worship of the feet

Ritual worship

Prostration

Being a slave to GOD

Being a friend

Self-surrender

Raja Yoga

Abstinence

Observance

Renunciation

Silence

Solitude

Proper use of time

Postures

Root Contraction (mula-bandha)

Strengthening the body

Straightening the body

Spiritual sight

Breath control

Pratyahara (Seeing divinity in all perceptible forms)

Contemplation ("The one changeless thought, I am the principle, the Brahman, with no other notion, is known under the name of contemplation and is the giver of Supreme Bliss."—*The Upanishads*)

Identification ("When the very notion of contemplation is forgotten, this is known as identification" –*The Upanishads*)

Jana Yoga

The Four States of Mind

The dispersed state

The past approach

The grasped state

The merging state

The Seven Obstacles

Good will

Reflection

Subtlety of mind

Perception of reality

Freedom from leaning toward the world

Disappearance of visible forms

The unmanifest state

Six Principles That Lead to Liberation

Discrimination

Renunciation

The three accomplishments (tranquility, sense restraint, actions totally in harmony with GOD)

Endurance

Mental collectedness

Faith

Mantra Yoga
(Repeating the Names of GOD)

Twelve Types

Daily Japa (repeating names of God) is usually done in the morning and evening.

Circumstantial Japa, which is usually done on Festival Days.

Japa that is done for some specific desired goal.

Forbidden Japa, which is done without discipline and with wrong pronunciation.

Japa that is done for penance.

Moving Japa, which is done through the day.

Voice Japa, which is done out loud.

Whispered Japa.

Bee Japa, in which the mantra is murmured so it sounds like the hum of a bee.

Mental Japa, which is done solely in the mind.

The uninterrupted Japa, (which is for those who have renounced the world) is done continuously.

Japa that is done with beads or a rosary.

The Sixteen Steps of Mantra Yoga

Devotion

Purity

Posture

Observances of the calendar which is based on Astrological under-standings and which defines Celebrations, fasts, and so on.

The way of conduct

Concentration

The search for the inner divine countries. These inner countries are considered the abodes of deities, masters, and gurus on the inner plane.

Breath control

Gesture

Water offerings

Fire offerings

Ritual Sacrifice

Ritual Worship

Repetition of mantras, words of power, and names of GOD

Contemplation

Identification

Kundalini Yoga

The Eight Steps

Observances and abstinences

Purification

Courage

Steadiness

Endurance

Subtlety

Direct evidence

Thoughtless identification

Shiva Yoga

The Five Parts

Knowledge of Shiva

Devotion to Shiva

Contemplation of Shiva

Observances of the austerities connected with Shiva

Ritual worship of Shiva

Hinduism and The Teachings of Sai Baba

There is only one religion, the religion of love.

There is only one language, the language of the heart.

There is only one race, the race of humanity.

There is only one GOD and He is Omnipresent.

10

My Favorite 157 Synthesis Names of GOD

I now officially recite and call forth:

GOD

GOD, CHRIST, and the HOLY SPIRIT

FATHER/MOTHER GOD

HEAVENLY FATHER CREATOR

PRIME CREATOR

GOD/GODDESS ALL THAT IS

I AM THAT I AM

I AM

THE MIGHTY I AM PRESENCE

BRAHMA, SHIVA, VISHNU (Creator, Destroyer, Preserver)

ALLAH

THE BUDDHA

RA

THE HIGHER SELF

THE OVERSOUL

THE ETERNAL SELF

THE COSMIC OVERSOUL

THE MONAD

THE COSMIC MONAD

LORD

ATMA

SUGMAD

YHWH (Yahweh)

THE ALL THAT IS

THE OVERSELF

THE COSMIC OVERSELF

ELOHIM

THE LOGOS

THE HOLY SPIRIT

SHEKINAH (Holy Spirit)

COSMIC SELF

TETRAGRAMATRON

JEHOVAH

THE DIVINE FATHER

THE ANCIENT OF DAYS

LORD GOD

SPIRIT

SUPERCONSCIOUS MIND

SUPREME GURU

EH HAY EH (I Am)

THE DIVINE PRESENCE

THE SUPREME BEING

THE ETERNAL FATHER

THE STILL SMALL VOICE WITHIN

THE VOICE OF THE DOVE

THE KING OF THE HEAVENS

THE MESSIAH OF THE MESSIAH

THE LORD OF LORDS

THE KING OF KINGS

THE LORD OF LIGHT

THE LORD OF LOVE

UNIVERSAL MIND

SOURCE

GODHEAD

DIVINE MIND

COSMIC MIND

FATHER

INFINITE SPIRIT

I AM, I WAS, I WILL BE

THE SELF EXISTENT ONE

OMNIPOTENT, OMNISCIENT, AND OMNIPRESENT ONE

I AM PRESENCE

THE SUPREME I AM

THE UNNAMED ONE

THE ETERNAL LIGHT

DEITY

ANCIENT-RECENT-FUTURE OF DAYS

THE LIVING LIGHT OF LOVE

THE AUTHOR OF LIFE

THE COMFORTER

THE TRINITY

SOVEREIGN LORD

THE HOLY GREAT ONE

THE HOLY NAME

LORD GOD OF HOSTS

SOVEREIGN LORD OF ARMIES

MOST HIGH GOD

LORD OF LORDS

LIVING GOD

GOD OF GODS

ETERNAL LORD OF LIGHT

ALMIGHTY ETERNAL LORD

DIVINE VOICE

GOD THE ABSOLUTE

THE PRESENCE OF GOD

THE TRINITY OF TRINITIES

SUPREME-ULTIMATE ABSOLUTE

SUPREME TRINITY

TRINITY ABSOLUTE

REVEALING FATHER

THE LIVING EVERLASTING LIGHT

LIVING FATHER

DIVINE SOURCE

SUPREME LORD

LIVING LORD

LIVING GOD

LIVING CREATOR

EXALTED ONE

ALMIGHTY GOD

KING OF THE UNIVERSE

OH LORD OUR GOD

FATHER OF THE ETERNAL LIGHT

LIMITLESS LIGHT

THE GREAT SPIRIT

SUPREME MANIFESTATION

LORD OF THE LORDS

LORD GOD

THE HOST OF THE HEAVENS

THE HOST OF DELIVERANCE

LORD OF THE HEAVENS

THE PRESENCE

THE ONE

THE ONE WHO IS AND WILL BE MANIFEST

DIVINE ETERNAL FATHER

ETERNAL PRESENCE

OH LORD

THE PRESENCE OF THE FATHER

SOURCE OF ALL LIFE

OH GREAT I AM

SUPREME FORM BEHIND ALL FORMS

LIVING GODHEAD

SACRED TRINITY LOGO

MOST HIGH

THE LORD GOD ALMIGHTY

SPIRIT OF TRUTH

GODSELF

HOLY NAME

THE DIVINE ARCHITECT

THE RIGHTEOUS KING

THE FLAMING NAME

DIVINE IMAGE

KING OF KINGS

THE DIVINE MIND OF ALL DIVINE MINDS

THE DIVINE NAME

THE LORD GOD OF HOSTS

THE DIVINE PRESENCE

KING OF UNIVERSES

CREATOR GOD

KING OF LOVE, JUSTICE AND RIGHTEOUSNESS

THE FIRST CAUSE

THE MAHADEVA

KU, KAN, KANOLA (Trinity in Hawaiian)

AUMAKUA

THE TAO

THE VOID

THE NOTHINGNESS

THE EVERYTHING

AME-NO-MI-MAKA-NUSHI (GOD in Shintoism)

AHURA MAZDA (Manifest Creator in Zoroastrian Religion)

ZEROANA AKERNE (Unmanifest Creator in Zoroastrian Religion)

UNMANIFEST AND MANIFEST CREATOR

THE UNIVERSAL SELF

THE MULTIDIMENSIONAL SELF

THE ALL

THE COSMIC MIGHTY I AM PRESENCE

KING OF THE OMNIVERSE

GOD OF THE COSMIC SOUL

11

The 275 Divine Spiritual Qualities of GOD

GOD IS LOVE

GOD IS OMNIPOTENT

GOD IS OMNISCIENT

GOD IS OMNIPRESENT

GOD THE VICTORIOUS

GOD IS LIGHT

GOD IS POWER

GOD THE ENLIGHTENER

GOD THE CREATOR

GOD THE PRESERVER

GOD THE DESTROYER

GOD THE SYNTHESIZER

GOD IS PEACE

GOD IS BLISS

GOD IS THE INEXPRESSIBLE ABSOLUTE REALITY

GOD IS JOY

GOD IS GREAT

GOD THE COMPASSIONATE ONE

GOD THE MERCIFUL

GOD IS FIXED DESIGN

GOD IS ONENESS

GOD IS WISDOM

GOD IS KNOWLEDGE

GOD IS ACTIVE INTELLIGENCE

GOD IS BEAUTY

GOD IS HARMONY

GOD IS SPIRITUAL SCIENCE

GOD IS DEVOTION

GOD IS CEREMONIAL ORDER AND MAGIC

GOD IS LIBERATION

GOD IS FAITH

GOD IS PATIENCE

GOD IS ALMIGHTY

GOD THE MOST HIGH

GOD THE LORD OF THE UNIVERSE

GOD THE LIMITLESS LIGHT OF THE ABSOLUTE

GOD THE DIVINE LORD OF LIGHT

GOD THE ALMIGHTY LIVING GOD

GOD THE LORD OF THE EARTH

GOD THE ANCIENT OF DAYS

GOD THE SUPREME GURU

GOD IS HE WHO DRAWS US TO HIM

GOD THE SUPREME WHO IS ONE BUT WHOSE NAMES ARE MANY

GOD THE BENEFICENT

GOD THE MAJESTIC

GOD THE FORGIVER

GOD THE OPENER

GOD THE INITIATOR

GOD THE SUPREME HIEROPHANT

GOD THE AUM

GOD THE OM

GOD IS THE DIVINE IMAGE

GOD IS THE DIVINE TRINITY

GOD THE RIGHTEOUS

GOD THE DIVINE PERSONALITY

GOD THE DELIVERER

GOD IS THE COVENANT

GOD IS THE ALPHA AND OMEGA

GOD IS THE ETERNAL LIGHT

GOD IS THE BEGINNING WORD OF LIFE

GOD IS SALVATION

GOD IS DIVINE JUDGEMENT

GOD IS SPLENDOR

GOD IS UNDERSTANDING

GOD IS LOVING KINDNESS

GOD IS DIVINE JUSTICE

GOD IS DIVINE ORDER

GOD IS THE PEACE THAT PASSETH UNDERSTANDING

GOD IS THE NAME OF NAMES

GOD THE UNFATHOMABLE

GOD THE UNLIMITED

GOD IS THE DIVINE COMMANDMENTS

GOD IS HOLY

GOD IS THE LIGHT AND THE POWERS

GOD IS THE PROVIDER

GOD IS THE WORD

GOD IS MY BANNER

GOD IS MY ADMONISHER

GOD IS MY HIGH STANDARD

GOD IS PERFECTION

GOD IS THE GREAT NAME

GOD IS THE GIVER

GOD IS THE COMFORTER

GOD IS THE GUIDE

GOD IS THE ANNOINTER

GOD IS THE INSPIRER

GOD IS THE INDWELLER

GOD IS THE QUICKENER

GOD IS THE REVEALER

GOD IS THE SANCTIFYER

GOD IS THE TEACHER

GOD IS THERE

GOD IS RIGHT FOCUS AND DEDICATION

GOD IS OUR RIGHTEOUSNESS

GOD IS OUR ETERNAL PROTECTOR

GOD IS GRACIOUS

GOD IS THE ESTABLISHER

GOD KNOWS

GOD SETS UP

GOD IS EXALTED

GOD IS MERCY

GOD IS THE WORD

GOD IS ABSOLUTE

GOD IS BENEVOLENCE

GOD IS WISDOM

GOD IS FAITH

GOD IS TEACHING

GOD IS ENDURANCE

GOD IS PURITY

GOD IS DEEDS

GOD IS NAMES

GOD IS EGOLESSNESS

GOD IS INCOMPARABLE LOVE

GOD IS MANIFESTATION

GOD IS DELIVERANCE

GOD IS MAJESTY

GOD IS REVELATION

GOD IS AWE

GOD IS GRANDEUR

GOD IS THE DELIVERER

GOD IS THE HELPER

GOD IS SUPREME TRUST

GOD IS MY REFUGE

GOD IS MY STRENGTH

GOD IS THE DIVINE LOVER

GOD IS REDEMPTION

GOD IS LIBERATION

GOD IS RESURRECTION

GOD IS TRANSLATION

GOD IS ASCENSION

GOD IS TRANSFORMATION

GOD IS ALCHEMY

GOD IS TRANSMUTATION

GOD IS TRANSFIGURATION

GOD IS RENUNCIATION

GOD IS REGENERATION

GOD IS HEALING

GOD IS ETERNITY

GOD IS IMMORTALITY

GOD IS INFINITE

GOD IS COMPASSION

GOD IS RANDOM ACTS OF LOVING KINDNESS

GOD IS THE DEFENDER

GOD IS THE KINGDOM

GOD IS THE GLORY

GOD IS RIGHT FOCUS AND DEDICATION

GOD IS THE INITIATOR

GOD IS THE INFINITE WAY

GOD IS RAPTURE

GOD IS THE REDEEMER

GOD IS EXPANDING

GOD IS CREATIVITY

GOD IS DIVINE ORDER

GOD IS RECONCILIATION

GOD IS THE IMAGE AND SIMILITUDE

GOD IS SYNTHESIS

GOD IS BEATITUDE

GOD IS COMPREHENSION

GOD IS REALIZATION

GOD IS ETERNAL LAW

GOD IS ALL KNOWING

GOD IS REVERENCE

GOD IS BENEVOLENCE

GOD IS CHARITY

GOD IS A FLAWLESS CHARACTER

GOD IS INTEGRITY

GOD IS ETHICS

GOD IS MORALITY

GOD IS HARMLESSNESS

GOD IS DEFENSELESSNESS

GOD IS INVULNERABILITY

GOD IS TRANSCENDENCE OF DUALITY

GOD IS EQUANIMITY

GOD IS PEACE OF MIND

GOD IS EVENMINDEDNESS

GOD IS SELFLESSNESS

GOD IS SERVICE

GOD IS GRATITUDE

GOD IS KINDLINESS

GOD IS APPROPRIATENESS

GOD IS COURTESY

GOD IS CLEANLINESS

GOD IS SELF-SACRIFICING

GOD IS VIRTUE

GOD IS FIRST CAUSE

GOD IS POSITIVITY

GOD IS HOLINESS

GOD IS FEARLESSNESS

GOD IS INNOCENCE

GOD IS RIGHT ATTITUDE

GOD IS PURIFICATION

GOD IS SIMPLICITY

GOD IS ONENESS

GOD IS THE HIGHER WAY

GOD IS TRANSCENDENCE

GOD IS DIVINE DETACHMENT

GOD IS RIGHT THINKING

GOD IS RIGHT FEELING

GOD IS RIGHT ACTION

GOD IS RIGHT MOTIVES

GOD IS RIGHT DESIRES

GOD IS IDEALISM

GOD IS COMMUNICATION

GOD IS CREATIVE ASPIRATION

GOD IS GOOD WILL

GOD IS SPIRITUAL COMMUNION

GOD IS SPIRITUAL BROTHERHOOD

GOD IS OBEDIENCE

GOD IS SURRENDER

GOD IS ACCEPTANCE

GOD IS NONRESISTANCE

GOD IS RITUAL

GOD IS SELF-DISCIPLINE

GOD IS SPIRITUAL FLOW

GOD IS SYNERGY

GOD IS INTEGRATION

GOD IS MODERATION

GOD IS BALANCE

GOD IS RADIANCE

GOD IS INCLUSIVENESS

GOD IS TOLERANCE

GOD IS ORGANIZATION

GOD IS SCIENTIFIC AND MATHEMATICAL

GOD IS DIPLOMACY AND TACT

GOD IS RIGHT TIMING

GOD IS CALMNESS

GOD IS CLEAR VISION

GOD IS EFFICIENT PERCEPTION OF REALITY

GOD IS CHRIST/BUDDHA/SPIRITUAL CONSCIOUSNESS

GOD IS ALL KNOWLEDGE

GOD IS INTUITION

GOD IS INSPIRATION

GOD IS CREATIVITY

GOD IS ALMIGHTY

GOD IS RIGHT DEMONSTRATION

GOD IS PRACTICING THE PRESENCE

GOD IS VIGILANCE

GOD IS INTROSPECTION

GOD IS KNOWING THY SELF

GOD IS COOPERATION

GOD IS SELF-LOVE

GOD IS SELF-WORTH

GOD IS RESPONSIBILITY

GOD IS PRAYER AND MEDITATION

GOD IS LOVE FINDING

GOD IS THE EYES OF LOVE

GOD IS NONVIOLENCE

GOD IS SPIRITUAL VOWS

GOD IS SPIRITUAL ATTUNEMENT

GOD IS LOVING YOUR NEIGHBOR AS YOU LOVE YOURSELF

GOD IS GRACE

GOD IS THE TAO

GOD IS SALVATION

GOD IS ENLIGHTENMENT

GOD IS BUDDHAHOOD

GOD IS CHRISTHOOD

GOD IS UNITY

GOD IS FAITH

GOD IS INCORPOREALITY

GOD IS ETERNITY

GOD IS REVELATION

GOD IS ETERNAL LIFE

GOD IS REVERENCE

GOD IS OBEDIENCE

GOD IS STRENGTH OF SPIRIT

GOD IS PIETY AND FAITH

GOD IS HEALTH AND PERFECTION

GOD IS RIGHT VIEW AND UNDERSTANDING

GOD IS RIGHT THOUGHT

GOD IS RIGHT SPEECH

GOD IS RIGHT ACTION

GOD IS RIGHT LIVELIHOOD

GOD IS RIGHT MEDITATION

GOD IS RIGHT EFFORT

GOD IS RIGHT MINDFULNESS

12

The 72 Most Important Power Names and Mantras of GOD: To Recite Daily and Meditate Upon

There are, in truth, infinite numbers of names of GOD, mantras, and power words of GOD; for GOD is infinite. However, from an Earthly perspective these are the 72 most powerful and profound I have found from an Earthly synthesis point of view and perspective. Use and enjoy them for each one will serve as a profound trigger point and activation to bring a stream and river of GOD into your being.

- GOD

- GOD, Christ, Holy Spirit

- Aum

- So Ham

- Be Still, and Know I Am God!

- Brahma, Shiva, and Vishnu

- Allah

- YHWH

- Jehovah

- Om

- Adonai

- Yod Hay Vod Hay

- Yod Hay Wah Hay

- El Shadai

- El Eliyon

- Elohim

- Om Namah Shivaya

- Om Shanti

- Om Tat Sat (Thou are the Inexpressible Absolute Reality)

- Sai Ram

- Rama (He who fills with abiding joy)

- Hong Sau (I Am He)

- Hari Om

- Hari Om Tat Sat (Om, the Divine Absolute Reality)

- Moses

- Om Sri Rama Jaya Rama Jaya Jaya Rama (Victory for the Spiritual Self)

- I Am That I Am

- Ehyeh Asher Ehyeh (I Am that I Am)

- Allahu Akbar (GOD is Great)

- Bismillah Al-Rahman, Al-Rahim (In the Name of Allah, the Compassionate and Merciful)

- I Am

- I am Love

- Sivo Ham (I am Shiva)

- Sat Nam

- Jesus Christ

- Hail Mary, Full of Grace! The Lord is with Thee. Blessed are Thou amongst Women, and Blessed is the fruit of thy womb, Jesus. Holy Mary, Mother of GOD, Pray for us now, and at the hour of our death.

- Om Mani Padme Hum (The Jewel of Compassion in the Lotus of the Heart)

- Om Ah Hum (come toward me, Om)

- Buddha

- Light, Love, and Power

- Love, Wisdom, and Power

- Quan Yin

- I am the Soul, I am the Light Divine, I am Love, I am Will, I am Fixed Design (Ascended Master Mantra)

- Areeeeeeoooommm (Edgar Cayce's Mantra of Universal Mind)

- Nuk-Pu-Nuk (I Am He I Am) Egyptian

- Ra

- Eck Ong Kar Sat Nam Siri Wha Guru (The Supreme is one, His Names are Many)

- Sh'Mah Yisrael Adonai Elohainu Adonai Chad (Hear, Oh Israel! The Lord Our GOD, the Lord is One!)

- Sai Baba

- Lord Maitreya

- Ha Shem (Blessed is His Name)

- Shekinah (Holy Spirit)

- Hu

- Barukh Ata Adonai (Blessed is the Lord)

- Kadoish, Kadoish, Kadoish Adonai Tsebaoth (Holy, Holy, Holy is the Lord GOD of Hosts)

- Ruach Elohim (Spirit of the Godhead)

- Melchizedek

- Mahatma

- Archangel Metatron

- Archangel Michael

- Divine Mother

- Holy Spirit

- Christ

- Ain Soph Or (Limitless Light of the Absolute)

- Layoo-esh Shekinah (Pillar of Light of the Holy Spirit)

- Yahweh Elohim (Divine Lords of Light and Learning)

- Shaddai El Chai (The Almighty Living GOD)

- Moshe Yeshua Eliahu (Moses, Jesus, and Elijah)

- Hyos Ha Koidesh (Highest Servants of the Ancient of Days)

- Atma (Eternal Self)

- Monad

- Mighty I AM Presence

13

The 72 Holy Masters of GOD: To Call on for Help in your Prayers and Meditations

My Beloved Readers, for your continued enjoyment and edification I share with you "The Holy Masters of GOD" to call upon for help in your Prayers and Meditations. There are obviously an infinite numbers of beings that can be called on in GOD's Infinite Universe; however, these 72 are the most common and well-known from a synthesis point of view. GOD is not limited and neither are you, so if more come to mind please feel free to add them to your list!

1. GOD, Christ, Holy Spirit, Your own Mighty I Am Presence, Your Higher Self

2. Melchizedek

3. The Mahatma (Avatar of Synthesis)

4. Archangel Metatron

5. Archangels Michael and Faith

6. The Divine Mother

7. His Holiness, the Lord Sai Baba

8. Lord Buddha, the Planetary Logos

9. Lord Maitreya, the Planetary Christ

10. Saint Germain, the Mahachohan

11. Allah Gobi, the Manu

12. Helios and Vesta, the Solar Logos

13. Melchior, the Galactic Logos

14. The Lord of Sirius, the Head of The Great White Lodge

15. The Lord of Arcturus and Lady of Arcturus, the Head of the Arcturian Civilization

16. Sanat Kumara

17. Vywamus, the Higher Aspect of Sanat Kumara

18. Lenduce, the Higher Aspect of Vywamus

19. Commander Ashtar and the Ashtar Command

20. The Archangels and Angels of the Light of GOD

21. The Elohim Councils of the Light of GOD

22. The Six Kumaras (Buddhas of Activity)

23. The Earth Mother

24. Pan

25. The Karmic Board

26. Mother Mary

27. Quan Yin

28. Isis

29. Moses

30. Mohamed

31. El Morya, Chohan of the First Ray

32. Kuthumi, Chohan of the Second Ray

33. Djwhal Khul, Head of the Inner Plane 2nd Ray Synthesis Ashram

34. Serapis Bey, Chohan of the Third Ray

35. Paul the Venetian, Chohan of the Fourth Ray

36. Hilarion, Chohan of the Fifth Ray

37. Sananda, Chohan of the Sixth Ray

38. Lady Portia, Chohan of the Seventh Ray

39. Pallas Athena

40. Master Lanto

41. Lady Nada

42. Babaji

43. Paramahansa Yogananda

44. The Great Divine Director

45. The Silent Watchers

46. Dr. Lorphan and the Galactic Healers from Sirius

47. Archangel Sandalphon

48. Lady of the Sun

49. Lady of the Light

50. Ganesha

51. Hanuman

52. Rama

53. Krishna

54. Ramakrishna

55. Mother Teresa

56. Thoth/Hermes

57. Second Ray Archangels, Jophiel and Christine

58. Third Ray Archangels, Chamuel and Charity

59. Fourth Ray Archangels, Gabriel and Hope

60. Fifth Ray Archangels, Raphael and Mother Mary

61. Sixth Ray Archangels, Uriel and Aurora

62. Seventh Ray Archangels, Zadekiel and Amethyst

63. First Ray Elohim, Hercules and Amazonia

64. Second Ray Elohim, Apollo and Lumina

65. Third Ray Elohim, Heros and Amora

66. Fourth Ray Elohim, Purity and Astrea

67. Fifth Ray Elohim, Cyclopea and Virginia

68. Sixth Ray Elohim, Peace and Aloha

69. Seventh Ray Elohim, Arcturus and Victoria

70. The Hyos Ha Koidesh

71. The 24 Elders that Surround the Throne of Grace

72. The Co-Creator Council of Twelve at the 352nd Level of Divinity

14

The 72 Higher Light Bodies of GOD

My Beloved Readers, for your enjoyment and edification I give you "The 72 Higher Light Bodies of GOD" to anchor and activate! GOD being as infinite and unfathomable as He is cannot be placed within any boundary. However, these 72 Higher Light Bodies are the main ones from an Earth perspective; and will serve as profound trigger points, anchorings, and activations for your Ascension and Initiation process.

1. The Anointed Christ Overself Body

2. The Zohar Body of Light

3. The Higher Adam Kadmon Body

4. The Lord's Mystical Body

5. The Monadic Blueprint Body

6. The Mayavarupa Body

7. The Causal Body

8. The Gematrian Body

9.   The Epi-Kinetic Body

10. The Aka Body

11. The Electromagnetic Body

12. The Physical Body

13. The Emotional Body

14. The Astral Body

15. The Mental Body

16. The Higher Mental Body

17. The Oversoul Body

18. The Chakra Grid Bodies

19. The Higher Self Body

20. The Buddhic Body

21. The Atmic Body

22. The Monadic Body

23. The Logoic Body

24. The Elohistic Lord's Body

25. The Overself Body

26. The Paradise Son's Body

27. The Planetary Body

28. The Solar Body

29. The Galactic Body

30. The Universal Body

31. The Multi-Universal Body

32. The Cosmic Body

33. The GOD Body

34. The Love Body of GOD

35. The Light Body of GOD

36. The Light Body of Archangel Metatron

37. The Light Body of Melchizedek

38. The Light Body of the Mahatma

39. The Light Body of the Divine Mother

40. The Light Body of Archangels Michael and Faith

41. The Cosmic Physical Body of GOD

42. The Cosmic Astral Body of GOD

43. The Cosmic Mental Body of GOD

44. The Cosmic Buddhic Body of GOD

45. The Cosmic Atmic Body of GOD

46. The Cosmic Monadic Body of GOD

47. The Cosmic Logoic Body of GOD

48. The Merkabah Body

49. The Love, Wisdom, and Power Body of GOD

50. The Light, Love, and Power Body of GOD

51. The Light Body of the Planetary Hierarchy

52. The Light Body of the Cosmic Hierarchy

53. The Love, Light, and Power Bodies of the Planetary Hierarchy

54. The Love, Light, and Power Bodies of the Cosmic Hierarchy

55. The Soul Body

56. Garment of the Archangels

57. The Garment of the Elohim

58. Synthesis Body of GOD

59. Earth Mother Body

60. Jeweled Vehicle of Ascension

61. Vehicle of the Dove

62. The Light Body of the Holy Spirit

63. The Light Body of GOD, Christ, and the Holy Spirit

64. The Light, Love, and Power Body of the Holy Spirit

65. The Light, Love, and Power Body of God, Christ, and the Holy Spirit

66. The Love, Light, and Power Body of Lord Buddha, our Planetary Logos

67. The Full Living Light Garment of the Christ

68. The Garment of Perfection

69. The Love, Light, and Power Body of Isis

70. The Full Garment of the Father

71. Infinite Garment of YHWH

72. The Love, Light, and Power Bodies of GOD, Christ, the Holy Spirit, and the entire Cosmic and Planetary Hierarchy; including all Archangels, Angels, Elohim Masters, and Christed Extraterrestrials

15

The 233 Spiritual Practices to Realize GOD

- DEMONSTRATION OF CHRIST/BUDDHA CONSCIOUSNESS IN DAILY LIFE

- TRANSCENDENCE OF NEGATIVE EGO, FEAR-BASED, SEPARATIVE, LOWER-SELF CONSCIOUSNESS AND THINKING

- MEDITATION

- PRAYER

- JOURNAL WRITING

- SPIRITUAL READING

- REPEATING THE NAME OF GOD

- AFFIRMATIONS

- VISUALIZATION

- CHANTING

- TONING

- VISITING THE ASCENSION SEATS

- STUDYING IN INNER PLANE ASHRAMS WHILE YOU SLEEP

- YOGA

- PHYSICAL FITNESS

- HEALTHY EATING

- SERVICE WORK

- SELF-INQUIRY (The constant, vigilant monitoring of one's consciousness)

- SPIRITUAL FELLOWSHIP AND COMMUNION

- FUN AND RECREATION TIME

- BREATH WORK

- ORGANIZING AND CLEANING YOUR DESK AND HOUSE

- PRACTICING THE PRESENCE

- GARDENING AND COMMUNING WITH THE EARTH MOTHER AND THE NATURE KINGDOM

- RUNNING ERRANDS AND TAKING CARE OF RESPONSIBILITIES OF EARTH LIFE

- ATTITUDINAL HEALING

- CREATIVE ARTISTIC EXPRESSION OF SOME KIND

- INTROSPECTION, SELF-EXAMINATION, SELF-INVENTORY

- SOUL TRAVEL

- DREAM INTERPRETATION

- "DEAR GOD" LETTERS

- MAINTAINING SPIRITUAL LOGS FOR CHARACTER DEVELOPMENT

- CREATING SPIRITUAL ALTARS IN YOUR HOME

- FENG SHUI, AND PROPER SPIRITUAL AND AESTHETIC DECORATION OF YOUR HOME

- WORKING WITH A PENDULUM TO COMMUNICATE WITH THE SUBCONSCIOUS MIND AND BODY ELEMENTAL

- ACTING "AS IF"

- DIALOGUE WORK WITH VARIOUS ASPECTS OF SELF TO CREATE PROPER INTEGRATION

- SPIRITUAL TRAINING AND SERVICE WORK WHILE SLEEPING

- SELF-HYPNOSIS, TAPES, OR SLEEP TAPES FOR PROGRAMMING SUBCONSCIOUS MIND

- BHAJANS, DEVOTIONAL SINGING, AND MUSIC FOR SPIRITUAL UPLIFTING AND TRANSCENDENCE OF NEGATIVE EGO

- POSITIVE SELF-TALK

- PUTTING ON ONE'S MENTAL AND EMOTIONAL CLOTHING EVERY MORNING

- PROPER SPIRITUAL HYGIENE AND SPIRITUAL DRESSING EACH DAY

- ASCENSION AND/OR AFFIRMATIONAL WALKS

- BI-LOCATION PRACTICE

- CHANNELING WORK AND PRACTICE

- LISTENING TO SPIRITUAL TAPES, OR WATCHING SPIRITUAL VIDEOS

- PRACTICING ASCENSION ACTIVATION TOOLS AND TECHNIQUES
- PRACTICING THE POWER OF THE SPOKEN WORD
- BUILDING LIGHT QUOTIENT
- CALLING IN THE TWELVE RAYS
- USING MANTRAS AND SPIRITUAL WORDS OF POWER
- USING INVOCATIONS AND DECREES
- SPIRITUAL TREATMENTS
- BUILDING LIGHT, LOVE, AND POWER QUOTIENT
- WORKING ON RAISING YOUR PSYCHOLOGICAL QUOTIENTS
- ECOLOGICAL AND ENVIRONMENTAL PRACTICES
- HEALING WORK
- INNER PLANE PERSONAL AND PLANETARY HEALING WORK
- WORKING WITH LIGHT, COLOR, AND SOUND
- FASTING
- MENTAL, EMOTIONAL, AND SPIRITUAL FASTING AND DIETS
- SILENCE
- THE CREATING OF SPIRITUAL VOWS
- RITUAL WORSHIP, CHURCH, TEMPLE
- TIME AND ENERGY MANAGEMENT
- CREATIVE THINKING
- PURIFICATION PRACTICES ON ALL LEVELS

- RIGHT THINKING

- RIGHT FEELINGS

- RIGHT ACTION

- RIGHT USE OF ENERGY

- RIGHT LIVELIHOOD

- SPIRITUAL POSTURE

- RIGHT NONVERBAL COMMUNICATION

- RIGHT SPEAKING

- CONTEMPLATION

- LISTENING TO THE INNER MUSIC OF THE SPHERES

- SEEING THE INNER LIGHT

- MEDITATING ON GEOMETRIC DESIGNS

- SPIRITUAL DEVOTION

- LECTURES, CLASSES, SEMINARS, AND WORKSHOPS

- SATSANG

- RECEIVING SHAKTIPAT FROM INNER PLANE ASCENDED MASTERS AND/OR SPIRITUAL TEACHERS ON EARTH

- DARSHAN

- CHARACTER DEVELOPMENT

- TEN COMMANDMENTS, FOUR NOBLE TRUTHS, EIGHT FOLD PATH

- OBEDIENCE TO GOD AND GOD'S LAWS

- PRACTICE OF FORGIVENESS TO SELF AND OTHERS

- PRACTICE OF UNCONDTIONAL LOVE AT ALL TIMES IN ALL SITUATIONS

- HOLY ENCOUNTER, CHRIST MEETING CHRIST EVERY TIME YOU SEE A BROTHER AND SISTER

- REMAINING IN THE TAO

- OPTIMISM AND POSITIVITY AT ALL TIMES

- THE USE OF I AM AFFIRMATIONS AND PRAYERS

- THE SPIRITUAL PRACTICE OF JOY AND HAPPINESS AT ALL TIMES

- PROPER PARENTING OF THE INNER CHILD

- RENUNCIATION OF MATERIALISM, NEGATIVE EGO, AND LOWER-SELF DESIRE

- MODERATION IN ALL THINGS

- BALANCED USE OF SEXUAL ENERGIES FOR MOST, AND CELIBACY FOR A FEW

- TAKING REFUGE IN GOD, THE INNER PLANE ASCENDED MASTERS, ARCHANGELS AND ELOHIM, CHRISTED EXTRATERRESTRIALS, AND CHRIST/BUDDHA TEACHERS ON EARTH

- TAKING REFUGE IN THE TEACHINGS

- TAKING REFUGE IN THE SPIRITUAL COMMUNITY

- THE PRACTICE OF RANDOM ACTS OF KINDNESS AND COMPASSION

- TITHING

- SEED MONEY

- SPIRITUAL PRACTICE OF INTEGRITY AND CONSISTENCY AT ALL TIMES

- RIGHT EFFORT, AND NEVER GIVING UP

- SPIRITUAL PRACTICE OF SELF-MASTERY AND CAUSING ONE'S REALITY AT ALL TIMES

- SPIRITUAL PRACTICE OF REMAINING IN BALANCE AT ALL TIMES.

- GIVING RIGHT COUNSEL

- DO NOT BREAK SPIRITUAL VOWS

- LOVE FINDER, AND NOT A FAULT FINDER

- MAINTAINING BALANCE AT ALL TIMES

- PROFESS BELIEF

- TO HELP AND GIVE TO THE POOR

- TAKE SPIRITUAL PILGRIMAGES AND VISIT SACRED SPIRITUAL SPOTS ON EARTH

- DEVELOPING AN EFFICIENT PERCEPTION OF REALITY

- SIMPLIFY YOUR LIFE

- MONITOR YOUR MOTIVES WITH DEVASTATING HONESTY

- STRIVE FOR PURITY IN ALL THAT YOU DO

- TREAT ANIMAL, PLANT, AND MINERAL KINGDOMS AS YOUR YOUNGER BROTHERS AND SISTERS

- RELINQUISHMENT OF FEAR, SELF-WILL, NEGATIVE SELF-ISHNESS, SELF-CENTEREDNESS, SEPARATENESS, NARCIS-

SISM, ANGER, BEING UPSET, DEFENSIVENESS, DEPRESSION, VICTIM CONSCIOUSNESS, NEGATIVE THOUGHTS, AND FEELINGS.

- STRIVE FOR UNCONDITIONAL LOVE, FORGIVENESS, NON-JUDGMENTALNESS, INNER PEACE, JOY, HAPPINESS, EVEN-MINDEDNESS, EQUANIMITY, TOLERANCE, FAITH, HOPE, CHARITY, PATIENCE, SELF-MASTERY, CENTEREDNESS, BEING A CAUSE, BALANCE, INTEGRATION, MODERATION, AND ALL POSITIVE CHRIST/BUDDHA THOUGHTS AND FEELINGS

- LET GO OF ALL ATTACHMENTS AND STRIVE TO ONLY HAVE PREFERENCES

- OWN YOUR PERSONAL POWER AT ALL TIMES

- PRACTICE UNCONDITIONAL SELF-LOVE AT ALL TIMES

- PUT YOUR GOLDEN BUBBLE OF PROTECTION ON EVERY MORNING TO START YOUR DAY SO AS TO LET OTHER PEO-PLE'S NEGATIVE ENERGY SLIDE OFF YOU LIKE WATER OFF A DUCK'S BACK

- LOOK AT EVERYTHING THAT HAPPENS IN LIFE AS A SPIRI-TUAL TEST AND LESSON

- KEEP YOUR MIND AND ATTENTION CONSTANTLY CEN-TERED AND FOCUSED ON GOD, YOUR MIGHTY I AM PRES-ENCE, AND THE CHRIST/BUDDHA CONSCIOUSNESS AT ALL TIMES

- MAINTAIN 100% PERSONAL POWER, ENTHUSIASM, DEVO-TION, AND PASSION FOR GOD AND YOUR SPIRITUAL PATH AT ALL TIMES

- "LOVE THE LORD THY GOD WITH ALL THY HEART AND SOUL AND MIND AND MIGHT, AND LOVE THY NEIGHBOR AS YOU LOVE YOURSELF"

- DENY ANY THOUGHT, IMAGE, OR FEELING NOT OF GOD TO ENTER YOUR CONSCIOUSNESS FROM WITHIN OR WITHOUT.

- CONSTANTLY THINK, AFFIRM AND VISUALIZE POSITIVE CHRIST/BUDDHA THOUGHTS, IMAGES, AND FEELINGS ALL DAY LONG.

- WORKING WITH GUIDANCE THROUGH TAROT, I CHING, RUNES, AND OTHER SUCH VEHICLES OF SYNCHRONISTIC GUIDANCE

- REMAIN GROUNDED AND CONNECTED TO THE EARTH

- MANIFEST YOUR SPIRITUAL MISSION AND PUZZLE PIECE IN THE DIVINE PLAN ON EARTH

- LOVE YOUR ENEMIES

- TURN THE OTHER CHEEK

- INTEGRATE THE TWELVE RAYS IN BALANCED PROPORTION

- INTEGRATE AND BALANCE YOUR TWELVE MAJOR ARCHE-TYPES

- INTEGRATE AND BALANCE THE TEN ASPECTS OF THE TREE OF LIFE

- HAVE YOUR NEGATIVE EXTRATERRESTRIAL IMPLANTS AND NEGATIVE ELEMENTALS REMOVED

- ANCHOR AND ACTIVATE YOUR HIGHER LIGHT BODIES

- ANCHOR AND ACTIVATE YOUR HIGHER CHAKRAS

- ACTIVATE YOUR TWELVE STRANDS OF DNA

- BALANCE YOUR FEMININE AND MASCULINE

- BALANCE HEAVEN AND EARTH

- BECOME YOUR MIGHTY I AM PRESENCE ON EARTH

- LEARN TO SEE LIFE FROM A FULL SPECTRUM PRISM AND NOT GET CAUGHT IN ONE OR A FEW SMALL LENSES

- INTEGRATE AND BALANCE THE TWELVE SIGNS OF THE ZODIAC REGARDLESS OF WHAT YOUR HOROSCOPE SAYS

- RECEIVE A RAY READING TO FIND OUT THE RAY TYPE OF YOUR MONAD, SOUL, PERSONALITY, MIND, EMOTIONS, AND BODY

- FIND OUT YOUR LEVEL OF INITIATION AND PERCENTAGE OF LIGHT QUOTIENT YOU ARE CURRENTLY HOLDING

- LEARN TO CHANNEL THE INNER PLANE ASCENDED MASTERS, ARCHANGELS AND ANGELS, AND ELOHIM MASTERS

- MAKE YOUR SUBCONSCIOUS COMPLETELY SUBSERVIENT TO YOUR CONSCIOUS MIND AND MAKE YOUR CONSCIOUS MIND COMPLETELY OF SERVICE TO GOD AND THE MASTERS

- PRACTICE DR. STONE'S ASCENSION ACTIVATION MEDITATIONS

- WORK WITH DR. STONE'S ASCENSION ACTIVATION MEDITATIONS TO BUILD YOUR LIGHT BODY

- CALL IN THE INNER PLANE ASCENDED MASTERS TO HELP HEAL YOUR PHYSICAL BODY

- WORK WITH THE CORE FEAR MATRIX REMOVAL PRO-GRAM TO REMOVE ALL FEAR FROM YOUR AURIC FIELD

- CALL ON THE HOLY SPIRIT TO UNDO ALL MISQUALIFIED ENERGY YOU HAVE SET IN MOTION IN THE PAST OR IN JAMS YOU FIND YOURSELF IN

- COME TO THE WESAK CELEBRATIONS HELD AT MT. SHASTA FOR 2000 FELLOW LIGHTWORKERS FROM AROUND THE WORLD

- USE THE HUNA PRAYER METHOD IN DR. STONE'S BOOK *BEYOND ASCENSION* TO MANIFEST WHATEVER YOU WANT OR NEED FOR YOUR SPIRITUAL MISSION

- WORK ON DEVELOPING A HIGH FUNCTIONING SPIRI-TUAL, PSYCHOLOGICAL, AND PHYSICAL IMMUNE SYSTEM

- STRIVE TO COMPLETE YOUR SEVEN LEVELS OF INITIATION IN AN INTEGRATED MANNER THIS LIFETIME, AND THEN STRIVE TO COMPLETE YOUR TWELVE LEVELS OF INITIA-TION IN AN INTEGRATED MANNER

- BE SURE TO INTEGRATE YOUR INITIATIONS INTO YOUR MENTAL, EMOTIONAL, ETHERIC, AND PHYSICAL BODY

- BE SURE TO DO YOUR PSYCHOLOGICAL WORK; OTHER-WISE YOUR SPIRITUAL WORK WILL BECOME CORRUPTED BY THE NEGATIVE EGO AND BECOME IMBALANCED AND OFF-KILTER

- HONOR AND SANCTIFY THE MATERIAL FACE OF GOD

- BALANCE AND INTEGRATE THE 72 ASPECTS OF THE MIND OF GOD

- BE SURE TO ANCHOR AND ACTIVATE YOUR ANNOINTED CHRIST OVERSELF BODY, THE ZOHAR BODY OF LIGHT, AND YOUR OVERSELF BODY!

- PRACTICE OUTER OR INNER POLITICAL AND SOCIAL ACTIVISM

- FOLLOW A PATH OF SYNTHESIS AND ONE OF AN ECLECTIC NATURE

- OWN YOUR PERSONAL POWER ON ALL LEVELS

- ASK FOR PROTECTION FROM GOD AND THE MASTERS EVERY MORNING TO START YOUR DAY

- PRACTICE SPIRITUAL DISCERNMENT AT ALL TIMES

- STRIVE TO MAINTAIN PERFECTION AT ALL TIMES, AND WHEN IT IS NOT MANIFESTING, SAY A PRAYER OR DO AN AFFIRMATION OR VISUALIZATION TO MAKE IT SO IN YOUR CONSCIOUSNESS

- FORGIVE YOURSELF FOR YOUR MISTAKES

- TRANSCEND CARNAL, LOWER-SELF SEXUALITY

- RELINQUISH ALL ATTACK THOUGHTS

- CULTIVATE CONSTANT REMEMBRANCE OF GOD

- BUILD YOUR ANTAKARANA BACK TO YOUR MIGHTY I AM PRESENCE AND THEN BACK TO GOD

- THINK GOD

- ABOVE ALL ELSE, TO THINE OWN SELF BE TRUE

- KNOW THY SELF

- DO NOT USE THE LORD'S NAME IN VAIN

- PRACTICE THE TEN COMMANDMENTS, FOUR NOBLE TRUTHS, AND EIGHT-FOLD PATH

- SEE YOURSELF ULTIMATELY AS THE INTEGRATED MIGHTY I AM PRESENCE, MONAD, CHRIST, BUDDHA, AND MELCHIZDEK LIVING FULLY IN YOUR PHYSICAL BODY ON EARTH, CREATING HEAVEN ON EARTH IN SERVICE OF THE ALL, AND LOVING IT

- RECEIVE OCCASIONAL CHANNELED OR SPIRITUAL PSY-CHIC READINGS FROM SELF, OR FROM PSYCHOLOGICALLY AND SPIRITUALLY CLEAR HIGH LEVEL INITIATES AND MASTERS ON EARTH

- BE A SPIRITUAL WARRIOR IN LIFE AND NEVER GIVE UP

- ANCHOR THE FIRE LETTERS, KEY CODES, AND SACRED GEOMETRIES OF GOD

- ANCHOR AND ACTIVATE THE LIGHT, LOVE, AND POWER PACKETS OF GOD

- ANCHOR AND ACTIVATE THE COSMIC TREE OF LIFE OF GOD

- STRIVE FOR SYNTHESIS AND INTEGRATION IN ALL THINGS

- STRIVE TO BECOME A FULL-FLEDGED MELCHIZEDEK

- CREATE A VICTORY LOG OF ALL YOUR SUCCESSES

- CREATE A GRATITUDE LOG FOR ALL YOU HAVE TO BE GRATEFUL ABOUT

- MAKE SPIRITUAL LISTS TO COUNTERACT THE NEGATIVE THINKING OF THE NEGATIVE EGO, FEAR-BASED, DOUBTING MIND

- LOVE THE EARTH AND EARTH LIFE

- ENJOY EARTH LIFE

- ENJOY THE BEST OF BOTH WORLDS

- CHANT AND LISTEN TO THE AUM

- CALL IN PLATINUM NETS FROM THE MASTERS CONSTANTLY

- CALL CONSTANTLY FOR THE BACTERIAL AND VIRAL VACUUM FROM THE MASTERS WHEN YOU FEEL YOURSELF WEAKENED OR YOUR RESISTANCE IS DOWN

- CALL THE MASTERS FOR WALLS OR PROTECTION WHENEVER NEEDED

- BUY FLOWERS FOR YOUR SPIRITUAL ALTAR AND HOME

- LIGHT INCENSE TO RAISE THE ENERGY IN YOUR HOME

- USE AROMATHERAPY AND BACH FLOWER REMEDIES

- PRACTICE MASSAGE; GIVING AND RECEIVING

- TAKE HOT BATHS AND USE THEM AS MEDITATION EXPERIENCES

- LIGHT BURNING POTS IN YOUR HOME A MINIMUM OF ONCE A MONTH TO CLEAN THE PSYCHIC ATMOSPHERE OF THE ROOMS IN YOUR HOME. (Find out how to do this in Dr. Stone's books).

- PRACTICE THE ASCENSION BUDDY SYSTEM

- TEACH ASCENSION CLASSES IN YOUR HOME USING DR. STONE'S BOOKS

- CONSTANTLY MAKE ATTITUDINAL ADJUSTMENTS WHERE NEEDED

- DON'T SWEAR

- REVIEW HOW YOU DID LEARNING YOUR SPIRITUAL LESSONS AND MAKE APPROPRIATE ATTITUDINAL, EMOTIONAL, AND BEHAVIORAL ADJUSTMENTS

- KEEP A MEDITATION LOG TO WRITE DOWN ANY INFO RECEIVED

- CONSTANTLY PRAY AND TALK TO THE INNER PLANE ASCENDED MASTERS AND ANGELS

- STRIVE TO INTEGRATE AND BALANCE THE 72 ATTRIBUTES OF GOD

- COMBINE YOUR PHYSICAL FOODS PROPERLY

- AVOID TOO MUCH SUGAR AND ARTIFICIAL STIMULANTS

- AVOID DRUGS OF ALL KINDS AS MUCH AS POSSIBLE, ESPECIALLY RECREATIONAL DRUGS

- USE HOMEOPATHICS AND HERBS FOR HEALING, AS WELL AS A REFINED DIET

- PURSUE EXCELLENCE IN EVERYTHING, BUT DON'T BE A NEGATIVE PERFECTIONIST AND OVERLY CRITICAL TO SELF OR OTHERS

- STRIVE TO MOVE INTO YOUR SPIRITUAL LEADERSHIP IN THE PUZZLE PIECE THAT IS RIGHT FOR YOU

- DEVELOP YOUR HEALING ABILITIES ON ALL LEVELS
- BE SURE TO BALANCE AND INTEGRATE THE 72 AREAS OF THE MIND OF GOD!
- RIGHT PERSPECTIVE AND UNDERSTANDING
- RIGHT THOUGHT
- RIGHT SPEECH
- RIGHT ACTION
- RIGHT LIVELIHOOD
- RIGHT MEDITATION
- RIGHT EFFORT
- RIGHT MINDFULNESS
- RIGHT CONCENTRATION

16

The 300 Advanced Ascended Master Abilities on a Spiritual, Psychological, and Physical/Earthly Level

My Beloved Readers, this is one of the most complete lists of advanced Ascended Master abilities ever put together! What is also unique about this list is that it focuses on advanced Ascended Master abilities on a Spiritual, Psychological and Physical/Earthly level! Many lightworkers often forget that some of the most advanced Ascended Master abilities occur on the Psychological Level, and even on the Physical/Earthly level. Examples of this would be: the ability to transcend your negative ego thought systems, achieving God purity, developing a flawless character, grounding your Spiritual Mission on Earth and fulfilling your puzzle piece in the Divine Plan on Earth, demonstrating the Presence of God on Earth in a balanced and integrated way, and unconditional love! There are a great many spiritual people who may have some of the classic Spiritual Gifts or Advanced Ascended Master abilities on a Spiritual or Psychic level; however, they often have not mastered the Advanced Ascended Master abilities on a Psychological and Earthly level! For this reason and purpose this list has been compiled to put together what, I humbly suggest, is the most complete list ever put together! I suggest marking the ones you are developed in and the ones that need development; and then set up a Spiritual Plan for how you might go about developing those areas that you are not as developed in so you can achieve your highest potential of God Realization and Integrated Ascension in this lifetime! Enjoy!

- BI-LOCATION
- MATERIALIZATION
- CLAIRVOYANCE
- CLAURAUDIENCE
- CLAIRSENTIENCE
- INNER SMELL
- INNER TASTE
- PAST LIFE MEMORY
- PHYSICAL IMMORTALITY
- MULTIDIMENSIONAL COMMUNICATION
- MULTIDIMENSIONAL CONSCIOUSNESS
- 22 SUPERSENSES OF GOD
- TRANSCENDENCE OF PHYSICAL LAWS
- WALKING ON WATER
- TURNING WATER INTO WINE
- DIVINE HEALING
- COMMUNICATING IN DIVINE LANGUAGES

- ABILITY TO SEE PAST, PRESENT, AND FUTURE

- ABILITY TO READ BOOKS ENERGETICALLY

- SHAPESHIFTING

- PROPHECY

- TELEPATHY

- SPIRITUAL WISDOM

- PSYCHOLOGICAL WISDOM

- PHYSICAL/EARTHLY WISDOM

- WISDOM OF SYNTHESIS

- SPIRITUAL LEADERSHIP

- PLANETARY WORLD SERVICE

- POWER OF THE SPOKEN WORD

- BALANCE AND INTEGRATION

- INTEGRATED ASCENSION

- BALANCING OF FEMININE AND MASCULINE

- BALANCE OF HEAVEN AND EARTH

- INTEGRATION OF VERTICAL AND HORIZONTAL

- TUNING INTO AKASHIC RECORDS

- SOUL TRAVEL

- TRANSCENDENCE OF NEGATIVE EGO CONSCIOUSNESS AND ESTABLISHMENT OF CHRIST CONSCIOUSNESS

- MASTERY AND INTEGRATION OF THE SEVEN RAYS

- COMPLETION OF YOUR 12 LEVELS OF INTEGRATION

- SOUL MERGER

- MONADIC MERGE

- SPIRITUAL MASTERY

- PSYCHOLOGICAL MASTERY

- PHYSICAL/EARTHLY MASTERY

- INTEGRATION OF SPIRITUAL, PSYCHOLOGICAL, EARTHLY MASTERY

- REALIZATION OF LIGHT BODY

- LUCID DREAMING

- DREAM INTERPRETATION

- GIFTS OF THE HOLY SPIRIT

- PROSPERITY CONSCIOUSNESS

- UNCONDITIONAL LOVE

- SPEAKING IN TONGUES

- BALANCING OF THREE-FOLD FLAME

- BALANCING OF INTEGRATION OF 12 MAJOR ARCHETYPES

- RAISING OF THE KUNDALINI

- MASTERY AND INTEGRATION OF 12 MAJOR SIGNS OF ZODIAC

- SOUL TRAVEL

- CHANNELING

- EARTHLY SUCCESS ON ALL LEVELS

- SYNTHESIS CONSCIOUSNESS

- BE AND DEMONSTRATE GOD

- MIND READING

- RAISING THE DEAD

- MATERIALIZING THINGS

- TRANSCENDENCE OF ALL PHYSICAL LAWS

- BEING IN 50 PLACES AT ONE TIME

- LANGUAGE OF LIGHT

- INTUITION

- KNOWINGNESS

- COMPREHENSION

- REALIZATION

- PERFECTION

- MYSTIC VISION

- OCCULT VISION

- PSYCHOLOGICAL VISION

- REMOTE VIEWING

- PHYSICAL ASCENSION

- SPIRITUAL DISCERNMENT

- RESPONSE TO GROUP VIBRATION

- IDEALISM

- DIVINE VISION
- MULTIDIMENSIONAL COMMUNICATION
- BEATITUDE
- ACTIVE SERVICE
- FULL SPECTRUM PRISM SEEING
- HEALING
- EFFICIENT PERCEPTION OF REALITY
- LIVING ON LIGHT
- PAST LIVE AWARENESS
- PSYCHOMETRY
- LEVITATION
- GROUND SPIRITUAL MISSION
- FULLY EMBRACE PUZZLE PIECE IN DIVINE PLAN
- MASTERY AND BALANCE SEVEN CHAKRAS
- SPIRITUALLY TEACH
- PSYCHIC
- COUNSELING
- UNDERSTANDING
- COMPASSION
- FORGIVENESS
- NONATTACHMENT
- HIGHER LIGHT QUOTIENT

- HIGHER LOVE QUOTIENT

- HIGHER POWER QUOTIENT

- ANCHORING AND ACTIVATION OF TWELVE STRANDS OF DNA

- ANCHORING AND MERGER WITH HIGHER LIGHT BODIES

- ANCHORING, ACTIVATION AND ACTUALIZATION OF HIGHER CHAKRAS

- INTEGRATION AND CLEANSING OF ALL YOUR SOUL'S EXTENSIONS

- BUILDING OF YOUR PERSONAL AND COSMIC ANTAKARANA

- TRANSCENDENCE OF GLAMOUR, MAYA, AND ILLUSION

- COMPLETING YOUR BARDO WHILE STILL IN A PHYSICAL BODY

- MASTERING AND INTEGRATION OF THE 12 RAYS

- PHYSICAL BI-LOCATION

- PURSUIT OF EXCELLENCE ON ALL LEVELS

- INTEGRITY

- EGOLESSNESS

- SELFLESSNESS

- CLEAR MOTIVENESS

- CLEANLINESS ON ALL LEVELS

- BEAUTY AND AESTHETICS IN ALL ASPECTS OF YOUR LIFE

- FREEDOM IN ALL ASPECTS OF LIFE

- DIVINE ORDER AND STRUCTURE IN LIFE

- MASTERY OF BUSINESS AND FINANCIAL ASPECTS OF LIFE

- POLITICAL, SOCIAL, AND PHILOSOPHICAL CONSCIOUS-NESS

- INNER OR OUTER SERVICE IN POLITICS

- MASTERY OF SPIRITUAL EDUCATION

- MASTERY AND INTEGRATION OF ARTISTIC AND CREATIVE ASPECT OF LIFE

- MASTERY AND INTEGRATION OF NEW AGE SCIENCES

- ABILITY TO HELP, REORDER AND RESTRUCTURE SOCIETY AND CREATE HEAVEN ON EARTH!

- ABILITY TO LIVE A LIFE OF SELFLESS SERVICE TO GOD, YOUR BROTHERS AND SISTERS, AND ALL KINGDOMS OF GOD

- POSITIVE THINKING

- ABILITY TO KEEP ATTENTION SPECIFICALLY FOCUSED ONLY ON MIGHTY I AM PRESENCE, SPIRIT, AND GOD!

- CREATIVE VISUALIZATION

- ABILITY TO ACT AS IF

- ABILITY TO TRANSCEND APPEARANCES AND SEE THE ESSENCE BEHIND ALL FORM

- RIGHT WITH SELF

- RIGHT WITH GOD

- RIGHT RELATIONSHIPS WITH PEOPLE

- DEMONSTRATION OF SERVICE MISSION

- SELF-DISCIPLINE

- ABILITY TO MEDITATE

- ABILITY TO PRAY

- HUMBLENESS

- HUMILITY

- ABILITY TO ADMIT MISTAKES AND APOLOGIZE

- GOOD SPIRITUAL, MENTAL, EMOTIONAL, ENERGETIC, AND PHYSICAL DIET

- BEING ORGANIZED

- RESPONSIBLE

- ENLIGHTENMENT

- SAMADHI

- DEVELOPMENT OF EIGHT MAJOR PSYCHOLOGICAL QUO-TIENTS

- DEVELOPMENT OF THE 72 PSYCHOLOGICAL SUBQUO-TIENTS AND VIRTUES OF GOD

- FLAWLESS CHARACTER

- ABILITY TO PROPERLY PARENT THE INNER CHILD

- MASTER ROMANTIC RELATIONSHIPS

- MASTER PARENTING

- ABILITY TO REPROGRAM SUBCONSCIOUS MIND

- MASTERY AND APPROPRIATE USE OF SEXUALITY

- ABILITY TO NOT MISUSE POWER

- ABILITY TO NOT BE TAKEN OVER BY FAME

- ABILITY TO NOT BE TAKEN OVER BY GREED

- ABILITY TO NOT BE TAKEN OVER BY LOWER-SELF DESIRE

- ABILITY TO MASTER SUBCONSCIOUS MIND

- ABILITY TO MASTER MIND

- ABILITY TO MASTER FEELINGS AND EMOTIONS

- ABILITY TO MASTER ENERGY

- ABILITY TO MASTER THE PHYSICAL BODY

- ABILITY TO MASTER EARTH ENERGIES AND EARTHLY LOVE

- LOVING EARTH LIFE

- ABILITY TO TRANSCEND ALL NEGATIVE THOUGHTS

- ABILITY TO TRANSCEND ALL NEGATIVE FEELINGS AND EMOTIONS

- ABILITY TO TRANSCEND OVERINDULGENCE AND GLUTTONY

- ABILITY TO TRANSCEND FALSE PRIDE

- ABILITY TO TRANSCEND SELF-GLORY FOR GODS GLORY

- ABILITY TO ACHIEVE GOD PURITY

- ABILITY TO TRANSCEND SELF-DECEPTION

- SPIRITUAL VIGILANCE

- ABILITY TO SEE AURAS

- LAYING ON OF HANDS

- ABILITY TO HEAL WITH THE EYES

- ABILITY TO BE HAPPY AND JOYOUS AT ALL TIMES

- INNER PEACE, EQUANIMITY, EVENMINDENESS

- TRANSCENDENCE OF DUALITY

- ABILITY TO MANIFEST

- ABILITY TO BALANCE YOUR KARMA

- ABILITY TO REMOVE IMPLANTS AND NEGATIVE ELEMEN-TALS

- ABILITY TO CO-CREATE WITH SPIRIT AND THE MASTERS

- ABILITY TO OVERCOME SEPARATION

- ABILITY TO OVERCOME SELFISHNESS

- ABILITY TO OVERCOME ANGER

- ABILITY TO OVERCOME FEAR AND WORRY

- ABILITY TO OVERCOME JEALOUSY AND COMPETITION

- ABILITY TO OVERCOME EGOTISM

- ABILITY TO CLIMB YOUR APPOINTED SPIRITUAL MOUN-TAIN

- ABILITY TO MAINTAIN GOD PURITY EVEN WHEN SPIRI-TUAL MOUNTAIN IS CLIMBED

- ABILITY TO LOOK AT EVERYTHING THAT HAPPENS AS A SPIRITUAL TEST AND LESSON

- PURIFICATION IN THOUGHT, FEELING, ENERGY, AND PHYSICAL BODY

- ABILITY TO INTEGRATE ANGELIC, ASCENDED MASTER, AND ELOHIM AS ASPECTS OF SELF

- ABILITY TO HEAR THE MUSIC OF SPHERES ON DIFFERENT LEVELS

- ABILITY TO SEE LIGHT OF GOD

- ABILITY TO FAST WHEN NECESSARY

- INVOLVED DETACHMENT

- ABILITY TO RAISE SEXUAL ENERGY INTO OJAS, OR BRAIN ILLUMINATION

- ABILITY TO PLAY AND HAVE FUN

- ABILITY TO TRANSCEND LAZINESS, PROCRASTINATION AND INDOLENCE

- ABILITY TO KEEP MIND STEADY IN THE LIGHT

- ABILITY TO LIVE OUT OF THE HEART

- ABILITY TO EXPERIENCE THE BLISS AND ECSTASY OF GOD

- ABILITY TO MASTER AND INTEGRATE THE 12 SEPHIROTH OF THE TREE OF LIFE

- ABILITY TO NOT GET CAUGHT UP IN EARTH LIFE

- ABILITY TO NEVER ATTACK

- ABILITY TO BE HARMLESS AND DEFENSELESSNESS

- FAITH, TRUST AND PATIENCE

- ABILITY TO BE CONSISTENT ON ALL LEVELS

- ABILITY TO BE DECISIVE

- ABILITY TO FULLY OWN 100% PERSONAL POWER, UNCON-
DITIONAL LOVE, AND WISDOM AT ALL TIMES

- ABILITY TO TRAVEL TO ASCENSION SEATS

- INTEGRATION OF THE COSMIC RAYS OF GOD

- ABILITY TO FULFILL EARTHLY MISSION

- ABILITY TO TUNE INTO EARTH MOTHER, PAN, NATURE
SPIRITS, AND DEVAS

- ABILITY TO BE SPIRITUALLY GROUNDED

- ABILITY TO HELP TRANSFORM OUR CIVILIZATION

- ABILITY TO TRANSCEND GLAMOURS OF THE SPIRITUAL
PATH

- ABILITY TO TRANSCEND NEGATIVE ASPECTS OF RAYS,
ZODIAC, TREE OF LIFE, TAROT, AND ARCHETYPES

- ABILITY TO COOPERATE WITH OTHER SPIRITUAL LEADERS
AND TEACHERS

- TRANSCENDENCE OF JEALOUSY AND ENVY

- ABILITY TO STAY ON ONE'S DHARMA

- ABILITY TO NOT GIVE INTO TEMPTATION

- ABILITY TO TRANSCEND LOWER-SELF

- ABILITY TO NOT GET CAUGHT UP IN PSYCHISM

- ABILITY TO CREATE HEALTH IN PHYSICAL BODY

- ABILITY TO TRANSCEND NEGATIVE EGO DUALITIES

- DEVELOPING AN INTEGRATED CONSCIOUSNESS
- ABILITY TO OVERCOME VANITY
- DEVELOPING A STRONG IMMUNE SYSTEM ON ALL THREE LEVELS
- PERSEVERANCE
- ABILITY TO TURN THE OTHER CHEEK
- ABILITY TO LOVE OUR ENEMIES
- HONOR THE MATERIAL FACE OF GOD
- MASTER AND INTEGRATE THE FOUR FACES OF GOD
- INTEGRATE THE INTUITIVE, THINKING, FEELING, AND SENSATION ASPECTS OF SELF
- ABILITY TO BALANCE FOUR BODIES
- ABILITY TO "TURN LEMONS INTO LEMONADE"
- INTEGRATE 12 MAJOR INITIATIONS INTO FOUR LOWER BODIES
- ABILITY TO TAKE ADVANTAGE OF SLEEP TIME
- ABILITY TO CHANT THE NAMES AND MANTRAS OF GOD
- ABILITY TO HEAL AND REPAIR ALL BODIES
- ASCENSION, RESURRECTION, TRANSLATION, RAPTURE, TRANSFIGURATION, RENUNCIATION
- MASTERY OF SPIRITUAL ALCHEMY
- ABILITY TO SPIRITUALLY, PSYCHOLOGICALLY, AND PHYSICALLY PROTECT ONESELF

- INTEGRATION OF THE SECRET RODS OF GOD

- ABILITY TO CREATE A SPIRITUAL/CHRIST/BUDDHA LIVING SPACE

- ABILITY TO CREATE AN ASCENSION ENVIRONMENT

- ABILITY TO BE SILENT

- ABILITY TO COMMUNICATE

- ABILITY TO LIVE IN THE TAO

- MASTERING THE SPIRITUAL SCIENCE OF THE RAYS, WHICH ARE THE PERSONALITY OF GOD!

- ABILITY TO DEVELOP SPIRITUAL, PSYCHOLOGICAL, AND PHYSICAL/EARTHLY VISION

- ABILITY TO PROPERLY MASTER AND INTEGRATE ONE'S FEELINGS AND EMOTIONS

- ABILITY TO TRANSCEND LIMITED LENS SEEING AND BLIND SPOTS

- ABILITY TO RESOLVE CONFLICT WITHIN SELF AND WITH OTHERS

- DEVELOPMENT OF THE MIDAS TOUCH

- DEVELOPMENT OF APPROPRIATE BOUNDARIES

- COMMON SENSE

- PRACTICALITY

- ABILITY TO OPEN CREATIVE CHANNELS

- ABILITY TO BALANCE GOD/GODDESS WITHIN SELF

- DEVELOPING A PROPER PSYCHOLOGY, PHILOSOPHY, AND OVERALL SPIRITUAL UNDERSTANDING AND VIEW OF LIFE

- ABILITY TO KEEP THINGS IN PERSPECTIVE

- ABILITY TO MAINTAIN BIG PICTURE AND LITTLE PICTURE SIMULTANEOUSLY

- ABILITY TO SURRENDER TO GOD'S WILL AND NOT NEGATIVE EGO'S WILL

- ABILITY TO DEAL WITH NEGATIVE EGO RUN PEOPLE AND NOT GET YOUR BUTTONS PUSHED

- ABILITY TO NOT TAKE A TUMBLE DOWN THE SPIRITUAL MOUNTAIN

- ABILITY TO NOT FALL FROM GRACE THROUGH UNCONSCIOUSNESS

- ABILITY TO NOT FALL INTO AUTOMATIC PILOT

- ABILITY TO DEAL WITH SPIRITUAL CRISES EFFECTIVELY

- ABILITY TO MAKE ATTITUDINAL, EMOTIONAL, ENERGETIC, PHYSICAL, AND EARTHLY LIFE ADJUSTMENTS

- ABILITY TO LEARN LESSONS AND NOT REPEAT THEM

- ABILITY TO PRACTICE THE PRESENCE OF GOD

- ABILITY TO PAY ATTENTION TO DETAILS

- ABILITY TO FOCUS AND CONCENTRATE

- DEDICATION

- PROPER DEVOTION

- ABILITY TO ACHIEVE LIBERATION AND SALVATION

- ABILITY TO OVERCOME SPIRITUAL WEARINESS AND FATIGUE

- ABILITY TO PRACTICE THE ART OF LOVING ON ALL LEVELS

- ENJOYING EARTH LIFE

- TIME MANAGEMENT

- ABILITY TO HONOR YOUR POINT OF BALANCE

- ABILITY TO NOT COMPARE WITH OTHERS

- ABILITY TO REMOVE ALL FEAR PROGRAMMING FROM ENERGY FIELDS OF FOUR LOWER BODIES

- ABILITY TO INTEGRATE THE HEAVENLY IDEAL WITH THE REAL WORLD

- ABILITY TO CHANGE NEGATIVE EXPERIENCES INTO POSITIVE ONES!

- LOOKING AT THINGS AS LESSONS

- SELF-MASTERY

- CAUSING YOUR OWN REALITY

- GOLDEN BUBBLE OF PROTECTION

- CHANNELING

- GOD-REALIZATION

- OMNISCIENCE

- OMNIPRESENCE

- OMNIPOTENCE

17

The 22 Main Power Numbers of GOD

1. The Number of Creation. A lucky number meaning beginning. Called "Original Substance." It indicates the Start, the "Commencement." It is Adam. The Way of Original Essence. The first step.

2. A favorable and/or unfavorable number. The Matrix of Numbers. Called "Isis." It indicates Occult Training and Knowledge. It is Eve and the Door of the Temple. The Way of the Completion of Creation.

3. A lucky number of Holiness. Called "Holy Intelligence." It indicates Tenderness and Strength of Mind, Mother. The Way of Original Wisdom.

4. A lucky number of Completion. Called "Cubic Stone." It indicates Firmness, Mastery, Power, and Willpower. Everything is formed by the 4. The Way of Essences and Powers.

5. The Number of Competition. Called "The Flaming Pentacle." It indicates The Quintessence, The Perfect Man, The True Magician, Advice. The Way of Fundamental Intelligence.

6. A doubtful number of Choice or Balance. Called "The Way of Ways." It indicates first Indecision, then Balance. It is Solomon's Seal. The Way of Mediating Influence.

7. A favorable number of Regality and Triumph. Called "The Conqueror." It indicates Intelligence (3), which dominates matter (4). Expansion. The Way of Occult Intelligence.

8. A doubtful number of Attraction and Repulsion. Called "The Rule." It indicates completion in The Law and a Balance struck. The Way of Perfection.

9. A lucky, sacred number of Prophecy. Called "The Sphinx." It indicates Vital Intuitions, Magical Power, Self-confidence, and Understanding of the Higher Cycles. The Way of Resplendent Intelligence.

10. A lucky number of Mystery and the Power of Silence. Called "The Oil Lamp." It indicates the Search for Inner Light. The Way of Pure Intelligence.

11. A neutral number of Energy and Courage. Called "The Passage." Indicates the Ardor of Freedom and the Desire for Light. Moral strength. The Way of Scintillating Intelligence, which produces Knowledge and the Ability to Dominate; even the Stars.

12. A neutral number of Suffering for Elevation. Called "Grace and Perfection." A sacred number. It indicates Experience, Suffering Expectation. The Way of Prophetic Vision.

13. A lucky number of Change. Called "The Key to Power." It indicates Transformation, Rebirth. The Way of Unity and Understanding of the True Knowledge.

14. A favorable number of incarnation. Called "Penetrating Energy." It indicates The Vital Energies and their Balanced Conservation. The Way of Preparation.

15. A neutral number of Action. Called "Baphometh," or "Solve et Coagula." It indicates the Power of Occult Knowledge, Passion, and/or Temptation. The Way of Darkness.

16. An unlucky number of Error. Called "The Tower of Bhabhel." It indicates Trial, The Error of Presumption, and The Victory of those who Overcome it. The Way of Glory in Rectitude.

17. A lucky Spiritual number. Called "The King's Star." It indicates Beauty and Hope for the Just. The Way of Reward for those who have "Sown" well.

18. An unfavorable number lacking in Clarity. Called the "The Twilight Path." It indicates the Danger of Mistaken Judgements, the Pains of Love and Deception or Bewilderment. The Way of the Senses.

19. A lucky number of Clarity. Called "The Reinstated Boy." It indicates Success and Harmony. Marriage, and honors Union, Agreement. The Way of the Spirit.

20. A favorable number of Knowledge. Called "The Awakening Angel." It indicates New Ventures in Social Life, Decision. The Way of Primordial Vision.

21. A lucky number of Overcoming. Called "The Cleansed One." It indicates Non-influenceability. Overcoming of the Human Dimension, Purification. The Way of Enlightened Purification.

22. A lucky number of Absolute Truth. Called "The Magician's Crown." It indicates Honor, Fulfillment, Progress, Elevation, and Success achieved through the Purification of Profound Energies. The Way of Total Enlightenment.

This information was gathered from a poster that someone gave me called "Ex Numeris Fortuna: Numeris Lucidus Ordo." I give credit to G. Tavaglione for compiling this information.

18

The 98 Names of Allah

1. Al-Musawwir: *The Fashioner*

2. Al-Bari: *The Maker*

3. Al-Khaliq: The Creator

4. Al-Mutakabbir: The Majestic

5. Al-Jabbar: *The Compeller*

6. Al-Aziz: *The Mighty*

7. Al-Muhaimin: *The Protector*

8. Al-Mu'min: *The Giver of Peace*

9. As-Salam: *The Author of Safety*

10. Al-Quddus: *The Holy*

11. Al-Malik: *The Sovereign*

12. Ar-Rahim: *The Merciful*

13. Al-Rahman: *The Compassionate*

14. Al-Sami': *The All-Hearing*

15. Al-Muzi'l: *The Dishonorer*

16. Al-Mu'izz: *The Honorer*

17. Al-Rafeh: *The Exalter*

18. Al-Khafid: *The Abaser*

19. Al-Basit: *The Expander*

20. Al-Qabiz: *The Constrictor*

21. Al-'Alim: *The All-Knowing*

22. Al-Fattah: *The Judge*

23. Al-Razzaq: *The Provider*

24. Al-Wahhab: *The Bestower*

25. Al-Qahhar: *The Dominant*

26. Al-Gaffar: *The Forgiver*

27. Al-Muqit: *The Maintainer*

28. Al-Hafiz: *The Preserver*

29. Al-Kabir: *The Most Great*

30. Al-Aliyy: *The Sublime*

31. Al-Shakur: *The Appreciative*

32. Al-Ghafoor: *The All-Forgiving*

33. Al-Azim: *The Great One*

34. Al-Halim: *The Patient*

35. Al-Khabir: *The Aware*

36. Al-Latif: *The Subtle One*

37. Al-Adl: *The Just*

38. Al-Hakam: *The Judge*

39. Al-Basir: *The All-Seeing*

40. Al-Wakil: *The Trustee*

41. Al-Haqq: *The Truth*

42. Al-Shahid: *The Witness*

43. Al-Ba'ith: *The Awakener*

44. Al-Maajid: *The Noble*

45. Al-Wadud: *The Loving*

46. Al-Hakim: *The Wise One*

47. Al-Wase': *The All-Embracing*

48. Al-Mujib: *The Responsive*

49. Ar-Raqib: *The Watchful*

50. Al-Karim: *The Generous One*

51. Al-Jalil: *The Glorious*

52. Al-Hasib: *The Reckoner*

53. Al-Maajid: *The Noble*

54. Al-Wajid: *The Finder*

55. Al-Qayyum: *The Self-Subsisting*

56. Al-Hayy: *The Alive*

57. Al-Mumit: *The Giver of Death*

58. Al-Mohyi: *The Giver of Life*

59. Al-Muid: *The Restorer*

60. Al-Mubdi: *The Beginner*

61. Al-Muhsi: *The Counter*

62. Al-Hamid: *The Praiseworthy*

63. Al-Wali: *The Protecting Friend*

64. Al-Matin: *The Firm One*

65. Al-Qawi: *The Most Strong*

66. Al-Barr: *The Source of All Goodness*

67. Al-Muta'ali: *The Most Exalted*

68. Al-Waali: *The Governor*

69. Al-Batin: *The Hidden*

70. Al-Zahir: *The Manifest*

71. Al-Akhir: *The Last*

72. Al-Awwal: *The First*

73. Al-Mu'akhir: *The Deferrer*

74. Al-Muqaddam: *The Forward Bringer*

75. Al-Muqtadir: *The Powerful*

76. Al-Qadir: *The Able*

77. As-Samad: *The Eternal*

78. Al-Wahid: *The One*

79. Al-Mane': *The Witholder*

80. Al-Mughni: *The Enricher*

81. Al-Ghani: *The Self-Sufficient*

82. Al-Jame: *The Gatherer*

83. Al-Muqsit: *The Equitable*

84. Dhul-Jalal-Wal Ikraam: *The Lord of Majesty and Bounty*

85. Malikul-Mulk: *The Lord of the Kingdom*

86. Ar-Ra'uf: *The Compassionate*

87. Al-Afuw: *The Pardoner*

88. Al-Muntaqim: *The Avenger*

89. Al-Tawwab: *The Acceptor of Repentance*

90. Al-Saboor: *The Patient*

91. Al-Rashid: *The Guide*

92. Al-Warith: *The Inheritor*

93. Al-Baqi: *The Everlasting*

94. Al-Badi': *The Originator*

95. Al-Haadi: *The Guide*

96. Al-Nur: *The Light*

97. An-Nafe: *The Profiter*

98. Ad-Darr: *The Distresser*

19

The 250 Golden Keys to Creating Perfect Radiant Health in Your Physical Body from the Soul's Perspective

- Physical diet

- Physical exercise and fitness

- Fresh air

- Sunshine

- Deep breathing

- Health affirmations

- Health prayers

- Stretching

- Yoga

- Aerobic exercise (walking, jogging, bicycling, swimming, rowing)

- Strength training (weights)

- Fasting (three-day raw apple fast, or green vegetable juice fast with a little bit of carrot juice or water)

- "Water of Life," which is available from the Academy for cleanings, energizing, and balancing chemical balance in physical body! Highly recommended!

- Have your implants and negative elementals removed by a trained initiate at The Academy.

- Channeled Ascension clearing session (Call Academy)

- Using a pendulum to test your food.

- Purple energy plates to energize and cleanse food.

- Read this book

- Find a good homeopathic, herbalist, and or naturopathic doctor!

- Have your mercury fillings removed!

- Buy and work with my Ascension Activation Meditation Tape called "The 18 Point Cosmic Cleansing Meditation." Available from the Academy.

- Call forth an "Axiatonal Alignment," three times a day!

- Call forth a "Golden Net" from your own Mighty I Am Presence, three times a day!

- Call forth from Archangel Michael and Faith, and your own Mighty I Am Presence, every day to start your day, a "Golden Dome" and/or a "Tube of Light of Protection"!

- Call Forth from the Lord of Arcturus for the Arcturian liquid crystals to be poured into your energy field to deactivate any and all negative energy!

- Call to Djwhal Khul for the anchoring of the "Prana Wind Clearing Device" to cleanse your meridians, nadis, and energy fields!

- Call to your Healing Angels to work on you every night while you sleep!

- Call forth help for Healing from Dr. Lorphan and the Galactic Healers from the Great White Lodge on Sirius!

- Call forth for the inner plane "Acupuncture Team" to do etheric Acupuncture on you!

- Find a good holistic Medical doctor you trust!

- Work with Bach Flower Remedies

- Always keep a good "Positive Mental Attitude"!

- Spiritualize all your negative feelings and emotions to positive ones!

- Find a good "Laying on of Hands" type of Healer for emergencies.

- Occasionally get a Chiropractic Adjustment

- Do positive creative visualization for five minutes every day for perfect radiant health!

- Work with Radionics to cleanse and balance energy fields (See Academy Website)!

- Eat a diet based on Principles of Proper food combining (See local health food store booklets)

- Eat lots of green leafy vegetables, vegetables, protein, starch.

- Drink lots of water

- Ask Spirit and the Masters to run Spiritual Current through you to start every workday!

- Call in Etheric surgeons to repair your etheric body from any past life or child trauma!

- Call in Healing Angels to repair any holes or leaks in your Aura

- Work with my 13 audio Ascension Activation Meditation Tapes on a daily basis to Spiritualize and Electrify your energy fields with Spiritual Current!

- Only allow yourself to eat a very small amount of sugar!

- Stop using all artificial stimulants, except on special occasions or emergencies

- Never use recreational drugs!

- If possible, try to use homeopathics and herbs, instead of drugs, for healing!

- Take extra Acidolphilus if you ever have used or use antibiotics

- Get enough sleep every night!

- Take a good food source vitamin and mineral supplement after meals every day (no factory made supplements, only natural food source)!

- Work with Aromatherapy.

- Ask Spirit and the Masters to Balance Your Chakras and Energy fields every day or even twice a day!

- Ask your Mighty I Am Presence to fully Anchor and Activate your Monadic Blue Print Body into your Four-Body System!

- Call to the Holy Spirit to undo and heal the cause of any physical health problem you are suffering from!

- Love your physical body and talk to it, for it has a form of consciousness!

- A Homeopthic Company called Futureplex has a number of homeopathic products for bacteria, viruses, immune system booster, and environmental detox. They are called "Bacterotox, Virotox, Envirotox, Prototox." You can read about these in my book! Call Homeopathic Pharmacy in Los Angeles to order them: (818) 905-8338.

- Never use a Microwave oven, it puts holes in the aura of the food!

- Create a Science of Mind Treatment for your health or have a Science of mind practitioner create one for you to say for your health, which you can say once a day!

- Say a prayer to Spirit and the Masters to remove all energy of disease from your mental body, emotional body, etheric body, and physical body!

- Call to the Lord of Arcturus and the Arcturians to clean and clear all energy of cancer from your mental, emotional, etheric, and physical bodies!

- Go for an affirmation walk doing physical health affirmations the entire time!

- Put your Health Affirmation on tape and play them as background music while you are just working around the house!

- Put your Health affirmations on an endless loop tape or endless play tape recorder and play it softy in the background all night while you sleep!

- Have a dialogue with your physical body in your journal to see if there is anything it wants or is trying to tell you!

- Realize GOD works through the physical body and if you have a health lesson GOD is trying to teach you something.

- Talk to the physical as you would a good friend and form a positive relationship to it, and thank it for all its good work on your behalf; for the physical body needs love, honor, friendship, and respect as well. There is a form of consciousness within it called the "body elemental"!

- Twenty times throughout the day give yourself a "Thymus Tap" to increase functioning of the Thymus Gland which is your immune system!

- Never use Aluminum Foil, or Aluminum pots and pans, for you can get aluminum poisoning.

- Do not overindulge in sexuality for it can drain your energy!

- Moderation in all things!

- Call in Spirit and the Masters to remove all Core Fear Programming, negative ego programming, and poor health programming from your subconscious mind and four-body system!

- Ask Spirit and the Masters to clear your Genetic line of any health problems or weakness!

- Ask Spirit and the Masters to clear all your Past Lives from health challenges, lessons, or problems that may be affecting you now!

- Ask Spirit and the Masters to clear, cleanse, and detach you from any health lessons being caused by bleed through from one of your 144 Soul Extensions from your Monad and Mighty I Am Presence!

- Ask your Soul and Mighty I Am Presence to help you create Perfect radiant health everyday!

- Call to Mother Mary and Archangel Raphael to have the Golden Angels live in any area of your body on a permanent basis that is chronically weak!

- For any person who is dealing with Chronic Health Lessons it is absolutely essential that you read my books *Soul Psychology, How to Release Fear-Based Thinking and Feeling: An In-depth Study of Spiritual Psychology*, and *The Golden Book of Melchizedek: How to Become an Integrated Christ/Buddha in this Lifetime!*

- Ask Spirit and the Masters for the Lower aspect of all your Rays to be cleansed from your energy fields!

- Ask Spirit and the Masters for the lower aspect of all your 12 major Archetypes to be cleansed from your energy fields!

- Ask Spirit and the Masters for the lower aspect of all 12 signs of the Zodiac to be cleansed from your energy fields!

- Once a month do a burning pot in each room of your home to cleanse the Spiritual, mental, emotional, and etheric atmosphere in your home!

- Be conscious, for Healing, of the color of clothes you wear each day!

- Use Colored lights for Healing!

- Play sleep tapes at night for Healing!

- Use Subliminal Music tapes for Healing!

- Read all my books in my Ascension Book Series to be completely transformed and to Achieve Spiritual Mastery on a Spiritual, Psychological, and Physical/Earthly level!

- Find the appropriate work/play balance!

- Ask Spirit and the Masters to bath you in any Color or Sound Resonance you need for healing!

- Call to Dr. Lorphan and the Galactic Healers to repair any chakras that may be damaged from past lives or this life!

- Call to Spirit and the Masters to completely cleanse and clear your 12-Body System, energy fields, aura, and all your Chakras!

- Call to Melchizedek, the Mahatma, and Archangel Metatron for a Viral Vacuum or Bacterial Vacuum any time there is any virus or bacterial energy in your system!

- Call to Spirit and the Masters to place an impenetrable Golden Bubble of protection around you if there is anyone who is sick around you, and ask that they be placed in the Golden Bubble as well and helped to heal!

- Fast on Beiler Broth as much as possible (Steam zucchini, green beans, and a little parsley and celery). Then blend it up and drink it! It is the panacea for all health concerns.

- Call to the Lord of Arcturus and the Arcturians to clear all energy of cancer from your mental, emotional, etheric, and physical bodies!

- Go for an affirmation walk doing physical health affirmations the entire time!

- Put your Health Affirmations on tape and play them as background music while you are working around the house!

- Put your Health Affirmations on an endless loop tape or endless play tape recorder and play it softly in the background all night while you sleep!

- Have a dialogue with your physical body in your journal to see if there is anything it wants or is trying to tell you!

- Realize GOD works through the physical body, and if you have a health lesson then GOD is trying to teach you something.

- Talk to the physical as you would a good friend and form a positive relationship to it. Thank it for all its good work on you behalf, for the physical body needs love, honor, friendship, and respect as well. There is a form of consciousness within it called the "body elemental"!

- Pray for a miracle healing every day from Spirit and the Masters!

- Be sure to stay grounded!

- Clean your house once a week!

- Keep really good hygiene!

- Ask Spirit and the Masters to have all past or present diseases or health problems be cleansed from your aura!

- Do not be a hypochondriac!

- Be open to traditional and nontraditional forms of healing!

- Six almonds a day is a cancer preventative (Edgar Cayce)!

- Enjoy and Love Earth life!

- Take time to rest!

- Ask Spirit and the Masters to fully anchor and activate your Mayavarupa body! (It is the Ascension Body—See my book *The Complete Ascension Manual*)!

- Forgive your physical body for not working well at times!

- Call Spirit and the Masters to remove all improper Soul Fragments and to bring back all Soul Fragments that do belong to you, as GOD would have it be!

- Call to Archangels Michael and Faith to cut all energetic cords with people in this life and past lives that are Spiritually inappropriate and draining your energy!

- Call to Spirit and the Masters to Cleanse and purify all your Karma!

- Try to keep your legs and arms uncrossed as much as possible, for it keeps the flow of electrical current from flowing smoothly through the body!

- Work with Crystals and Gemstones!

- Honor your body's natural rhythms!

- Live in the Tao and conserve your energies!

- Keep proper self-boundaries!

- Keep a proper selfish and selfless balance!

- Study holistic health!

- Clear your spouse of implants and elementals as well! (See Revised Edition of *Soul Psychology* on how to do this!)

- Clear your pets of all negative implants and elementals!

- Take catnaps if you are tired!

- Cosmic Cellular Cleansing (See my book *Cosmic Ascension!*)

- Be sure to look at everything that is going on with your physical body and everything in your life as a Spiritual Test!

- Be sure to learn how to fully be grounded at all times! (See the book *Empowerment and Integration of the Goddess,* available from the Academy!)

- Strive and affirm for physical immortality!

- Strive and pray for Physical Ascension!

- Pray to Spirit and the Masters to have your 144 Soul extensions cleansed, cleared, and integrated within your being! (See my book *Cosmic Ascension!*)

- Sit in Ascension Seats of GOD! (See my books *The Complete Ascension Manual, Beyond Ascension,* and *Cosmic Ascension,* for this can greatly increase health and vitality as well!)

- Ask Spirit and Masters to help you fully establish your Antakarana to your Higher Self, Mighty I Am Presence, and back to GOD!

- Ask Spirit and the Masters to Widen your Antakarana to allow more Spiritual Current to flow through!

- Pray to Spirit and the Masters to increase the amount of Spiritual Current that is coming in!

- Pray to Spirit and the Masters for an increase in energy any time you need it!

- Learn to fully honor and sanctify the Material Face of GOD! (See my books *The Golden Book of Melchizedek* and *Empowerment and Integration of the Goddess,* which are available from the Academy!)

- Create a Huna Prayer for Perfect physical Health!

- Take time to "Be," instead of always being so active!

- Spend time in nature!

- Spend time meditating leaning up against a tree!

- Take time to smell the flowers!

- Pray to Spirit and the Masters to deactivate and clear any electrical or geopathic energy imbalances in your home!

- Do not keep your feet too close to a color television, for your feet chakras will soak up the radiation!

- For any Health Problem for self or others, send prayer requests to the Academy and I will place them on our "Interdimensional Prayer Altar" for this purpose!

- Call to Spirit and the Masters twice a day for a Love and Light Shower to cleanse your energy fields and aura!

- Call to Saint Germain for the Violet Transmuting flame, to transmute any health concerns!

- Ask Spirit and the Masters to remove any gray fields in your aura!

- Call to Spirit and the Masters to remove any astral dross, mental dross, or etheric dross from your aura and energy fields!

- Call to the Lord of Arcturus for the "Golden Cylinder" to remove any and all negative energy from your energy fields!

- Get an occasional massage, professionally or from a friend!

- If you are sick, go and get a colonic, for it will do you wonders!

- Take a lot of extra vitamin C every day!

- Call Spirit and the Masters to remove all negative thoughts and emotions from your energy fields that may be causing you to have health lessons!

- Ask Spirit and the Masters to remove all "etheric needless, darts and/or bullets" from your organs and energy fields from people who have sent you negative energy and anger in the past!

- Be sure at all times to have a good physical, mental, emotional, energetic, and Spiritual diet!

- Anchor and Activate all your "Higher Light Bodies and Higher Chakras into your energy fields"! Doing this will enormously increase your physical health and vitality! (See *The Complete Ascension Manual, Beyond Ascension, Cosmic Ascension, Revelations of a Melchizedek Initiate,* and *The Golden Book of Melchizedek,* all available from the Academy)

- Ask Spirit and the Masters to implement all the ideas and suggestions listed in this chapter, at night while you sleep!

- When you start to worry about your health, "pray instead"!

- To all health lessons, be they temporary or chronic say, "Not my will but thine, thank you for the lesson!"

- Some health lessons of a chronic nature may be "For the Glory of GOD," so don't give your power to your body and live your life thanking GOD for this Spiritual Test!

- Use sage in your home and a little incense to cleanse atmosphere!

- Anchor the Secret Rods of GOD in your four-body system and chakras (See my book *Golden Book of Melchizedek: How to be an Integrated Christ/Buddha in this Lifetime!*)

- Do not give your personal power to your physical body!

- Be sure to wash your vegetables well, to cleanse all pesticides!

- Ask a homeopathic doctor or homeopathic pharmacist for homeopathics to remove all heavy metals and chemicals from your body! Furtureplex has some products for this as well!

- Ask Spirit and the Masters to place you in "Color Baths," on the inner plane!

- Pray to Spirit and the Masters to clear and cleanse the lower aspect of all 12 Sephiroth in the Cosmic Tree of Life!

- Ask Spirit and the Masters to balance your feminine and masculine aspects within self!

- Ask Spirit and the Masters to balance your Heavenly and Earthly Aspects!

- Ask Spirit and the Masters to help you to master, balance, and integrate all Seven Rays, and Ray attributes and qualities!

- Ask Spirit and the Masters to help you develop a Full Spectrum Consciousness Vision and Perspective!

- Ask Spirit and the Masters to cut any etheric cords in regard to people who are currently draining you!

- Ask Spirit and the Masters to cut any etheric cords of people who you have had past sexual involvement with from this life or past lives that need to be cut or that are causing you to be drained of any energies!

- Ask Spirit and the Masters to remove any and all unwanted entities from hanging around your energy fields that are not of an Ascended Master nature, if this prayer be in harmony with GOD's Will!

- Ask Spirit and the Masters to help you to learn to always think and feel only from your Spiritual/Christ/Buddha Consciousness and never from your negative ego/fear-based/separative mind!

- Ask Spirit and the Masters to help your stay balanced and integrated at all times!

- Call on Mother Mary and Archangel Raphael any time you need healing help!

- Call on Sai Baba any time you need healing help!

- Call on Sananda any time you need healing help!

- Call on the Lord of Arcturus and the Arcturians any time you need healing help!

- Call Melchizedek, the Mahatma, and Metatron to establish an impenetrable wall of protection around you at all times!

- Pray to and ask for help from Djwhal Khul with his Holographic Computer for help with any Health lessons and challenges!

- Call to the Lord of Arcturus and the Arcturians for Balancing and/or tightening your grids if necessary!

- Call Forth from Archangel Metatron for the anchoring of any fire letters, key codes and sacred geometries needed to accelerate healing!

- Call to the 14 Mighty Archangels for healing!

- Call to the Archangels for sound tones of healing!

- Ask for Healing to be given to you at night while you sleep!

- Pray to Spirit and the Masters to imprint programs of perfect radiant health into your subconscious mind at night while you sleep!

- Pray to Spirit and the Masters to imprint the "Virtues and Qualities of GOD into your four-body system while you sleep"!

- Pray to GOD, Christ, and the Holy Spirit for help with any Health problems you have!

- Pray to Spirit and the Masters to remove all glamour, maya, and illusion from your being!

- Pray to Spirit and the Masters for guidance and more ideas on how you can heal your self!

- Ask to be fully merged and integrated with your Higher Self and Monad on Earth!

- Be sure to breathe deeply!

- Practice Tai Chi, Qui Gong, or Aikido

- Repeat the Names of God, Mantras, and Words of Power, to increase physical health and vitality!

- Practice self-hypnosis to give suggestions of perfect health!

- Give suggestions of perfect health to subconscious after Meditations!

- Give suggestions of perfect health to your subconscious at night while you sleep if you wake-up, or as you are falling asleep or just waking-up!

- Pray before you eat your physical food, and ask GOD and the Angels to bless it and cleanse it of all energetic impurities!

- Pray to Spirit and the Masters to increase your light quotient so you have more energy in your energy and light fields to heal with!

- See your true identity as God, the Christ, the Buddha, and the Eternal self and realize that Sickness is a defense against the truth! You are God and Christ and hence cannot get sick! Affirm this!

- Realize most health crises are cleansings, which are good!

- Also, realize many health crises are signs of accelerated Spiritual Growth and the physical manifestation of the Ascension process!

- Practice Ecology!

- Be sure to manifest your Spiritual Mission on Earth in a physical sense, which will help run more Spiritual current through you physically!

- Do not be afraid of asking your Brothers and Sisters for help, for that is what we are here for. Remember that we are all just incarnations of GOD, so this would just be God helping God!

- Do not accept pat answers in regard to physical health lessons. Some health lessons are just Spiritual Mutational symptoms and signs of Spiritual refinement in the physical, so don't let people lay trips on you! Keep your Golden Bubble of Light up at all times and let other people's trips slide off you like water off a duck's back!

- Be compassionate towards others who are sick, but not empathetic where you take on their stuff. Pray to Spirit and the Masters to clear it if you have done this or are doing this!

- Occasionally take time to sleep separately from your Spouse or mate if you feel a need to regenerate your energies!

- Fulfill your Spiritual puzzle piece on Earth, this will help your health!

- Work with my Meditations in *The Golden Book of Melchizedek* to anchor and activate the "72 Higher Light Bodies of GOD" and to anchor and activate your "Love/Light and Power Bodies of GOD"!

- Use the 25 programming techniques in my book *Soul Psychology*, to program the subconscious mind to create perfect radiant health in the physical body!

- Grow your own vegetables if possible!

- Buy organic vegetables if you can!

- In my book *How to Achieve Perfect Radiant Health,* study the first chapter, which is about eating a good physical diet. It will give you hundreds of excellent physical and Spiritual suggestions on diet that I have practiced and gathered together from all my studies and work in Holistic Health and from suggestions on diet from Spirit and the Ascended Masters. You won't find this information in any physical health book on the planet! That is why I have called my book *How To Achieve Perfect Radiant Health From The Perspective of the Soul*! This is the Soul and Spirit's perspective on physical health not the personality or just mind! Tell all your friends that need a major health upgrade about it! It is available at this time only from the Academy!

- Develop a Christ/Buddha Living Space in your Home! (See *The Golden Book of Melchizedek*)

- Consider having a Feng Shui expert come to your home!

- Play music in the background that you find healing to your physical body and soul!

- Have your "Earth Crystals" removed! (See *The Golden Book of Melchizedek)!*

- Call to Spirit and the Masters for the full anchoring and activation of your Higher Adam Kadmon Body!

- Call to Archangel Metatron to program your Gematrian body with all the codes for Perfect Radiant Health!

- Call to Archangel Metatron to program your Electromagnetic body for perfect radiant health!

- Call to Spirit and the Masters to fully anchor and activate your Anointed Christ Overself Body, your Zohar Body of Light, and your Overself body, which will bring more Light and perfect blue-print bodies into your field!

- One of the best things you can do for your physical health is to develop a Psychology, Philosophy, and Belief System that perfectly matches that of GOD, Christ, the Holy Spirit, your Mighty I Am Presence, your Higher Self, and the Inner Plane Ascended Masters. This can be achieved by carefully reading and studying my books *Soul Psychology* and *How to Release Fear-Based Thinking and Feeling: An In-depth Study of Spiritual Psychology.* These two books will have an enormous impact on your physical health as well!

- The other key to increase physical health is to develop Self-Mastery and Self-Realization on the Spiritual Level, which will then have an imprinting effect on the etheric and physical level. To achieve this, study my books *The Complete Ascension Manual, Beyond Ascension, Cosmic Ascension, The Golden Book of Melchizedek: How to Become an Integrated Christ/Buddha in this Lifetime, Revelations of a Melchizedek Initiate,* and *The Golden Keys to Ascension and Healing!*

- Call to Spirit, the Masters, and the Angels to imprint, at night while you sleep; thoughtforms, images, and suggestions of perfect health!

- Every night before bed, ask and pray to Spirit and the Masters to work all night long on your physical body for healing in whatever area you need it. The key is in the asking, for they are not allowed to help unless you ask and pray!

- Go to a Health Farm for a week as a gift to the physical body.

- Take an Epson Salt bath.

- Take a bath with Water of Life products.

- During all the hours you are consciously awake, call and pray to Spirit and the Masters for help any time you have any symptoms, be they energetic or physical, and they will come and instantly begin working on you!

- Get acupuncture treatments from a trained doctor!

- Call to Spirit and the Masters to fully repair the electrical system in your etheric and physical body!

- Master your mind and emotions! (See *How to Release Fear-Based Thinking and Feeling: An In-depth Study of Spiritual Psychology* and *Soul Psychology*, available from the Academy!)

- Be sure to take responsibility for "Mastering the Earth, Earth Energies, and fully Integrating the Material Face of GOD!" (See *The Golden Book of Melchizedek*, available from the Academy!)

- Be sure to integrate the God/Goddess aspects of self (See new book *Empowerment and Integration of the Goddess*, available from Academy!)

- Learn to "Dine with GOD"! (See *The Golden Book of Melchizedek*)

- Learn how to call on Spirit and the Masters to help you eat a good physical diet but also live on Light as a dietary supplement!

- Pray to Spirit and the Masters for etheric vitamin and mineral shots!

- Pray to Spirit and the Masters to etherically give you any medicine you need that GOD also wishes you to have for help in your healing!

- Read chapter in *The Golden Book of Melchizedek* on health lessons caused by "Spiritual Mutation and Ascension Acceleration process!"

- Read my book *Ascension and Romantic Relationships* to make sure that you are 100% clear on relationship issues. Make sure that you are not improperly bonding in your Romantic or any other type of relationships that may be pulling on your energies inappropriately!

- Call to Spirit and the Masters to clear and cleanse any energy from group karma, racial karma, planetary karma, and ancestral karma!

- Ask GOD, Christ, and the Holy Spirit, to cleanse and purify your Oversoul, Monad and entire being, all the way back to your original Covenant with GOD!

In extreme health cases, if you do all these things and you are still not recovering, go to a skilled Spiritual Channel, Spiritual Psychic, Clairvoyant, and/or Intuitive Medical practitioner and see if they can pick up any karmic reasons or any other psychological lessons that need learning. I will say, however, if you do all the things I have mentioned in this chapter and in my books *How to Achieve Perfect Radiant Health from the Soul's Perspective, The Golden Book of Melchizedek: How to be an Integrated Christ/Buddha in this Lifetime, How to Release Fear-Based Thinking and Feeling: An In-depth Study of Spiritual Psychology*, and *Soul Psychology (Revised Edition)*, that 99% of the time, in my humble opinion, you will be able to create with the help of GOD, Christ, the Holy Spirit, the Masters, the Archangels and Angels, and the Christed Extraterrestrials, the healing, balancing, and repair of just about any and all health lessons on a Spiritual, mental, emotional, etheric, and physical level! In this program and outline that Spirit, the Masters and I have set up for you, is one of the most comprehensive health programs ever put forth in any book on physical health, for it is not just focusing on the physical level, it is also focusing on the Spiritual level, Mental level, Emotional level, Etheric level, Physical/Earthly level, and Interpersonal or Relationship level. It is only when you approach Healing from this "Integrated Health Full Spectrum Prism" approach from the Soul and Spirit's Perspective that physical health can really even be understood! My Beloved Readers, most doctors and practitioners approach health from a purely physical level, which is great! It needs to be understood; however, that 90% of all health problems and concerns have their origins and initial cause in the mental body, emotional body, and etheric body! The program here that Spirit, the Masters, and I have set up for you; along with a little extra reading on your part to insure full training is achieved on a Spiritual, Psychological, and Physical/Earthly Level; will completely purify, cleanse, and heal not only your physical body, but the etheric, emotional, mental, and all your Spiritual bodies! This will not only cause a much greater increase in your health and overall vitality, but Spirit, the Masters and I are also helping you to achieve God Realization and Integrated Ascension! This, my Beloved Readers, is why you have the health lessons you have! It was GOD, Christ, the Holy Spirit, your Mighty I Am Presence, and Higher Self's way of motivating you to seek truth, so that you would see that achieving God Realization and Integrated Ascension is the key to achieving Perfect Radiant Physical Health as well! My Beloved Readers, trust in the guidance and suggestions that Spirit, the Masters, and I have given you here; for I tell you that these suggestions work! If you follow the guidance given in this chapter, this book, and in the few books I have mentioned, you will become a "Crystal Clear Diamond of GOD" on a Spiritual, Mental, Emotional, Physical, and Physical/Earthly Level! When you are this purified and refined on every level, there will be no place for disease or health lessons to manifest! If they ever do manifest, it is because of some lessons that need to be learned. For there is no judgment in this and this is part of the Spiritual Path. You will have the Spiritual Knowledge and tools as contained in this chapter and the books I have mentioned, to heal yourself of any and all health concerns on a Spiritual, Psychological, and Physical/Earthly level!

My Beloved Readers, did not that Bible say "Seek ye the Kingdom of GOD and all things shall be handed unto thee"? This includes, my Beloved Readers, "Perfect Radiant Health"! In those very few cases where the health lesson is karmic, I will teach you through my books how to use whatever health lessons you have "for the Glory of GOD!" Spirit, the Masters, and I will show you how to maintain 100% inner peace regardless of any health lessons you have! For your physical body does not cause your reality, your thoughts do! In those extremely rare instances where a health lesson is karma; Spirit, the Masters, and I will show you how to enormously increase your overall physical health and be at total inner peace with any health challenges you do have, so all will achieve the 100% inner peace they seek! If you follow this overall program as Spirit, the Masters, and I have presented in this chapter and the books I have recommended, you will, I humbly suggest, achieve "an inner peace and overall general good health and Spiritual vitality that passeth understanding" regardless of what health lessons you are dealing with.

So let it be Written! So let it be Done!

20

The Five Dispensations of Ascended Master Teachings

My Beloved Readers, I am writing this chapter upon request of my dear friend Master El Morya, who thought it would be helpful to lightworkers to have an overview of the Ascended Master Teachings, Dispensations, and Organizations of the past, present, and future. Because of my great Love and respect for Master M, when he asked me to do this I was very happy to oblige and to make manifest on this Earthly plane this most wondrous legacy of Ascended Master Dispensations on the Earthly plane! There are five basic dispensations of Ascended Master teaching in our present age that have been and will be brought forth to this planet! This is not to say that a great many others have not greatly added and contributed to the knowledge brought forth to the present learning and understanding of Ascended Master Teachings. For especially in this present modern era, there has been a great many contributions in writings to the legacy of the Ascended Masters. These Dispensations I am speaking of here are a large series of Ascended Master Teachings books brought forth to lay the foundation for the Ascended Masters Work!

The First Dispensation was, of course, by the great Madam Blavatasky, now known on the inner plane as Lady Helena. She was, of course, the founder and main channel and scribe for Kuthumi, Saint Germain, El Morya, and the Ascended Masters for the first Dispensation of Ascended Master Teachings in the late 1800's and early 1900's. She wrote a voluminous amount of channeled material on the Ascended Masters. Madam Blavatasky was one of the greatest channels of our time. She founded the Theosophical Movement! She worked very closely with another wonderful teacher by the name of C.W. Leadbeater, who was also instrumental in later stages of the Theosophical Movement and wrote some wonderful easier to read books on the Ascended Master Teachings. One that stands out in my mind is a book called *The Masters and the Path*! Both Madam Blavatsky and Leadbeater worked very closely with Colonel Henry S. Olcott who was kind of like Madam Blavatsky's right hand man and a great healer in his own right! Later Annie Besant joined the group and took on much of the work of the Theosophical Movement. It was this organization, The Theosophical Movement, under the leadership of Madam Blavatsky and C.W. Leadbeater, that took on the assignment of finding a suitable candidate on the Earthly plane for Lord Maitreya, the Planetary Christ on the inner plane, to "Overlight" in a similar vein as he did for the Master Jesus 2000 years previously! Five candidates were selected; however, only one was chosen. This was Krishnamurti! Krishnamurti was a totally uneducated and refined Indian boy who Madam Blavatasky and C.W. Leadbeater took under their wing, so to speak, and trained to become the next "Christed Vehicle" for the Earth. This training went on for a great many years and the Theosophical Movement developed a tremendous following around the world because of the collective efforts of these valiant souls who were really the ground breakers of the first Ascended Master Dispensation! Madam Blavatsky was clearly the head of the organization and wrote I believe over 20 books that, still to this day, hold the testament of time.

Krishnamurti upon entering adulthood changed his mind, as did Lord Maitreya and the Spiritual Hierarchy, as to the original plan of Overlighting, and Krishnamurti left the Theosophical Movement and chose to cut himself off from the Ascended Masters, which was a long story in itself. He chose to follow his own path, which of course was his Divine Right, and continued his work until his passing in the not so distant past in the Ojai, California area! For those interested in learning more about Madam Blavatsky, C.W. Leadbeater, Colonel Henry Olcott, Krishnamurti, and Annie Besant, I would humbly recommend reading my book *The Ascended Masters Light The Way*! I have written four most wondrous chapters on the highlights of the life of Madam Blavatsky, C.W. Leadbeater, Colonel Henry Olcott, and Krishnamurti. This is indeed a most wondrous story of the First Dispensation of Ascended Master Teachings.

It is also very interesting to note that Madam Blavatsky had personal physical contact with the Ascended Masters Kuthumi, El Morya, and Djwhal Khul; who were all physically incarnated and at that time living in Tibet! I also believe she had physical contact with Saint Germain as well. Actual photographs were taken of them all together, which I believe many of you have seen! For those who have not read these four chapters in my book, I think you would find this first Dispensation of Ascended Master Teachings quite interesting reading! I would like to take this time to honor Madam Blavatsky (Lady Helena) and those great souls who helped to lay the First Dispensation of Ascended Master Teachings on the Earth!

The Second Dispensation of Ascended Master Teachings were the incredible books written by the Ascended Master Djwhal Khul! As you all know from reading my books, Djwhal Khul is a very dear friend and close mentor of mine! Djwhal Khul was the Master Kuthumi's main disciple, initiate, and friend at the time of the Theosophical Movement. He appeared physically to Madam Blavatsky on at least one occasion I can remember for sure. Djwhal Khul in his past life was Confucius, the great Sage of China. He was also one of the Three Wise Men in the Story of Jesus, along with El Morya and Master Kuthumi! Saint Germain was Joseph, the husband to Mother Mary! So, they all met up again 2000 years later to lay the very early initial foundation for the next 2000 year cycle! Quite interesting wouldn't you say, my Beloved Readers! I believe at the time of the Theosophical Movement even Lord Maitreya may have made some physical appearances, for El Morya, Kuthumi, Saint Germain, and Djwhal Khul were all very close and at least three of them were living in Tibet very close together. The Ascended Master Djwhal Khul was also in a past life Kleinias, a disciple of Pythagoras, who of course was Master Kuthumi in a past life. Master Kuthumi in past lives has also been Saint Francis, the architect of the Taj Mahal, John the Beloved, and a disciple of Jesus. El Morya was Balthazar of the Three Wise Men, I believe, with Kuthumi being Melchior and Djwhal Khul being Casper. El Morya was also Abraham, the founder of the Jewish religion, and Lord Maitreya was Krishna in a past life. Saint German was in his past lives Columbus, the Prophet Samuel in the Jewish religion, Francis Bacon (Shakespeare), and Merlin. So this is quite an interesting crew we have here!

Djwhal Khul telepathically channeled 22 volumes of Ascended Master Teachings through Alice Bailey who was also one of the greatest channels of our present day! It is to this day one of the most comprehensive dispensations of Ascended Master Teachings ever brought forth to the Earth! They stand as a tremendous Spiritual monument to the work of the Spiritual Hierarchy and Ascended Masters!

Djwhal Khul physically ascended in the late 1940's, which means in this case he turned his physical body into light and returned to the spiritual world! There, Master Kuthumi gave him Spiritual Leadership of the "Inner Plane Synthesis Ashram" which is a sub-ashram of the Second Ray Ashram of Master Kuthumi. This ashram is in charge of training all the disciples and initiates on the Earth in the area of Spiritual Education and Synthesis training in the Seven Rays. It is the only ashram on the inner plane that's specific purpose is the synthesis of all Seven Rays! The Second Ray is the Ray of Love/Wisdom and its focus is "Spiritual Education"! This is such a big job on Earth and that is why Lord Maitreya and Master Kuthumi decided to create the Second Inner Plane Ashram. It is also because Master Kuthumi, who is the Chohan of the Second Ray, is training to take over the position of Planetary Christ when Lord Maitreya moves to his next Cosmic Position! Master Kuthumi is so busy with this other work that he needed a trustworthy Master to train a great many of the Second Ray disciples and initiates and all disciples and initiates needing spiritual education and training in how to integrate all Seven Rays! Djwhal Khul has taken on a great many of Master Kuthumi's students so Master Kuthumi could focus on the cosmic work that he is involved in! Master Kuthumi and Djwhal Khul are extremely close friends, as is Master El Morya, Lord Maitreya, Saint Germain, and all the Ascended Masters!

On the inner plane the Second Ray Ashram is a three story building complex of immense size and beauty! Djwhal Khul runs the first floor, known as the inner plane Synthesis Ashram! Master Kuthumi runs the second floor as the Chohan or Lord of that Ray, and Lord Maitreya, the Planetary Christ, runs the third floor! These are the three main Masters that run the Second Ray Department of Spiritual Education and the Love/Wisdom Ray for this planet! El Morya is the Chohan of the First Ray of Power focusing on the political arena on Earth! Serapis Bey is the Chohan for the Third Ray of Active Intelligence, which deals with the business side of Earth life! Paul the Venetian is Chohan for the Fourth Ray which is Harmony, Beauty, and the Arts! His job is the harmonizing, beautification, and training in the spiritual side of the Arts! The Chohan for the Fifth Ray is Master Hilarion, with the focus on the Concrete Mind and New Age Science. The Sixth Ray Chohan is

Sananda. This is also quite an interesting story, for Sananda in past lives was of course Jesus, Amilius, Adam, Melchizedek teacher of Abraham (El Morya), Enoch, Zend the father of Zoroaster (Buddha), Ur, Asapha, Apollonius of Tynnia, Jeshua, and Joshua, who took over for Moses and led the Jewish people into the Promised Land. Isn't this interesting? The Seventh Ray is Lady Portia and Saint Germain in the area of Ceremonial Order and Magic, Freedom, Transmutation, Alchemy, the Violet Flame, and the Restructuring, Organization and Grounding of the Divine Plan on Earth! Allah Gobi is the Manu of the First Ray. Lord Maitreya the Planetry Christ, as I said. Saint German is also serving now as the Mahachohan! Lord Buddha has taken over the position of Planetary Logos, or President of the Planet, from Sanat Kumara who has moved to his next higher Cosmic Position and is overlighting Lord Buddha in his work! Lord Buddha in past lives was, of course, Orpheus, the great Greek Master. He was Arjuna, disciple of Krishna (Lord Maitreya). He was Thoth/Hermes, the great Egyptian Master, builder of the Pyramids and the author of the Great Hermetic laws; Vyassa, the Scribe for the Bhagavad-Gita; and Zoroaster, the Great Persian Spiritual Master!

So my Beloved Readers, I think you can see that, in truth, this story of the Ascended Masters really began much earlier than this First Dispensation of Ascended Master Teachings with Madam Blavatsky and the Theosophical Movement. It has its first antecedents in all the religions of the Earth!

My Beloved Readers, I have a few more things I wish to say about Djwhal Khul and Alice Bailey; however, before I do this I want to share the Third Dispensation of Ascended Master Teachings which are the "I Am Discourses" channeled by Godfre Ray King. This is also, my Beloved Readers, a most interesting story, for Godfre Ray King in his past life was none other than George Washington, the first President of the United States! Is it not fitting that he would be the channel to bring forth the "I Am Teachings" for Saint Germain to the United States and the world? This was another 18-volume series of books that, I believe, brought forth another fantastic Dispensation of Ascended Master Teachings to the planet. Beloved Saint Germain brought forth the most wondrous teachings of the "The Mighty I Am Presence"! These are most wonderful books! Very easy to read and to bring forth the Science of Invocation and Affirmation using the "I Am" as only Saint Germain can! These books blend very nicely with the 22 volumes written by Alice Bailey and Djwhal Khul!

As the story goes Saint German physically materialized to Godfre Ray King in the 1930's, which began a whole story and series of books channeled by Saint Germain and other Ascended Masters! Godfre King is another one of the great channels of our time! Saint Germain has made a wonderful contribution to this planet again as he has in the past in bringing forth these teachings!

In addition, around this time it is noteworthy to say, not in the sense of a Dispensation, but as a very great contribution to the collected work of Ascended Master Teachings, Master El Morya through Nicolas Roerich brought forth another series of books on Agni Yoga. I believe there were around 15 or 16 books in this series, which was another catalyst to the legacy of the Ascended Masters' Dispensations!

Also, in this vein of noteworthy contributions by the Ascended Masters is the set of books written in the 1970's by the Master Jesus known as *A Course in Miracles*. The Master Jesus took on the Spiritual Assignment as only he could do, of explaining the difference between Christ thinking and egotistical thinking in this three volume set: Text book, Lesson book and Teacher's Manual! Truly one of the most incredible set of books and Divine Revelations of Ascended Master Teachings of our time! Jesus channeled these books through a Jewish woman, who when asked why she was chosen for this assignment the Master Jesus said, "…because she would do it and would not put a lot of her own interpretations and opinions into the work"! She indeed did as Jesus requested!

One other noteworthy contribution is Djwhal Khul returning in the 1970's with Vywamus, the Higher Aspect of Sanat Kumara, to found the Tibetan Foundation. This was done through the channeling work and books of Janet McLure! I believe she passed on in the late 70's or early 80's, but brought forth some wonderful channelings from Djwhal Khul and Vywamus to continue this Ascended Mastery Legacy. The Tibetan Foundation is no longer in operation; however, I would like to take this time to honor Janet McLure for her wonderful contribution to this legacy!

Djwhal Khul in the 1940's, after "Physically Ascending" and turning his body to light, continued to telepathically communicate with Alice Bailey from the inner planes. Before that, he was living in Tibet and was telepathically channeling the books from there to Alice Bailey. I would also at this time like to honor Alice Bailey and Djwhal Khul for the wonderful contribution they both have made through these writings to this Ascended Mastery Legacy!

To continue this most interesting story of the Ascended Mastery Dispensations, organizations, writings and legacy; Djwhal Khul in 1996 graciously asked me if I would consider taking over his "Inner Plane Synthesis Ashram" in the not too distant future, for he was preparing to get ready to leave for his next Cosmic Position! At the time of his making this request I had published my first five books: *The Complete Ascension Manual, Soul Psychology, Beyond Ascension, Hidden Mysteries,* and *The Ascended Masters Light the Way*! I had also just completed my first Wesak Celebration in Mt. Shasta! I had been working very closely with him for many years and he had helped me, along with other Ascended Masters, to write many of my books. I was extremely well-versed and well-studied in all the previous Dispensations and contributions of Ascended Master Teachings. I had been a Spiritual Teacher, Spiritual Psychologist, and Channel for many years for the Masters, and had always felt an enormous attunement and kinship with the Ascended Masters' lineage and teachings! I was greatly honored by Djwhal Khul's and the Spiritual Hierarchy's invitation to take on this Spiritual Leadership Assignment. The idea of being able to run the first floor of this inner plane ashram with Master Kuthumi and Lord Maitreya was most intriguing! Since 1996, I have been in training with Djwhal Khul, Melchizedek, the Mahatma, Archangel Metatron, and the Core Group of Masters I work with in preparation to take over this "Inner Plane Synthesis Ashram"! In the meantime, I was guided at that time to open the Melchizedek Synthesis Light Academy! This was the anchoring on Earth of the Inner Plane Synthesis Ashram overlighted by Djwhal Khul, Melchizedek, the Mahatma, Archangel Metatron, and the Planetary Hierarchy I have mentioned in this chapter, and others such as the Divine Mother, Mother Mary, Quan Yin, Isis, Helios and Vesta, the Lord of Arcturus, the Lord of Sirius, the Ashtar Command, Sai Baba, and others. It has grown over the years and I humbly and lovingly call them all "Core Group"!

Anyway, to continue this story, I had already started writing, as I previously mentioned, my "Easy-to-Read Encyclopedia of the Spiritual Path"! I have completed 27 volumes in this series of books. They are based upon the Ascended Master Teachings of the past, present, and future! They are both co-creative writings of my own and the Ascended Masters, creating a "Synthesis of all Ascended Master Teachings, Religions, Spiritual Paths, Mystery Schools, Sacred Writings, Spiritual Texts, Spiritual Teachers, and Gurus"! It has its foundation, however, in the writing of the Ascended Masters! However, because of my humble unique gift in the area of "Synthesis," I have tied the Ascended Master Teachings in with this synthesis effort to show the unification of all teachings! In truth, all teachings have their origin in the Universal Logos Melchizedek and what has been called the "Ancient and Sacred Order of Melchizedek"! In truth we all are connected with this sacred order for we all live, move and have our being in the "The Melchizedek Universe" of which Melchizedek is the head. The name Melchizedek is one a great many people have called themselves or named themselves! Just because someone names himself or herself Melchizedek, does not make them one. A Melchizedek in Ancient Teachings is considered a Seventh Degree Initiate! It is a Priest- and Priestesshood! This is why a great many people on our Earth have taken on this name or are taking on this name, which is fine and beautiful! The Melchizedek I am speaking of here is Melchizedek, the Universal Logos and President of our entire Universe! So all of us, my Brothers and Sisters, are part of His sacred order!

I have plans to complete 34 volumes in my book series, and then this book series will be complete and I will have completed my Spiritual Assignment and mission in this specific regard! The unique things about these books are the comprehensiveness and scope of the work and how easy to read and practical they are. How they synthesize all that I have spoken of. How they address not just Spiritual Mastery, but all Psychological Mastery and Physical/Earthly Mastery, and how to integrate the three! Also, they bring forth from the Ascended Masters, I humbly suggest, some of the most cutting-edge Ascended Master Teachings in the area of Ascension, Spirituality, Psychology, Earthly Mastery and Healing ever brought forth! Djwhal Khul told me approximately three years ago that this 34 volume series of books, of which I have completed 27 volumes, is the "Fourth Dispensation of Ascended Master Teachings" that he prophesied would come at the turn of the century and which he wrote about in the Alice Bailey books in the 1940's! I am very humbled and honored to have taken on and almost completed the assignment, and to have been offered the position of taking over the "Inner Plane Synthesis Ashram" when Djwhal Khul moves on to his next Cosmic Position. At this time I am very much enjoying anchoring the Synthesis Ashram and Academy on Earth under the guidance of Djwhal Khul, Melchizedek, the Mahatma, and the Core Group of inner plane Ascended Masters! When my mission on Earth is complete, I will take over this aforementioned Spiritual Assignment, for which I am receiving great training and practice here on Earth! I feel an incredible love and connection with the Ascended Masters. They feel like my home, so to speak! I am greatly honored and humbled to be a link in this chain of Ascended Masters Teachings, Dispensations, and Legacy! It is my great hope and prayer that this current 27 volume series of books will bring forth the profound wonderment and enlightenment of this most rich Ascended Master tradition in a past, present and cutting-edge future sense on all levels!

My Beloved Readers, this now brings me to the Fifth and final Ascended Master Dispensation! This one is the future one which has not yet come to pass! It has been my job to lay the foundation and revelation for the New Millennium. It is my great honor under the guidance and direction of the inner plane Ascended Masters at this time to give a "bird's eye view" of what we are now preparing for in terms of the next Ascended Master Dispensation upon entering this New Millennium. The writing about this is one of the most enjoyable Spiritual Assignments I have ever taken on, for it truly is the Spiritual Vision of the Seventh Golden Age! On this note, I will begin!

My Beloved Readers, in the not too distant future a great change and transformation will be taking place on this planet which, in truth, has already just begun. The previously hidden esoteric and hidden Mystery School Training will be made Exoteric! The Externalization of the Spiritual Hierarchy will be made fully manifest on the Earth! The "Houses and Temples of Light" will be reopened! Instead of the Pyramids being monoliths of past spiritual greatness, they and many other edifices of a like nature will be reopened to the greatness of their past! The inner plane ashrams of the Christ will be made manifest on the Earth. The Melchizedek Synthesis Light Academy and Ashram is one of the first of these to be made manifest! It has been my Spiritual Assignment and those of my fellow Masters and High Level Initiates and many others of you all over the world, to lay the groundwork and foundation for this to take place! Those members of the Spiritual Hierarchy on Earth will fully claim their rightful positions. The Seven Ashrams of the Christ will be fully anchored and headed by Masters and High Levels Initiates on Earth. Actual initiations will be performed on Earth as they are on the Spiritual Plane! The traditions and secrets of the Mystery Schools will no longer be hidden! There will be open instruction and teaching. The inner mysteries will be totally revealed! The full Externalization of the Hierarchy will not just manifest in the area of Spiritual Education, but in all aspects of society. Masters and High Level Initiates will openly claim their positions in Politics, Government, Business, Economics, the Arts, Music, Architecture, all the New Age Sciences, Religion, and the complete reorganization and restructuring of society! Our educational system will be completely reformed and the Soul and Spirit will be reintroduced in a Universal and synthesis manner that honors and is inclusive of all religions and alienates no one! Our prison systems will be reformed along spiritual principles. Violence and lust will be removed from our movies and media for the people won't stand for it! Our legal system will be transformed. Partisan politics will be a thing of the past and a new form of civility, honor, and Spiritual/Christ/Buddha Consciousness will re-enter this most noble profession.

The veil between the inner plane Ascended Masters and the outer plane Externalization of the Hierarchy will be lifted! The Spiritual Government on the inner plane through its externalized Masters on Earth will begin to government-ally and politically lead the nations of the Earth!

The United Nations will be revamped to truly reflect all countries on the Earth! We will truly have a confederation of nations on Earth all working together under the Spiritual Leadership of the Ascended Masters and Spiritual inner plane Government! This will lead to the admission by all governments of the existence of Extraterrestrials! This will lead to the open entering, en masse, of Christed Extraterrestrials to the Earth! This will cause an acceleration on our planet, the likes of which it has never known! They will help us rid our planet of pollution! They will help us get rid of all illness and disease! They will help us rebuild the "Houses and Temples of Light"! The Ancient Temples of Atlantis and Lemuria in their golden past ages will re-emerge! The Ancient Order of Melchizedek will be made manifest on Earth! The Extraterrestrials in conjunction with the inner plane Ascended Masters will bring new technologies and ideas to every aspect of our society. These are civilizations on other planets that have solved these issues and lessons hundreds and thousands of years ago! As we show ourselves responsible and prepared, more and more will be given! Every aspect of Society and Civilization will be reorganized and re-formed under the Divine Plan of the inner plane Ascended Masters, under the Divine Plan of Lord Buddha, Lord Maitreya, the Manu Allah Gobi, the Mahachohan and the Seven Chohans, Saint Germain, Djwhal Khul and the Synthesis Ashram! There will be much more open and direct contact and much clearer communication between the inner plane Ashrams, Masters, Initiates, and Government and Political Leaders! We will begin to slowly but surely return to how it was in Lemuria before the fall and densifica-tion of matter occurred! Matter is now in the process of slowly but surely becoming more etheric in nature as it was in the beginning! The next 1000 years will continue this process until eventually we will return to a place where it was in the beginning, in the Garden of Eden of Lemuria! We are the Light Bearers for a New Age! Sai Baba will reincar-nate again for his third incarnation in his triple avatar incarnation! The Archangels and Angels will also be part of this New Revelation! They will be more openly honored, revered, and accepted as the noble Servants of GOD they are. They will reveal themselves much more openly and their mysteries and teachings will be unfolded! The Elohim line of evolution will be added to this mix as well! There will be an integrated working together of the Inner Plane Ascended Masters, Archangels and Angels, Elohim Councils, Christed Extraterrestrials, Masters and Initiates on Earth! Adding to this mix will be the complete returning of the Divine Mother and the Goddess to Earth. The Goddess energies have been abused and banished from the Earth for eons of time! This will completely change! Total equality will reign! Women will be paid as much as men! Women will take over governmental and political positions! The end of the Patriarchy will have come! All prejudice and racism will be removed from our society! The Divine Mother and the Goddess energies will finally be given their proper honor and Reverence! Brotherhoods and Sister-hoods of Light will reign supreme! The Goddess path will be revered as highly as the God path! The Goddess will take over more and more positions in the Spiritual Government as well! In truth, they already have, they are just not known about!

As part of this process, the Mother Earth will finally be honored as the living, Sacred Being she is! Honoring and sanctifying the Earth will be one of our biggest priorities. The Earth will be removed of all pollution and returned to her pristine Edenic State! There will also be much greater honoring of the Animal, Plant, and Mineral Kingdoms! They will be seen as our younger Brothers and Sisters and will be seen as the incarnations of God that they are!

Part of this Transformation will also see the honoring of the Nature Kingdom, Pan, the Nature Spirits, Plant Devas and Elementals! There will be an open communication between the people of the Earth and these etheric beings that control all of nature! They will again fully return to Earth and all Her gardens and farms!

There will be the open communication of all these different beings I have mentioned in this chapter under the guidance of the "inner plane Ascended Masters"! Lord Buddha who holds the Divine Plan for our planet, which he receives from Helios and Vesta, which they receive from Melchior, which he receives from Melchizedek, which he receives from GOD, Christ and the Holy Spirit! It is stepped down at each level so the entire Universe unfolds according to GOD's Plan! Lord Buddha will give the Divine Plan to the Manu, the Christ, and the Mahachohan, as well as the Seven Chohans, Djwhal Khul and the Synthesis Ashram. They will then disseminate this Divine Plan to all Masters and Higher Level Initiates on Earth in all aspects of Earth life! Each of the Seven Ashrams of the Christ and the Synthesis Ashram will be in charge of a different aspect of the Divine Plan to Manifest on Earth both in a Heavenly and Earthly sense!

The Religions of the world will also be revamped to free them from the contamination of negative ego programming and dogma. As negative ego is cleared from the religions, they will become much more united and inclusive in nature, and all competition and self-righteousness will end! They will also be seen as pathways to GOD that are equally valued! There will always be different Religions and this is good! However, they will cooperate much more in the future under the Spiritual Leadership of the Ascended Masters!

As time progresses, the governments and political leaders of our world will be Spiritual Masters and High Level Initiates! The Ascended Masters will have led us to build a new Utopian civilization! It will be a Fifth Dimensional civilization not a third dimensional civilization! One of the blueprints the Inner Plane Ascended Masters will use is the blueprint of the Arcturian civilization! Arcturus is the most advanced civilization in our Galaxy. They are approximately 3000 years ahead of us! They will bring their Technologies and Spiritual Wisdom, in conjunction with the

Ascended Masters, to help us more quickly solve all the great pressing issues of our times! The rain forests will be saved! The ozone level repaired! All pollution will be removed! Greenhouse effect repaired! Pesticides stopped! New forms of energy based on principles like that which Nikola Tesla brought to the planet, will come, and we will no longer burn fossil fuels for energy! Free forms of energy will be created! With free forms of energy, all pollution will end! Control of our worlds by Power Elite and Secret Governments will end! Abuse of all kinds will end! All war will end! The Earth will join its rightful conscious place in the Confederation of Planets of our Solar System, Galaxy, and Universe. With the help of extraterrestrial technology, space travel to other worlds will actually be a possibility!

There will be open Spiritual, Scientific, and Technological exchange! All Spiritual Paths, Mystery Schools, and Spiritual Traditions will be honored under the rulership of Ascended Masters! Great Spiritual Masters from the inner plane will incarnate on Earth! Lord Maitreya may incarnate again in 700 years as the new Cosmic Christ!

With the society totally changed under the direct leadership of the Ascended Masters, it will not be such a major decision for inner plane Ascended Masters to choose to come to Earth as it is now!

So, in conclusion, this fifth Dispensation of Ascended Master Teachings and Organization will be a most glorious one! My Beloved Readers, we are not that far away I am happy to see, and yet there is much work to be done! It is all of our jobs as the Light Bearers for the New Age, to lay the foundation and ground work for all of this to take place! We are living now on the brink of one of the most glorious times in the history of this Earth! We are literally on the brink of the Realization of the Seventh Golden Age on this Planet! It is my sincere hope and prayer that you have enjoyed the Masters and my sharing of rich Spiritual Tradition, Legacy, Present Condition, and Future

Dispensation of the Ascended Masters on Earth! It has been my great honor and joy to share this past, present, and future Story of the Ascended Masters on Earth with you!

21

The Incredible Love, Wisdom, and Power of GOD, the Godforce, and the Sons and Daughters of GOD on Earth!

My Beloved Readers, I feel very inspired this afternoon to write this chapter! Very often lightworkers do not feel they have much power to make a change in this world! My Beloved Readers, never give into this thought or feeling, for nothing could be father from the truth! Even just one person, let alone many, can have an enormous effect on people's lives!

There are so many examples. Let us look at the life of Jesus! The example of one man, who only lived on this planet until the age of 33 years old, may be one of the most influential in the history of our planet! Look at the effect Lord Buddha has had, not only when he lived, but for 2000 years later! Look at the effect one man, Mahatma Ghandi, had in India. His only weapon was his faith, his love, and his loincloth! One man brought down the British Empire!

Look at Mother Teresa, an average nun who had an idea about helping the poorest of the poor! Edgar Cayce, a nondescript, simple man who became one of the greatest prophets and channels in the history of the Earth! Confucius in China! Thoth in Egypt! Orpheus in Greece! Zoroaster in Persia! Krishna in India! Rama in India! Moses in the Middle East! Mohammed in the Arab world! Pythagoras, Mother Mary, Plato, and the list goes on and on! Look at the incredible Spiritual Power and impact that these people had!

It is not just the famous Prophets and Saints, however! Look at the incredibly inspiring example of Christopher Reeves! Look at the enormous impact on the world by Dr. Martin Luther King! Look at the effect of Nelson Mandela in South Africa. Living in prison for 25 years and coming out to be President of South Africa, and the Christed loving example he set!

Djwhal Khul said something very interesting in the Alice Bailey books, that sometimes the average man ends up achieving much more than the genius because of his or her personal power, faith, work ethic, self-discipline, and love!

My Beloved Readers, there are so many examples of average men and women who have done extraordinary things to affect this world! Look at some of the inventions! Look at the inventions of Nikola Tesla or Thomas Edison! They completely changed the way we live our lives! Discoveries in medicine have stopped disease! Look at the example Gorbachev set; and Yeltsin when there was that coup in the Soviet Union. If Yeltsin had not held strong against the coup he would never have become President, and the Cold War would not have ended! Look at the example of leaders such as Lincoln, Washington, John F. Kennedy, and Ronald Reagan. You don't have to be a Republican or a Democrat to appreciate the example these men set. Let the examples that were set by the soldiers in World War II to stop the tyranny of Nazi Germany be an example to us all, for their sacrifice on our behalf is what allow us to have the freedom we have today. This world would be quite a different place if we had lost that war!

Sometimes the vote of a Senator or Congressman can be the differ-ence between a crucial issue passing or not. One that can affect millions of people's lives! Look at what an effect a President of a country or a Congressman can have! Look at the effect a good spiritual book can have on millions of people's lives. Look at the inspirational effect a movie can have. Look at the effect that even a conversation can have on someone's life!

I humbly and with deep humility have seen the effect my books have had on people's lives. There is no a better feeling in the world than to know that you have helped someone and made them happier, brought them greater inner peace and helped them become closer to GOD and the Masters! One person can liter-ally change the world. They can do it in politics, spiritual education, through service work in the world, maybe feeding starving children, curing AIDS, helping the homeless, saving the rainforest, stopping child abuse, combating drunk driving, the list of possibilities is endless. They can do it through the arts. Maybe through architecture, like Michelangelo and the Sistine Chapel. Maybe the Taj Mahal. It could be through music! Look at the effect of Beethoven, Bach, current musicians, singers, and New Age artists! It could be spiritual education through doing workshops and seminars! It could be doing big spiritual events like Wesak! It could be through Spiritual counseling, healing, channeling sessions, writing articles, through television, radio, Websites, or the Internet! In this day and age, the world is actually very small. With a phone, fax, e-mail, a Website, and letters, one can literally affect the whole world and not leave their office. Do not underestimate the effect one person can have. In writing this 30 volume series of books, starting the MSLA, the Website, doing Wesak, making meditation tapes and videos, enormous numbers of people can and are being reached. I honestly do not share this for any egotistical reasons. I am just giving examples of what Sons and Daughters can do, and the enormous impact they can have. In this day and age with fax machines, phones, Websites, the Internet and e-mail, the entire world is a click away! Do not ever think you are powerless! Look how many people in a lifetime you have contact with. What if you dedicated every encounter with another person as one that is dedicated only to GOD! Imagine what an impact you would have! Look at the effect your words can have! Look at the effect even just your spiritual energy field can have! Look how many people you can reach by the phone and fax and e-mail! We can even travel so easily now around the world! The key is having pure motives and doing everything you do truly only for the glory of GOD and not for any selfish reason!

I am reminded of Peace Pilgrim; who would walk back and forth across the United States, with no money, just with her little backpack and faith! Look how a book someone writes, even 2000 years ago, can live on for thousands and thousands of years!

So far, I have just talked about the examples Sons and Daughters of GOD are setting all the time and the enormously profound effect they have!

I would like to change course here and now switch focus to the Power of Prayer that one Son and/or Daughter of GOD can have! This point was unbelievably brought home to me personally by the Masters one time, and I never forgot it. I have a great interest in politics and the social causes of our beloved planet Earth. Many of you are familiar with the Huna Prayer method that I have spoken about in my books *Beyond Ascension* and *How to Release Fear-Based Thinking and Feeling*! I am a man who is very big on prayer and meditation! I love GOD with all my heart and soul and mind and might, and I love the inner plane Ascended Masters, Archangels, Elohim, and Christed Extraterrestrials as well! I talk to them all of the time. I am constantly, and I mean constantly, praying. I pray to GOD, Christ, the Holy Spirit, and the Masters literally all of the time. I invite them into every aspect of my life! When anything is going on with other people and the world, I invite them in as well! I am a firm believer in what the Universal Mind said through Edgar Cayce! The Universal Mind said, "Why worry when you can pray"! Anytime I see anything negative going on I either pray, bless the situation, send love and light, do an affirmation or positively visualize! In this way, I try to be a positive force in the world. I try both to be an outer plane activist through my books, articles, public speaking, and an inner place activist through my inner plane work. So one of my favorite tools is doing Huna Prayers, or just calling in all the Masters and praying! A Huna Prayer, I should explain, is where you write out a prayer to GOD, all the Masters and Angels and so on. You then read the text of the prayer, and lastly ask and command the subconscious mind to take the Prayer to GOD and the Godforce with all the mana and vital force that is needed and necessary to manifest and demonstrate this prayer! This is all written or typed out on paper and said three times! It is extremely powerful and one of the most powerful prayer techniques I have ever found. If you have not been turned on to this before, check out the chapters on this subject in one of my two books that I mentioned! Anyway, to continue this story, this one particular time there was a stock market crash and in one day the stock market crashed over 500 points! It was a real melt down! Now I don't even own stock, but that is not the point. I knew this was very bad for the country and we had been having such incredibly good economic times, I knew the power of fear and how these things have a way of taking on a life of their own. So I immediately called in all the Masters and did a really big prayer calling in GOD, Christ, the Holy Spirit, and almost every Master in the Cosmic and Planetary Hierarchy by name to help turn this around! I think I may have done this a number of times over a two or three day period. Anyway, lo and behold, panic did not set in, the market recovered, and the stock market recovered all the points lost and started climbing again! I didn't think much of it for I am not one to look back, for I am too focused on the present and the future and too busy with nine million creative ideas and projects I am always trying to work on and get done in my Service work! So I knew that Spirit and the Masters helped, and that I was sure of. Anyway, I happened to be talking to the Masters a couple of days later and I was already on to something new as I always am, and they stopped the conversation and thanked me for praying for the stock market. To my total surprise, they said that my prayers had really had quite an impactful effect along with a few others on the planet that also prayed. My Beloved Readers, you must understand that Spirit and the Masters are not allowed to help unless asked. This is the "Prime Directive"! They are not allowed to interfere with the free choice of Sons and Daughters on Earth unless asked! So my simple prayer, along with others like me who called upon Spirit and the Masters, apparently had a big effect! They said it really did help turn around that which could have been a real downturn in the nation's economy, and as everyone knows the United States economy has a great effect on the world's economy. So, the fact that a small group of people on the Earth prayed really turned things around! I know for a fact that this was the case with people who prayed during World War II and during many other situations! Sometimes the fate of great events hangs in the balance on Earth and it is the prayers of a simple housewife, child, group of people, church group, group of lightworkers, disciple, initiate or Master, or Masters that may turn the tide! My Beloved Readers, I never forgot this! My Beloved Readers, the entire Power of GOD and the Godforce can be called in! This is what we do at Wesak! The Wesak Celebrations I hold at Mt. Shasta, the Masters told me, are overlighted by over one million inner plane Masters! You can imagine how powerful these events are! You know why there are a million Masters present. Not because I am special, but because over the years I kept calling them in! I was so persistent like Jacob in the Bible who would not let go of the Angel until he was blessed! Well that was the way I was! I kept praying and asking unceasingly; and I would not take no for an answer, and I would call them all in at home in my prayers and at Wesak, and you know what, my Beloved Readers, eventually they all came! Does not the Master Jesus say, "Ask and you shall receive; knock and the door shall be opened"! I have never forgotten the lesson from this story I told you, and I humbly suggest that you do not forget it either. A housewife living at home just raising her children can change the fate of the entire world through the power of her consistent, egoless, selfless, pure, heart-felt prayers for the world! Never forget this! Do not focus on the fruit of your prayers, for you must leave that to GOD and the Godforce! Just keep calling them in as Jacob of old, until they bless you and the whole world, which you live and breathe only to serve!

I would humbly like to share one other story about the power of meditation and prayer that brought this lesson home! I have never shared this story with anyone since it happened! I never really like to share these stories for I never ever want to come across as being egotistical. I try to keep all my books very clean of all this stuff and just give all the information and tools. There is enough self-promotion in the world and I have always been very sensitive on this point. This chapter, however, cannot be written without sharing a few personal experiences, so please forgive me for this fact! For this was the other experience that tuned me on to the power of prayer and meditation for all Sons and Daughters of GOD on Earth!

In this particular experience I was creating and channeling one of my Ascension Activation Meditations for Wesak. One where I do a type of Soul travel experience to the 352nd level of Creation to the Seat of the Throne of Grace, to have a type of council meeting with GOD and the Godforce with the 2000 lightworkers at Wesak, under the Wesak full moon and the mountain of Mt. Shasta! This particular Ascension Activation Meditation I was channeling was extremely powerful! When I am creating these meditations, I am in a meditative/channeling state! As I am typing or writing it down, I am actually going through it myself! So I had written this whole meditation where we all traveled to the Throne of Grace and there we were all seated before the Cosmic Council of 12 and the 24 Elders that surround the Throne of Grace! The entire Cosmic and Planetary Hierarchy were present because I had called them all in! I leave nothing to chance as you see! Anyway, while going through this meditation and Cosmic Activation, I called to the Cosmic Council of 12 and the 24 Elders that surround the Throne of Grace for their help in anchoring the "Cosmic Monad." Now I am not talking about our Mighty I Am Presence. That is our individualized Monad! I am talking here about the "Cosmic Monad," which in a sense contains all the Monads of all Creation! Now I don't claim to fully understand this; however, I had received some inner guidance that such a thing existed and leave it to me to leave no stone unturned. If it is out there or in there I should say, the "Sherlock Holmes of the Universe" will find it! So I asked the Cosmic Council of 12 and the 24 Elders that surround the Throne of Grace to bring forth their Spiritual Light Rods and anchor the Cosmic Monad onto and into the Earth. Now I swear to you on a stack of Bibles that the very second I had them do this in my meditation, in terms of bringing forth their Spiritual Light Rods instantaneously while sitting at my desk, there was a sizeable earthquake! Now, my Beloved Readers, I suppose this could have been a coincidence; however it occurred literally at the simultaneous instant their light rods came down! I was extremely humbled by this experience and this was the second experience I had that made me appreciate the effect that one Son or Daughter's Prayers can have! I promised myself I would never speak of this to anyone. This occurred about three years ago and I have not spoken of it to a single person until this moment! I share this for the sole purpose that next time you don't think you can have an effect on the world by your demonstration or your prayers think of this chapter! Literally, the demonstration and prayers of one soul with a pure, selfless, egoless heart can change the course of the history of this Earth!

Since all good things seem to come in threes, I will end this chapter by sharing one last story as to why I felt inspired to share this story. I love the Earth as I told you, and I feel a responsibility to help in the political and social affairs of the Earth. After having these experiences and seeing the effect I can have by my own demonstration and the power of prayer, I feel even more of a responsibility to take an active role. So today I was watching the news; there is a presidential election going on. I have very strong feelings and Spiritual passion on who I think is more in line with the Hierarchy's viewpoints. I have often talked to the Masters about political issues; the many social and philosophical issues this world is currently dealing with! As you all know the first ray department of the Spiritual Hierarchy is specifically in charge of Spiritual politics. The third ray and seventh ray departments also deal with the grounding of the new Spiritual Paradigms and Institutions on the Earth! Anyway, the election is very close now and could go in either direction. Fully knowing and understanding the power of prayer and past experience of calling in the full Power of GOD, Christ, the Holy Spirit, all the inner plane Ascended Masters, the Archangels and Angels of the Light of GOD, the Elohim Councils, and the Christed Extraterrestrials, I created just before I wrote this chapter one "humdinger" of a Huna Prayer to ask the full power of GOD and the Godforce for a Divine Dispensation, Divine Intercession, and Divine Intervention, 24 hours a day, seven days a week, 365 days a year until the election is over, to help the candidate of my choice win! I have also e-mailed twenty trusted Spiritual Masters and High Level Initiates this prayer, and asked them to join me if they feel so guided to help in this particular piece of Planetary World Service Work. I have also placed this prayer in the Academy on my Interdimensional Prayer Altar Program, which all of you are welcome to use for free as well. Just send me what-ever prayer you want and I will place it there for you! My Beloved Readers, I humbly state to you with total humility that I think my prayers to GOD and the entire Godforce who I have painstakingly and with great detail called in one by one will help! I hope and pray it will! I will not be attached to the "fruit of my actions" as Lord Krishna so eloquently stated in the Bhagavad-Gita in explaining the Path of Yoga and/or Service. However, my feeling is, my Beloved Readers, I could not live with myself if I did not at least try to do my part! If there is any chance that twenty Spiritual Masters and Initiates could consistently pray over the next three months to turn the tide of the election to the Spiritual Hierarchies' favor then I and we must try! Being a true believer in miracles, and having absolute unwavering belief and knowingness in the Love, Wisdom, and Power of GOD, Christ, the Holy Spirit, and the entire Godforce, we are humbly going to try and turn this election around in the favor of the candidate of our choice! It is after doing this and being filled with the love, wisdom, and power of GOD and the Godforce that I felt Spiritually guided to write this chapter!

My Beloved Readers, you are now being Spiritually challenged in total unconditional love to claim your full "Mantle of Christ," "Rod of Moses," and "love, wisdom, and power of God"; and dedicate your life from this moment forward to making your every specific thought, word, and deed the rest of this lifetime to demonstrating only the practice of the Presence of God, and making the largest mark on this world you can make for only the Glory of GOD! In doing so you not only demonstrate God in your every thought, word, deed, and every interaction with your Brothers and Sisters and all Kingdoms of GOD; but you also dedicate yourself in this moment to use your incredible power of prayer to call in GOD, Christ, the Holy Spirit, and the Godforce to help heal all personal and planetary situations that you come across! With your love, wisdom and power, your light, your love, your affirmations, your positive visualization, you Spiritual/Melchizedek/Christ/Buddha Consciousness, your Divine right action, your miracle-mindedness, and the power of your prayers to GOD and the Godforce, you can and will humbly perform miracles both known and unknown! Be not attached to the fruits of your actions, leave this to GOD, Christ, the Holy Spirit, and the Godforce, for all that is important is that you practice the presence of God!

So let it be Written! So let it be Done!

22

The Incredible Importance of Mastering, Loving, and Taking Responsibility for the Earth and Earth Energies

It is very interesting to me that there is so much focus on loving GOD and our Brothers and Sisters, which of course, is the most wonderful thing in the whole world, however there is not as much talk about loving the Earth and Earth life! In my humble opinion, if Jesus was on the Earth again in this New Millennium 2000 years later I think he would add a "New Commandment"! I think he would say, "Love the Lord thy GOD with all your heart and Soul and Mind and Might; love your neighbor as you love yourself; love all the Kingdoms of GOD and love Earth life!" For as I have said in this book many times, there are *four* Faces of GOD! All four need to be loved: Spiritual, Mental, Emotional, and Material! One will not realize God fully without mastering, integrating and fully loving Earth life!

Now it is a common belief among many people and may lightworkers on Earth to not like the Earth. Some look at it as a prison. Others look at it as being not important and only the Heavenly Worlds and

Celestial Dimensions as being important! Others still do not see the Material Universe as one of the Seven Heavens of GOD that it truly is! Others still think that matter is lower and unimportant and all that matter is good for is that we use this world to free us from the wheel of rebirth! Others still do not recognize that GOD exists as much in the Material Universe as he does in the Mental, Emotional, or Spiritual Dimensions of GOD! Others still do not recognize that if they do not learn to master, integrate, and fully love the Earth, Earth Energies, and Life, they will literally be missing one quarter of God Realization! A lot of lightworkers also do not realize that part of God Realization is integrating and balancing the God/Goddess within. One can never fully integrate the Divine Mother and the Goddess energies if you do not fully Love and integrate the Material Face of GOD!

Now my Beloved Readers, I am not just talking about here just loving the Earth Mother, and loving the Animal Kingdom, the Plant Kingdom, and the Mineral Kingdom. I am also not just talking about loving Pan, the Nature Spirits, the Plant Devas and Elemental Spirits. I am not just talking about mastering, integrating and loving the Earth and Earth energies! I am also not just talking about loving Nature, which is one of the easier aspects of Earth life to love. I am also talking about loving even Earth life! I am not saying there are not negative things that go on and a lot of negative people! I am not saying that it does not take a lot of courage! I am not saying it is not a difficult school! Maybe one of the most difficult! However, I am saying that if you do not learn to master, integrate and fully love the Earth and Earth life you have not fully learned your full lessons in regards to the Earth in terms of your reason for coming!

I have always been a very Spiritual person. This was always my greatest passion. I also incarnated in to a family of psychologists so I had a very strong connection to understanding working with psychology as well. Over the years, however, I have come to also have an unbelievably

242 / The Golden Book of Melchizedek

strong mastery, love, and connection to the Earth, Earth energies and Earth life! I really have come to more fully understand the Material Face of GOD! My single greatest passion in life deals with the understanding and recognition that to fully Realize God, that it must be done so on three distinct levels. It must be done on the Spiritual Level, the Psychological Level, and the Physical/Earthly Level! Each level is equally important! One is not better then another. Each level is a doorway to God Realization! I have always appreciated the Spiritual and the Psychological levels of GOD! I have always functioned well on the Earth and have had great mastery over Earth energies. However, it has just been in the last 10 years that my full appreciation of how God may be realized through the Earth has been fully appreciated and realized within me! It has opened a whole new window to GOD and appreciation of GOD! The profundity of GOD on the Spiritual Level goes without saying! The profundity of GOD on the Psychological Level, as you can see from reading this book and my other books on the subject, is equally as profound! Both of these levels of God Realization are so profound that they defy description! This book gives you a real appreciation of the Psychological and Spiritual profundity of GOD! What I want to share with you, my Beloved Readers, is that GOD is equally profound on a Physical/Earthly Level! I really have come to fully know and understand this! I incredibly appreciate the concept of mastering Earth energies as I do mastering the mind, emotions, and/or things of the Spirit! I also incredibly the Love and appreciate the concept and experience of grounding Spiritual energies, ascension, and the Mighty I Am Presence into my physical body and fully onto the Earth! As I have said many times: Ascension is descension. The purpose of life is not to leave the Earth, but to ground ones Mighty I Am Presence, Higher Self, and Soul fully into ones physical body and fully into the Earth and Earth Life!

The purpose of this chapter is to convey the importance of seeing the Material Face of GOD as an integral part of God realization. In truth, literally one third of God Realization would be missed. We would never even consider not loving the Spiritual dimensions of Reality. We would also not consider not loving the mental and emotional aspects of life. Yet, a great many people and lightworkers do not love the Earth and Earth life for many of the reasons I mentioned earlier in this chapter! This, my Beloved Readers, with no judgement intended, is faulty thinking! The Material Universe and the Earth is "GOD"! Earth life is GOD! To not fully Love the Material Universe and the Earth and Earth Life is to not Love GOD! To not learn to enjoy Earth life, and be happy on Earth, and to Love Earth life, is to not fully learn your Spiritual Lessons! Many lightworkers do not want to hear this, however it is the truth! There is a classic saying in Spiritual thought that says you never leave a situation until you have become happy in that situation, for if you haven't, you have not learned the lessons of that situation and are likely to repeat them. This applies to the Earth as well! As I started this chapter, to fully learn our lessons we must Love GOD, our Brothers and Sisters, All Kingdoms of GOD (Animal, Plant and Mineral, Nature, Etheric Nature spirits and Devas, Mother Earth, God/Goddess and last but not least the Earth and Earth life!) All of it must be loved! We must love and care for Earth life! Many Spiritual people are not political, or don't care about social issues or changing our society, for they believe it is not important. Only the Heavenly world is important, not what is going on in the Earthly world. This, of course, is faulty thinking! It is our purpose to love this world and turn it into a fifth dimensional society, a utopian society. This is why Sai Baba has said, "Hands that help are holier than lips that pray"! Cleaning up the pollution is important. Politics is important. Saving the whales is important. Saving the rain forest is important. Repairing the ozone layer is important. Picking up trash off the ground is important. Beautifying your home is important. Having a garden and taking care of it is important. Planting trees is important. Spiritually educating our world is important. Manifesting Spirituality on Earth is just as important as any Spiritual pursuit. Even more important, in truth, for that is why we have come; not to Ascend and leave, but to descend and build a new Spiritual Civilization on Earth. Creating beauty in this world in architecture and in all ways through the Arts is important. Helping to bring through new scientific discoveries on Earth is important. Revamping the religions of our world so they are free from negative ego contamination is important. Creating new structures on the Earth to make society run better is important. Being a gardener is important! Picking up trashcans is important! Cleaning toxic waste dumps is important. Every profession on Earth is important! Changing out society is incredibly important. Grounding your Spiritual mission on the Earth is incredibly important! Many lightworkers never ever ground their Spiritual Mission. Why have a physical body if you are not going to Spiritually Ground your mission. You could have done Spiritual and Psychological work without a physical body! You have come here to transform Earthly civilization. You did not come here to ascend and turn into light and leave this world. This is illusion. You have come here to become an Integrated Ascended Master and remain on Earth and transform this Earthly world! To think that you just came here to achieve your own personal ascension and leave is actually selfish, in an egotistical sense of the term. You are here to become an integrated Ascended Master and be of Service on the Earth. You are here to fulfill your Spiritual puzzle piece on Earth, not in Heaven! It is time for lightworkers to get out of the clouds, come back to Earth, and fulfill their Spiritual mission; which is to bring their unique abilities and talents to change this world! We are here to create a God civilization on Earth as it is in Heaven. We are here to create Heaven on Earth! I am not saying it is an easy job! I am the first to admit all the corruption and all the negative ego-run institutions in our world. Almost every institution on this planet is run backwards and is corrupt! Look at our prison systems. Is this how GOD would have us run them? Look at our educational system, is this how GOD would have us run them? Look at our political system and the partisan politicians and corruption, and negative ego spinning. Is this how GOD would have us run things! Almost every institution on the planet is run from the personality and negative ego, and not from the soul and Spirits perspective! We are here to fix all this! An enormous number of Lightworkers are not fulfilling their responsibilities and are not focusing on what they need to be focused upon. Massive numbers of lightworkers are focused on their own Spiritual growth and are not focused on the service work that they Spiritually contracted to do! Massive numbers of lightworkers have their head in the clouds and are too ungrounded! Massive numbers of lightworkers are too much in their mental bodies and focusing too much on esoteric knowledge, and are not fulfilling their Earthly/Spiritual responsibilities of Service work. A great many lightworkers are too much in their emotional body and not focusing on the Earth and loving the Earth and Earthly civilization! If we do not Master the Earth, Love the Earth and Earth life, be happy living on the Earth, and take responsibility for the Earth, we will not achieve full God Realization. If we do not fulfill our Spiritual mission, purpose and puzzle piece "on the Earth," we will not achieve God Realization! Framing it in this way is what lightworkers need to hear and understand because it is the truth, and something not that many Spiritual Leaders and Teachers are talking about!

So, the first step is that we master the Earth and Earth energies within our own being. Then we must always love the Earth, Earth energies, and Earthly Life! Then we must take responsibility and fulfill our Spiritual mission, purpose, and puzzle piece on Earth! This is an indisputable Spiritual Lesson every lightworker must fulfill if they wish to achieve God Realization! The time of living in a Spiritual world and not being part of Earth and the Material Universe is over. The time of being ungrounded and not fully loving and appreciating the Earth and Earth life is over! The return of the Goddess has finally come! It is time for lightworkers now to get their acts together. Lightworkers are the caretakers for Mother Earth and Earthly Civilization. Our civilization is still backwards in a great many ways! If lightworkers do not fix it, who is going to fix it? It is our responsibility! To just focus on one's own Spiritual Growth is selfish! It is time to call a spade a spade! We each have a Spiritual responsibility of making changes in this world and making changes in this society. For some it will be through Politics, others through Spiritual Education, others through Active Service in the world, others through the Arts, others through the Sciences, others through Religion, and others through Business, Economics and changing the institutions of our civilization! It does not matter what you chose to do or how you do it, what is important is your are doing something!

I am not saying there is not a phase where it is important to work on oneself for there is. This is a crucial phase. However, at some point it is necessary to be of service. At some point it is necessary to do service work and make some contribution and give back to the people of the Earth, the Earth herself and the Civilization we were brought up in. At some point, it is necessary to help others! If we truly have unconditional love and compassion how can we sit around and focus only on our own Spiritual Growth when people all over the world are suffering Spiritually, mentally, emotionally and in an Earthly sense! The Mother Earth has been enormously abused! If we are truly God's and everything is all part of us, how can we not want to get our hands dirty and help! How can we not dedicate our lives to service!

How can you love the Divine Mother and Goddess energies without loving Mother Earth, the people of the Earth, and the Civilization of the Earth and want to help contribute to heal it!

So, it is essential to master all aspects of Earthly life. It is as important to learn to master all aspects of Earthly life as it is to master all aspects of one's Spiritual Life, Mental Life and Emotional Life! All Four Faces of

GOD must be mastered! Then we must fully unconditionally Love the Material Universe, the Mother Earth and Earthly civilization! The Mastery is the First Ray influence in relationship to the Material universe! The Second Ray influence is the need to Unconditionally Love every aspect of Earth life! Out of these first two Rays then comes the Third which is Active Intelligence, which takes the Power and unconditional love, and grounds the power and love into the Earth in the form of active physical service. One of the reasons that a great many lightworkers are not mastering Earth energies and are not taking responsibility for the Earth, is they are not balanced in the Seven Rays. They are weak in Third Ray energy. For example a lot of second ray souls or Monads have all this Love and Wisdom, but it never makes it to the Third Ray where it is grounded into the Earth in the form of active physical service! This is what the Third Ray is about, grounding Spiritual Energy physically into the world in the form of active physical service! In a lightworker who is primarily Second Ray, the Spiritual energy floats above the Earthly Plane but never gets grounded! It is time for lightworkers to really wake up on this point. Another reason such an unbelievable number of lightworkers have difficulty grounding their Spiritual missions is that they are not only weak in the Third Ray of Active Intelligence, they are weak in their First Ray as well! They have not been trained how to fully own their 100% Personal Power at all times! This inability to own your Personal Power will of course make you completely unable to master Earth Energies or any other type of energies for that matter. It will make you a victim of your mind, feelings, emotions, physical body and the Earth life, while will also cause you to be ungrounded and floating all the time! Life will push the person around instead the person mastering life and they will of course be unsuccessful! Many who are strong in the Fourth Ray have a physical connection though the Arts and usually appreciate the Beauty of the Earth, but most souls usually incarnate with a ray configuration of 2/4/6 or 1/3/5. The 2/4/6 pattern makes one more emotional and if the person is heavy in the Forth Ray we have the classic starving artist type; who has enormous creative energies but cannot fully master Earth life. If they don't have third ray, which most don't, then the business side of life will be very weak. This is very common in artist types. So, we have the inability to master Earth energies. If a person has too much First Ray, they may be able to master Earth energies but not enough 2/4/6 to fully love the Earth! The predominately Second Ray type may have the ability to love the Earth, but can't master it from lack of Personal Power and Mastery of the First Ray, and can't ground their Spiritual Energy because of lack of Third Ray! The emphasis upon the Fifth Ray has the scientific mind to master Earth life and maybe take some responsibility for it; however, may not have enough 2/4/6 to fully love it and appreciates its beauty! Six Ray is very devotional and idealistic. When this predominates and continues in the 2/4/6 pattern, mastery of Earth Energies will be extremely weak. Business and grounding of Earth Energies will be very weak, and grounding of one's Spiritual mission may be very weak because of lack of first ray, third ray, and fifth ray! When Seventh Ray predominates, it could bring mastery and responsibility for Earth; however, danger of lack of love from the strong influence of Divine structure and order!

I would subtitle this last section as "The Lack of Integration of the Seven Rays and its Effect on One's Relationship to the Earth and Earth Life!" The Rays are not the only thing that is causing Lightworkers to not Master, Love, and take Responsibility for the Earth. It is also their Psychologies and Philosophies. It is their Spiritual Training as well!

My Beloved Readers, the title of this book is *The Golden Book of Melchizedek: How to Become an Integrated Christ/Buddha in this Lifetime!* You will not become a full Melchizedek, Christ, or Buddha if you do not Master, Love, and take responsibility for the Earth and Earth life! It is as important to take care of a person's physical needs as it is to take care of their Spiritual needs, mental needs, and emotional needs!

In truth, even more important. If a person is physically ill, it is hard to focus on Spiritual growth! If a child or person is starving and malnourished, it is hard to focus on Spiritual concerns. If a person is homeless, it is hard to focus on Spiritual Concerns. If a person is living on survival mode, it is hard to focus on Spiritual Concerns. If a person has no money, it is hard to focus on Spiritual concerns when they can't pay their rent, buy food, take care of their family, and get medication if they need it! My Beloved Friends, how is this world ever going to change if we each don't master Earth Energies, totally and completely love every aspect of the Earth, and physical take action to heal it! GOD and the Masters aren't going to do it. They can't, they don't have physical bodies! Don't you see, that is why we are here! We are instruments and channels of GOD and the Masters to make changes in this Earthly world. GOD's Divine Plan is to make this world function here, as does civilization in the higher worlds! This world is not just here as a Spiritual School to achieve Ascension and then we leave! GOD wants this world to have a fifth dimensional civilization! This is what creating Heaven on Earth really means! The Purpose of Life is to achieve Integrated Ascension and then remain on Earth and turn this world and its Civilization into the Seventh Golden Age on Earth! It is not the easiest job; however, it is what we have volunteered to come to do. So this chapter is a clarion call from Spirit and the Masters to achieve Integrated Ascension; and in the process of doing so to begin focusing more on service work and on fully grounding your Spiritual Mission and puzzle piece, and doing your part to bring the Seventh Golden Age onto this physical/Earthly Plane! This chapter is a clarion call for lightworkers to now get their priorities in order, and to fully master the Earth and Earth energies, to fully unconditionally love the Earth and Earth life on every level, and to take responsibility for doing your part to heal Mother Earth and help build the New Jerusalem on Earth!

So let it be Written! So let it be Done!

23

What Does Spiritually Mastering the Earth and Earth Energies Really Mean?

Again, it must be remembered that to achieve God Realization you must become a Spiritual Master on all three levels. These three levels are the Spiritual Level, the Psychological Level, and the Physical/Earthly Level! These are the three levels of God Realization that must be mastered, integrated, and balanced to achieve full God Realization. I have spoken extensively in this book and my others books about Spiritual, mental, emotional, and energetic mastery.

Spiritually mastering the Earth and Earth energies is just like Spiritual mastery, mental mastery, emotional mastery, energy mastery: however, this is mastery in regards to the mastery of the physical body, Earthly Energies, and Earthly life! The best way to describe this to give examples! To begin with, this deals with mastering the physical body: learning to physically eat right, taking care of physical fitness, developing good sleep habits, mastering the understanding of your body rhythms and learning to work with them. Mastering you sexuality and not being run by lower-self desire, yet integrating your sexuality in a Spiritually balanced way! Mastery of Earth energies deals with mastering money and developing prosperity consciousness and not poverty consciousness. Spiritual Mastery of Earth energies deals with staying organized in your Earthly life and having proper time management, Spiritual, and Earthly structure, and prioritizing your goals and projects.

Mastering Earth Energies deals with getting all the work done you need to do, getting your errands done, taxes done, accounting, book keeping, banking, grocery shopping and so on! Keeping up with returning phone calls, letters, e-mail, and correspondence! Being successful in your business! It has to do with keeping your house and office clean and organized! Taking care of your home and garden! Taking proper care of your animals! It means beautifying your home and environment. Paying attention to aesthetics. It means proper grooming, and paying attention to the clothes and colors of the clothing that you wear! It means pursuing excellence in every aspect of Earth life just as you purse excellence in your Spiritual life and Psychological life! You want to strive to be Spiritually immaculate on all levels!

Earthly mastery means learning to be grounded. I have dedicated an entire chapter to this in this book; for it is a Spiritual Practice that many lightworkers have lost sight of, or have forgotten how to do and what the mechanics of staying grounded really are! Earthly mastery means flossing your teeth and taking care of your gums and all aspects of your physical body that need maintenance. It means going to the dentist, or doctors when need to be, and not looking at the care of the body as being of lesser importance than that of your Spiritual, mental, emotional, or etheric bodies! It means also taking your car in for maintenance, doing maintenance on your computer, printer, and any other machines you have! It means taking proper care and sanctifying Matter as an aspect of GOD! It means doing the dishes as a Spiritual devotional practice instead of seeing it as drudgery. Since the Material Universe is a Face of GOD, it means all dealings with matter are a Holy Encounter as well! To beautify and clean matter is to polish the Diamond that is

GOD! It is to like our your physical body as the temple of God! It is to look at your home as a Temple of God as well! It is to create shrines and altars in your home. It is possibly the practice of feng shui, or the art of Spiritual design and balance in your home! In our home we have Spiritual Statues, Pictures, Gemstones, and Spiritual objects adorning the grounds both outside and inside!

Physical/Earthly Mastery means taking care of one's Physical/Earthly needs, not just Spiritual, mental, emotional and energy needs! When you have guests, making sure they are comfortable and have something to drink and eat is an example of taking care of Physical/Earthly needs! Making sure the inside temperature is pleasing is another example! It is possibly giving money to charities, or tithing. It is paying attention to politics and all the social issues concerning the Earth, and raising consciousness and contributing to their healing through physical actions or inner plane Spiritual work such as prayer! It means voting in your elections! A great many lightworkers' information banks are filled with Spiritual knowledge and some with Psychological knowledge; however, some are very weak in Earthly knowledge! Earthly knowledge is important as well. What if a person did not know how to read, write, speak or spell, or know any arithmetic? This would be a great disadvantage in your Spiritual mission. There are a lot of other forms of Earthly knowledge that are similar. Watching the news and/or reading the newspaper and keeping up with Earthly current events! You want to be Spiritually knowledgeable, psychologically knowledgeable, knowledgeable of your physical body, and knowledgeable of Earthly life!

Other aspects of Earthly mastery are: remembering birthdays and anniversaries, meeting family obligations, keeping up with friendships, paying your bills, making sure your car has gasoline and oil, vacuuming the house, watering the plants, dusting, sweeping, putting food in the bird feeder, etc! My Beloved Readers, these are all Spiritual practices to the sanctification and Glory of GOD! They are just as important as meditating, praying, saying affirmations, visualizations, or any other Spiritual and Psychological practice! Do you see the attitudinal shift Spirit and the Masters are asking you to make! See all these things as "holy acts of God and Spiritual practices!" Whether you choose to look at them this way or not, this is what they are! They are literally Spiritual practices! By doing so your are honoring and sanctifying the Material Face of GOD! What can be more holy or more beautiful? When life is looked at from this manner then everything you do is a "holy act and Spiritual Practice and exercise"! Lightworkers have commonly spoken of this as being Zen-like. I do not practice Zen; however, the idea is to live in the now and give your full attention to whatever you are doing! So if you are washing the dishes then stay in the now! Spirit and the Masters are adding to this concept to do all physical acts on Earth as a Spiritual Practice and as a Devotion or Sanctification to GOD! When you are Mastering and taking care of the Physical/Earthly things you are mastering and taking care of literally one third of what GOD really is! The Spiritual aspect is one-third, the Psychological is one-third, and the Physical/Earthly is one-third of GOD! Living life in such a manner makes every Earthly thing you do become a Spiritual practice and form of Sanctification, honoring, and caring for the Material Face of GOD!

When you live this way, everything you do then Spiritually, Mentally, Emotionally, Energetically, and in a Physical/Earthly sense becomes a Spiritual practice and form of Spiritual Service! Seeing the Material Face of GOD and mastering it will give you a much greater sense of self and being a Spiritual Master! To be a Spiritual Master on all three levels; Spiritually, Psychologically and Physical/Earthly, in a balanced and integrated manner, will give you a tremendous sense of love and appreciation for GOD! You will literally see GOD in everything you do! There will no separation between levels! Literally every action you take in life will be a Spiritual Practice, a Sanctification and Act of Service! Is this not a most wonderful way to live? No level will be seen as better then any other. All four Faces of GOD; Spiritual, Mental, Emotional, and Material, will be honored. All you will see is GOD in everything you do. You will be paying your rent to GOD on all levels. Spiritual practices will not be seen as better then Psychological practices or Physical/Earthly practices. Don't you see, my Beloved Readers, that they are all the same! They all are equally important! They are all GOD! People and lightworkers have fallen into the trap of thinking that one level is better or more important than another! Some think Spiritual energies are better. Some favor Psychological energies over Spiritual energies. Some are too Materialistic! Some are more Spiritual and Psychologically focused! Some are more Psychologically and Materially focused! Some are more Spiritually and Materially focused and disown the Psychological! Don't you see, my Beloved Readers, this is all faulty thinking and fragmentation! How can one Face of GOD be better than another? Do not let the negative ego mind confuse you or fragment you in such a way. It is all one, and each Face of GOD must be honored equally! To not do so would be as absurd as saying one of our bodies is better then another. All four bodies must be balanced! We have a Spiritual body, mental body, emotional body, and physical body! If you do not integrate, balance, and honor all four bodies equally you will have disease and discomfort, for you will be defying the Laws of GOD. You will get an immediate lesson pointing this out to you! The same is true of the Four Faces of GOD if you do not honor all Four levels equally you will be hounded by the level you disown! You will be given intuitions, signs, signals, dreams, and clues. If you don't pay attention, you will start being given karmic lessons! Spirit and the Masters are giving you the opportunity here in reading this chapter to learn by grace and not karma! Honor and Sanctify all Four Faces of GOD, and this includes, of course, the Physical/Earthly level! The negative ego tells you that focusing on the Physical/Earthly level will take you away from GOD! This is only true if you overidentify with it and let it become a form of "Materialism"! Lightworkers have gone to the other extreme and have "thrown the baby out with the bath water"! They have rejected and disowned the Material Face of GOD, and then abused Mother Earth and defiled the Goddess energies! It is now time for the Divine Mother, the Goddess energies, and Mother Earth to be properly honored and cared for as well! I am sure all of you, my Beloved Readers, agree!

Part of Mastering the Earth and Earth Energies means anchoring your Spiritual Mission on the Earth and not just talking about it, not just thinking about it, not just visualizing about it, not just getting excited about it, and not just meditating and praying about it! "Hands that help are holier than lips that pray"! As of the year 2000, it is time to manifest on the physical. All this other stuff is fine, but it is time to deliver on the physical! Just manifesting on the Spiritual Plane and the Mental and Emotional Plane does not cut it any more! It is time to integrate all Seven Rays, not stay stuck in just a few of them. It is time to master money, master business, and master Spiritual leadership! It is time to fully own your First Ray and Personal Power 100% so you can do what you need to do on the Physical/Earthly Plane! It is time to master the Third Ray so you can take physical action in the physical world. It is time to own your Fourth Ray so you can beautify the physical world in Honor and Sanctification of GOD! It is time to integrate your Fifth Ray so you can make all these changes in your Physical world, scientifically and logically! It is time to own and fully integrate the Seventh Ray so you can put the Spiritual, Psychological, and Physical/Earthly structures into place in the Physical/Earthly world. It is time to make the changes that need to take place in our Earthly Civilization to create the Spiritual, Psychological, and Earthly Freedom that we are all striving for as a society!

Part of Mastering Earth Energies is embracing your Puzzle Piece in GOD's Divine Plane and manifesting it on the Earth. It is now time to do your Service work. It does not matter what it is, but it is time to do it.

Do not wait for GOD to conk you over your head with a hammer and tell you what it is. Start doing something! Life is a co-creation and it is not Spirit and the Masters job to just tell you what to do. It is also your job to tell yourself what to do with the incredibly creative God mind you have been given! GOD helps those who help themselves! It is time to fully anchor and integrate your Seven Levels of Initiation into all your bodies including your physical body! It is now time to physically ground your Ascension! It is now time to fully Ground your Mighty I Am Presence on Earth! It is now time to become an Integrated Ascended Master on Earth! It is time to pay attention to physically details and not let them slip by so easily as if they are not so important!

It is time to express your love physically, not just mentally, emotionally or Spiritually! This may mean buying flowers or sweet gifts for your Spouse or friends! This may mean expressing love through hugs and physical touch! This means loving your physical body in all ways and caring for it properly. It may mean not throwing trash on the ground, and picking up trash to keep GOD's body clean! It means giving love to animals, plants, and the mineral kingdom, and caring for our younger animal, plant and mineral Brothers and Sisters! It means honoring, respecting, loving, and integrating Pan, the nature spirits, and the plants devas, and inviting them back into our gardens, farms, forests and the Earth!

Mastering the Earth and Earth Energies means conservation and ecology practices! It means being aware of not ingesting into the physical, chemicals, pollution, heavy metals, and toxic substances. It means not using recreational drugs! It means cutting back on medical drugs and using more homeopathics and herbs. It means learning more about holistic health, naturopathy, homeopathy, herbal medicine, and the many forms of health and healing practices.

Earthly mastery means becoming aware of all the political and social causes, and helping to raise consciousness, send money, or physically help. It means possibly writing letters to your congressman, participating in marches, political and social action, or inner plane Spiritual Activism! It means doing everything you can, every moment of your life, that is within your power to make this world a better place for our children. It means praying not just for yourself, but for all the Political and Social Causes! This means educating yourself on all these issues. I would humbly suggest reading my book *Manual for Planetary Leadership*, which gives the Spiritual Hierarchy's views on a great many of the political and social issues of our time. It is fascinating reading and totally debunks this myth that Spirit and the Masters are not 100% involved with every aspect of Earth Life! The main purpose of the inner plane Spiritual Government and inner plane Ascended Masters is to create Heaven on Earth! We are GOD's mouth, hands, and feet to make this happen. Always recognize, however, that Life is a co-creation and that it is not just GOD and the Masters working through us, but it is also us with our own personal power, will and creativity with our free choice doing our part as well! It is the sparking of our full 100% personal power, unconditional love, and active intelligence; grounding our personal power and love on Earth in conjunction with GOD, Christ, the Holy Spirit, our Mighty I Am Presence, the Higher Self, and the inner plane Ascended Masters, Angels, Elohim and Christed Extraterrestrials overlighting and guiding us in this process; and using all the love, wisdom and power at their disposal as well that really makes things happen! It is the full co-creation of both. Enormous numbers of lightworkers are waiting for GOD, Spirit, the Masters, or Angels to do it for them! This will never happen! You must help yourself! The responsibility is yours. As you own your full 100% personal power, unconditional love, active intelligence, and the rest of your Seven Rays at the 100% level; and move into Earth life as best you know how, GOD and the Masters will overlight the process and help to guide you! When you run into roadblocks or obstacles, immediately pray for GOD and the Masters help and it will be forth coming! As the Universal Mind through Edgar Cayce said, "Why worry when you can pray"! Therefore, it is now time, my Beloved Brothers and Sisters, to "Be about the Fathers business on Earth"! My Beloved Brothers and Sisters, it is also time to "Be about the Divine Mother's and Goddess' business on Earth"! No more procrastinating, no more being lazy, no more not owning your full 100% personal power, no more not 100% loving the Earth and Earthly life and honoring and sanctifying the Earth Face of GOD! No more disowning the Third Ray of Active Physical Action and Service on Earth! No more waiting for God to tell you what to do! Think of something and just start doing it! If you need to change forms of service then do so! No more living in a cave! No more living in a monastery! No more living on a mountaintop! Those phases of your life were 100% appropriate and honorable! It is now time to physically ground your Ascension and your Spirituality! It is now time to integrate the horizontal plane of life, not just the vertical plane of life! It is now time to become balanced in the God/Goddess energies! It is now time to give back to the Mother Earth as she has so graciously given to you! It is now time to give the Divine Mother the honor, respect and love she so richly deserves! It is now time to live in the marketplace as the Master Jesus did! It is now time to enter Earth life fully! It is now time to Demonstrate your Divinity, not just on the Spiritual Plane, or the Mental Plane, or the Emotional Plane, but on the Physical/Earthly Plane! It is now time to fully Practice the Presence of God on Earth! It is now time to Be God on Earth! It is now time to Be Melchizedek on the Earth! It is now time to Be Christ on Earth! It is now time to Be the Buddha on Earth! It is now time to Be the Eternal Self on Earth! It is now time to cure aids, cure cancer, save the whales, save the rain forest, repair the ozone layer, stop all polluting and abusing of the Earth, return the Earth back to its Edenic State, stop all war on Earth, create a lasting peace in the Middle East, stop all partisan politics, unify all religions, revamp and Spiritualize the prison system, bring the Soul and Spirit in a universal way back into the educational system, have food for everyone, stop homelessness, provide proper health care for everyone, stop gang violence, provide better care for the aged, stop child abuse, stop abuse of animals, stop spousal abuse, stop all crime, stop all disease, help and honor the veterans, properly dispose of nuclear waste, end terrorism, bring the knowledge of the Extraterrestrials to the Earth, stop all drug abuse and alcoholism, clean up all pollution and develop new non-polluting energy sources, to name a few!

My Beloved Readers, this is just the tip of the iceberg of some of the changes that need to be made in our world! It is now time we each take on the "Earthly Mantle of Christ" that we Spiritually contracted to do before we came; and work arm and arm, shoulder to shoulder, and Heart to Heart, to turn our civilization into the Seventh Golden Age, the New Jerusalem, the thriving City and World of GOD that is its destiny to become! It is time for the cities and countries of Light to be anchored and physically manifested and demonstrated on Earth and around the world. It is now time to fully understand and welcome the Christed Extraterrestrials to the Earth, for they will be of invaluable help in making a lot of these changes. No need to reinvent the wheel when other Christed Races have solved a great many of these issues thousands of years ago. This has already begun to happen and will happen openly very soon. So, my Beloved Readers, do not feel burdened by the job at hand!

GOD, Christ, the Holy Spirit, our Mighty I Am Presence, our Higher Self, the inner plane Ascended Masters, the Archangels and Angels, Elohim Councils, and the Christed Extraterrestrials will help every step of the way. Allah Gobi and El Morya are helping on the Political Front from the First Ray Ashram of the Christ. Melchizedek, the Lord of Sirius, Lord Maitreya, Master Kuthumi, and the Ascended Master Djwhal Khul are helping with Spiritual Education for the planet from their inner plane Planetary and Cosmic Second Ray Ashrams! Master Serapis Bey is helping in the area of active physical service and business issues on Earth from his Third Ray inner plane ashram! Master Paul the Venetian is helping with Spiritualizing the Arts on Earth through his Fourth Ray inner plane ashram! Master Hilarion is helping with bringing forth all the New Age Sciences to the Earth from his Fifth Ray inner plane ashram! Sananda is helping integrate and reform the world's religions from his Sixth Ray inner plane ashram! Saint Germain and Lady Portia are spearheading the reform of our civilization and all its institutions from the inner plane Seventh Ray ashram! Lord Buddha, as our Planetary Logos, is holding the Divine Blueprint Vision in his mind's eye for all the changes that are to come on the Earth as the Spiritual President of this Planet at this time, while simultaneously being overlighted by Sanat Kumara!

The Archangels and Angels are working overtime to now restore the Divine Plan on Earth in every aspect of Earth life! By the Grace of GOD, the Archangels and Angels are here in force!

The Christed Extraterrestrials, such as the Arcturians and the Ashtar Command, are also here in force protecting this planet, and help to bring new light technologies to the Earth. There are many other Christed Extraterrestrial Races who are circling our planet and who will soon be more fully revealing themselves to the Earth! The Love, Information, and Knowledge they will bring will accelerate our world at an unimaginable speed. Our civilization will advance more from the years 1980 to the year 2025 then it did in the last 3.1 billion years!

So my Beloved Readers, do not feel burdened, for the amount of Spiritual, Psychological, and Physical/Earthly/Technological/Scientific help in every aspect of Earth life will be absolutely staggering! This planet, however, is *our* home! We are its Spiritual Leaders! We are its caretakers! We are the light bearers for the New Age to bring in this New

Heaven and New Earth. We are, my Beloved Readers, the Externalization of the Hierarchy!

It is time for all Earthlings to step forward in Spiritual Leadership and Planetary World Service! It is time to now 100% fully claim your love, wisdom, power, Spiritual leadership, Planetary World Service, and physically master, unconditionally love, anchor, and ground your Spiritual mission and puzzle piece on Earth! It is now time to fully become a Spiritual Master, a Psychological Master, and Physical/Earthly Master in an integrated and balanced manner! It is now time to 100% Demonstrate GOD on Earth and 100% rebuild the civilization of GOD on Earth, and fully own our reason and destiny for physically incarnating into physical bodies and into this world! The clarion call now goes forth from Spirit and the Cosmic and Planetary Hierarchy to mobilize their energies, and fully now manifest and demonstrate the Spiritual service mission and purpose for coming on Earth now at this momentous time in Earth's history! GOD, the Masters, the Archangels and Angels, the Elohim Councils and Christed Extraterrestrials are now gathering the Sons and Daughters of GOD on Earth to make the final big push to transform this Earthly World and Civilization into the "Shining diamond and clear bright star" it is meant to become!

So let it be Written! So let it be Done!

24

The Importance of Loving and Enjoying the Earth and Earth Life!

My Beloved Readers, one of the most important lessons of the Spiritual path is learning to love the Earth and Earth life! As we have already talked about in this book, Matter is one of the Four Faces of GOD! Matter is literally the Temple of GOD! The Earth is part of GOD's material Universe! The Earth is a like a molecule in the Physical Body of GOD! To not love the Earth is to not love GOD, for the Earth is part of GOD! The Earth as you all know is a living being! This is "Mother Earth"! Mother Earth has been greatly unloved and abused in the history of this planet! Her essence or Spirit has been abused and her physical body has been abused! This has been part of the defilement of the Divine Mother and the Goddess energies on Earth by a patriarchal, negative ego-run history! This is now changing! We have finally reached a point in history where is it is time for the return of the Divine Mother and the Goddess energies to return to their rightful place! This balance is imperative for the Seventh Golden Age to be realized! So when I say love the Earth and Earth life, I am not just talking about Mother Earth, nature, Pan, the Nature Spirits, Plant Devas, Mineral Kingdom, Plant

Kingdom, Animal Kingdom and so on. Yes, this is all part of loving the Material Face of GOD and loving the Earth! These are, in truth, our Brothers and Sisters. When Jesus said the whole law could be summed up as "Love the Lord thy GOD with all your heart and soul and mind and might and love your neighbor as you love yourself"! Your neighbor is also animals, plants, minerals, nature Spirits, plant devas, elements of nature, elementals, and so on. These are our younger brothers and sisters who are in our care, who we have not always cared for as we should in our planet's history! These beings are incarnations of GOD! This is a fact! To not 100% love all of them in physical and etheric form is to not love GOD, for they are God!

Now we need to take this issue of loving the Earth and Earth Life one step further! This means loving Earth life itself! Lightworkers commonly think of Earth has unimportant, a prison, just a means to achieve liberation. They think only Heaven and the Celestial realms are important. This is completely untrue. The Earth is one of the Seven Heavens of GOD as I have already said in this book! The material universe is literally a heaven. Everyone wants to get to Heaven, and I tell you we are already in one of GOD's Heavens! The outer world is really just a reflection of the inner world. The inner worlds actually look a lot like the outer world except more refined! There are a great many things on Earth which one cannot experience in Heaven. Eating food is quite an interesting experience. Making love is quite an interesting experience! The five physical senses are quite an interesting experience! Nature is quite an amazing experience! The experience of living in a physical body and experiencing Earth life is quite an interesting experience! Enjoy it while you can for once you achieve liberation you may never ever experience this again! There are enormous numbers of souls on the inner plane who are quite fascinated with the material universe and the opportunity to experience GOD through a physical body! This is also a most amazing time to be incarnated! Maybe one of the most amazing times in the History of the Earth! Souls are literally lining up trying to get into a body for the potential for Spiritual growth and evolution is greater at this time than maybe ever in the history of the Earth!

This issue of loving Earth, I would now like to take one step deeper, which is the importance of loving your physical body! You physical body is part of GOD as well! It is your temple! It is made of the substance of GOD! It is Divine! Honor it and sanctify it! There is an intelligence within the physical body called the body elemental! Honor and try to communicate with it. Many do this through the use of a pendulum! To not love your physical body is to not love GOD, for all matter is made up of GOD!

Now let's take this discussion one step deeper. It is not enough to just love all that I have said so far to achieve God Realization, you also must love Earth life itself. Again, a great many people do not think that Earth life is important. They think it is a lower level, or just again a means to achieve liberation. They see no value in trying to reorganize, restructure and rebuild our earthly society and world! This, my Beloved Readers, is "Faulty thinking"! This is the negative ego sabotaging that person. GOD's Divine plan is to create "Heaven on Earth"! GOD wants this Earthly Civilization to become a utopian society! He wants it to become a fifth dimensional society! The purpose of life is not, I repeat, is not to just achieve liberation and ascension and leave and say, "who cares about the Earth and Earth life, good riddance!" This is not loving GOD! Earth Life is a part of GOD, my Beloved Readers! You will not achieve God Realization in the fullest sense of the term if you do not learn to enjoy life on Earth and fully take responsibility for and love Earth life! GOD's Divine Plan is to that we just love the Heaven realms and look at the Earth and Earth life as some lower class citizen! It is all one! GOD wants all Seven Heavens to fully reflect His Glory! Remember what I have said about the importance of "consistency and integration"! GOD wants His Glory to reflect on all seven levels not just the first six heavens and leave the bottom one as a garbage dump! The Divine Plan is to reflect GOD's full glory on the earthly plane! Are not the Pyramids on Earth a glorious thing? Is not the Taj Mahal a glorious building that truly reflects the profundity that is GOD? Are not the Sacred Sites of the world glorious places? GOD wishes every aspect of Earth life to fully reflect His Glory! So GOD does not want people to just ascend and see Earth as just a lower class world to be used as a means to an end and then discarded like a piece of trash! This is GOD's Body we are talking about! Is not the Sistine Chapel a fitting Tabernacle of GOD? GOD wishes the entire world to be a Sistine Chapel! GOD wants all his Glory to be outpictured in and on the Earth in every aspect and in all rays and ray functions! GOD wants a God Civilization on the Earth!

Mother Earth, who is a living being, is taking her initiations as well! Her mission and purpose will not be complete unless this takes place! The Planetary Logos or President of this Planet is now Lord Buddha! His aura literally embodies this planet! His Spiritual mission will not be complete until this takes place. What are we wanting to take place, you ask. What we want to take place is the Seventh Golden Age on this Planet! What we want to take place is the return of this world to the "Edenic State" that it was in the time of Lemuria before separation occurred!

We all know that when we go camping it is always important to make our campsite when we leave even more beautiful than when we arrived! My Beloved Readers, it is time the six billion souls on Earth return the Earth back to its pristine state! It is time to rid the Earth of all pollution! It is time to give back to Mother Earth who has cared for and nurtured us! The whole purpose of the Spiritual Government on this planet and all the Ascended Masters and Planetary Hierarchy and Seven Ashrams of the Christ is to bring the Earth back to this Edenic State on all levels in terms of how our society operates. The First Ray Department is in charge of getting the governments and politics of the world back to operating on a Spiritual wavelength! The Second Ray Department is in charge of getting all the people of the Earth spiritually educated, psychologically and Physically/Earthly educated, integrated, and balanced, and to have right relationships with each and all aspects of Earth life. The Third Ray Department is in charge of getting all the business and economics of the world operating from a God Perspective. The Fourth Ray Department is getting all the arts, music, architecture, plays, and dance to attune and reflect the profundity and beauty of GOD! The Fourth Ray Department is also for beautifying the Earth! The Fifth Ray Department is to bring all the New Age Sciences to the Earth to solve all the Earth's problems. The Sixth Ray Department is to unify all religions and cleanse them from the contamination of negative ego thinking! The Seventh Ray Department is in charge of completely reorganizing and restructuring civilization from a personality-based, negative ego run society to a society based on Soul and Spiritual principles in every aspect of civilization!

My Beloved Readers, the purpose of life is not just to achieve Spiritual Growth! It is to achieve Spiritual Growth and fulfill your Spiritual Mission and Purpose. Every person on Earth, every single one, works out of one of these seven ray departments! Every person has a Spiritual Assignment and a puzzle piece to fulfill in GOD's Plan to create Heaven on Earth! I think you all can see this quite clearly now! Taking care of the rainforest, planting trees, helping the homeless, stopping drug addiction, stopping child abuse, cleaning the environment, stopping animal cruelty, repairing the ozone layer, stopping the greenhouse effect, saving the whales, and restructuring and reordering society, are as important Spiritual practices as meditation, prayer, channeling, and chanting the names of GOD! As a matter of fact, they may be even more important, for this is why you have come! You are not here to be obsessed with your initiation level! You are here to unconditionally love and serve all Kingdoms of GOD! People and lightworkers thought it was enough just to be loving to their Brothers and

Sisters! This is the wake-up call of the Divine Mother and the Goddess energies and the Material Face of GOD! It is not enough! To achieve full God Realization you must serve all of GOD, not just part of GOD! GOD is in all Kingdoms, and in the material universe, and in earthly life, society, and civilization. It is time to see and serve all of GOD, not just a part of GOD! I have it on good authority that Jesus' New Commandment is "Love the Lord thy GOD with all your heart and soul and mind and might and love your Neighbor as you love yourself; and love the Material Face of GOD, all your younger brothers and sisters, Mother Earth, Pan and all the nature spirits and plant devas, your physical body, nature, and Earth life; and fulfill your Spiritual mission, purpose, Divine puzzle piece, and create Heaven on Earth in every aspect of earthly civilization and society! My Beloved Readers, I have it on good authority that this is Master Jesus' New Commandment for the Aquarian Age and this next 2000-year cycle! This is also the New Commandment of the Divine Mother and the Goddess energies to bring balance and harmony back to the Earth and to bring the proper God/Goddess balance back to the Earth and the Seventh Golden Age!

People think they have been realizing GOD just focusing on the heavenly realms! With no judgement intended, they have blind spots to GOD! If you think GOD is glorious in the heavenly realms, wait until you see the glory of GOD in the psychological realms and in the physical/earthly realms! To be perfectly honest, most lightworkers only know a third of GOD! They are highly developed on the Spiritual level, but are not fully trained in Spiritual psychology and do not fully appreciate the absolute profundity of GOD on the physical/earthly/material level! If you think you have known the ecstasy of GOD on the Spiritual level, wait until your experience the ecstasy of GOD on the psychological and physical/earthly/material plane as well! These makeup the Four Faces of GOD! The Spiritual, mental, emotional, and material. The mental and emotional making up the psychological aspect of GOD! For those who want to realize the psychological level of GOD in all GOD's Glory, read my books *Soul Psychology* and *How to Release Fear-Based Thinking and Feeling: An In-depth Study of Spiritual Psychology*! This chapter is another key to help you adjust your consciousness and perspective to fully love the material, earthly, physical and earthly life aspect of GOD!

Getting back to earthly life and society for a moment. This is why Sai Baba has said, "Hands that help are holier then lips that pray"! This is a very profound statement! Is God Realization only demonstrating God on the Spiritual plane? Is this consistency and integration of all levels of God and your own four-body system: Spiritual, mental, emotional, and physical? Is this paying your rent to GOD on all levels? Your physical body is as Divine as is your mental body, emotional body, and Spiritual body! Until you see this, you are blinded to understanding the full Glory of GOD! Do you know who fully taught me this? This is going to surprise my readers! The Mahatma! The Mahatma helped be to fully understand and appreciate the full Glory of GOD on the physical/earthly level! The Mahatma is a group consciousness being of all 352 levels of GOD! There is no higher Cosmic Energy coming to the Earth than the Mahatma!

Beloved Readers, it is just as important that when you have company that their physical needs are met as well as their Spiritual, mental, or emotional needs! Maybe even more important! If people on the Earth are starving or homeless and on survival, how are they supposed to focus on GOD? The Masters have told me that no person on Earth will achieve full God Realization and Integrated Ascension unless they fully enjoy Earth life and fully love the Earth and Earth life! When you do physical things, do it as a sanctification of GOD! If you wash the floors, you are washing GOD's body! How would you treat your Spiritual Teacher or Guru if they came to visit! What if they were dirty from a long trip and big storm? How would you care for their physical needs! Do the same for GOD! For the material universe is GOD's Body! When you honor, sanctify, and love the material universe, you honor, love, and sanctify GOD! If you go to church or temple would you want to go to a church or temple that is filthy dirty! Do you want a physical body filled with toxins that is sick all the time? How about Mother Earth's Body or GOD's Material Body? When we dump toxic wastes and pollute the Earth, air, and water we are polluting GOD's Body! We are polluting Mother Earth's Body! The same is true in regard to civilization! Civilization is a part of GOD! Everything is a part of GOD! When we don't care for our earthly civilization and let it be run by the personality and negative ego, it is like the surface life of GOD's body has skin cancer! Is this the proper way to honor and sanctify GOD?

We have incarnated into the world not only to achieve liberation and ascension, but also to be and demonstrate God on Earth! GOD does not want us to ascend and leave, it wants us to ascend and remain on Earth and demonstrate God on Earth! As I said in a previous chapter, to just ascend and not give anything back to GOD on all levels is selfish! It is not fulfilling the Spiritual Mission, Purpose, and Puzzle Piece you came to fulfill! You came to create Heaven on Earth! You came to be God on Earth! You came to reorder and restructure Earthly life, civilization, and society in the area of expertise you have in one of the seven Ashrams of the Christ! I myself have a Second Ray Monad; and my Spiritual mission is to Spiritually educate lightworkers as to how to achieve God Realization, integrated ascension, psychological and physical/earthly mastery, and how to fulfill their Spiritual contracts, Spiritual mission, and puzzle piece in a grounded way on Earth! For too long, lightworkers have not been able to ground very much! They can't even ground themselves let alone their Spiritual Missions! This is not meant as a judgment, just a Spiritual observation and statement of fact! During the 2000-year Piscean Age, much growth occurred, but it did not make it very much to the physical/earthly plane. It remained on the Spiritual plane, or on the mental, or emotional plane! As the political speeches on the Earth often say, "It is time for this to end!" It is time for light-workers to "Ground" their Higher Selves and Mighty I Am Presence fully into their physical body and fully into Earth life! It is time for lightworkers to master Prosperity consciousness, and to master Earth life and Earth energies in service of GOD! It is time "now" for light-workers to fully "Demonstrate God" on Earth, fully in Earth life! It is now time that we as the collective lightworkers on Earth stand together arm in arm and heart to heart to do the Spiritual mission we came here to do! This is to recreate our society and civilization according to GOD's design. All the plans how to do this have already been set up! Lord Buddha, our Planetary Logos, has all this knowledge! The blueprints for every aspect of our new God Society have been figured out in every detail. GOD gives the Divine Plan to Metatron; who gives it to Melchizedek, our Universal Logos; who gives it to Melchior, who gives it to Helios and Vesta, who gives it to Lord Buddha; who gives it to Lord Maitreya, the Head of the Spiritual Hierarchy; who gives it to Allah Gobi and Saint German, the "Manu" and the "Mahachohan," who all give it to the seven Chohans or Lords of the Rays (El Morya, Kuthumi, Serapis Bey, Paul the Venetian, Sananda, and Lady Portia and Djwhal Khul)! Djwhal Khul runs the eighth Ashram of the Christ, called the "Synthesis Ashram," under the Second Ray. This is because Spiritual education is so important, an extra ashram was created under Kuthumi's Second Ray Ashram, and holds the focus of Spiritual educa-tion and also synthesis of all the rays! This focus on Synthesis of all Seven Rays is also why it was created as well! This is the Ashram I work out of, and Djwhal Khul has asked me to take over this inner plane Ashram when he moves on to take his next Cosmic position. Melchizedek, the Mahatma, Archangel Metatron, and Djwhal Khul have also asked me to anchor this Ashram and Academy on Earth! This was why I created the Melchizedek Synthesis Light Academy! It is a real life inner plane Ashram and Teaching Academy that has been manifested on this earthly plane to extend the Divine Plan of the second ray ashram! This is why I speak so Spiritually passionately on these things, and why I am so well versed in the importance of integration and synthesis on all levels!

The Mahatma is the Avatar of Synthesis on the Cosmic level for all Creation! The Mahatma embodies all 352 levels of GOD! The Mahatma knows and understands that the first level of GOD is just as Holy, Sanctified and Divine as the 352nd! To ignore one is like saying "I only love my head but I am going to dislike and hate my legs or feet"! It is like saying the seventh chakra is good, but the first chakra is bad, no good, unimportant, and not holy! All chakras, all bodies, all Faces of GOD, all 352 levels of GOD are, in truth, equally Divine! One cannot realize God unless all levels are equally honored, loved, and sanctified!

Anyone who has had a garden understands the Glory of GOD on the physical/earthly level! To see each morning how flowers, plants, buds, and leaves grow is absolutely unbelievable! Anyone who has gotten very attuned to nature knows the Glory of GOD! However, the Glory of GOD can be experienced everywhere on the Earthly Plane: I remember when I went to see the *Phantom of the Opera* in Los Angeles, I thought it was one of the most profound Spiritual experiences of my life! I felt like I was lifted up into the fifth dimension for three hours! Traveling in Europe to visit the Sistine Chapel, Louvre Museum, the Acropolis, the Holy Land, and other sacred sites! Watching the birds, rabbits, butterflies, chipmunks from my window where I work in the mornings! Watering the garden and tuning into the plant spirits and devas! Communing with nature! GOD is everywhere! Looking into the clouds and blue sky! Wistancia and I sometimes sit out at night and just look at the stars above the vast open piece of land behind our home! Our dog Brianna is literally an angel from Heaven in a dog's body! She is the embodiment of love. God is everywhere!

All the colors in the garden! All the incredible smells of nature! Seeing the roses bloom! Feeling the wind and the sun! Watching the birds eat from our bird feeders and listening to them chirp! All the little bees and insects flying around doing their thing and all working in harmony! Having a vegetable garden and seeing overnight how a zucchini plant pops out these gigantic zucchinis in a matter of days! It is really incredible to watch and witness.

I can honestly say I really love and enjoy Earth life! I recognize I am visiting here and that my ultimate destiny is to return to the seventh heaven; however, I really do see this material universe as the first heaven it is! It really is incredibly beautiful. We have decorated our home and the Academy with hundreds of Spiritual statues of Masters, Angels, and Saints! We have hundreds and hundreds of pictures of the Masters! We have many crystals, gemstones, and Spiritual objects! We even have all these things in the garden as well! We have all kinds of ascension columns and pillars of light and ascension technologies that also blend with all the beautiful earthly things and nature things! Our garden may be the center of our home and what draws us the most!

In writing this chapter on loving the Earth and earthly life I was tuning into Spirit to see the best way to convey this message of Spirit and the Masters on the importance of loving the Earth and earth life! The guidance I received was that the most effective way to help people appreciate this process of God Realization and love of the Material Face of GOD and the earthly/physical level was to share from my personal experience! Sometimes I have been hesitant to do this too much for sometimes this can be misinterpeted, so although my books are very personal and I write like I am speaking to each one of you in my living room, I am always very careful to not get carried away. In the rest of this chapter, however, I am consciously choosing to share my personal experience on this matter to try and give you my experience of loving earthly life rather than theoretical knowledge! I feel this is the most effective way to help people feel and experience the profundity and love of the material/physical/earthly Face of GOD! When you open to God's Vision on this level as well, then everything in life on a Spiritual, mental, emotional, and physical/earthly level becomes a sanctification, love, enjoyment, and communing with GOD! GOD can be communed with, loved, and enjoyed on all faces! This chapter is dedicated to the material face of GOD communion, love, and enjoyment!

So, to share my experience of loving and enjoying the Earth and Earth life on a personal level, I would like to speak from a spontaneous flow that comes to mind. I love eating! Although, in truth, I do not eat very much and I mostly live on Light, I do eat some food! When I do, I really enjoy it! I eat very pure food when I do; it gives me enormous pleasure and joy! This is something I might miss at times when I no longer have a physical body! Very often when I eat I like to watch the news! I love watching the news! I love being kept up to date on everything that is going on in the world. I do not see earthly affairs being separate from my Spiritual path! It is all one! When I hear of some injustice on the news I pray about it and ask GOD and the Masters to enter that situation. In the Academy, we have an Interdimensional Prayer Altar. I often will write down prayers for worldly events, people, and situations! Just as I enjoy gaining Spiritual knowledge and psychological knowledge, I also very much enjoy gaining earthly knowledge! Much of what I write about I get from watching the news or educational television programs. Everything is grist for the mill, so to speak! I keep a list of ideas and I am constantly writing little notes to myself when I get ways to serve, pray, or ideas for chapters! So eating in combination with the news I greatly enjoy! CNN was made for me!

I love hot showers. This is something I will miss if I don't have a physical body! I do some of my best channeling work in the shower! I love the computer! What an incredible invention. I get up every morning at around 4:00 and take a hot shower and begin my processing and channeling work! Then I go to my computer and start working! I love the early mornings when no one is up and it is totally quiet! I have about five hours to myself before my employees arrive! This is my favorite time every day. I get some of my best writing done! I love starting these days getting organized! The great thing about a computer is I have my entire life and all my books organized in it! I work at lightening speed, whipping around the computer with all my ideas and inspiration pouring in a mile a minute! I absolutely love e-mail! What an incredible invention! It goes instantly, no postage stamps. I thought faxes were great until I got into the computer world!

Then there is the Internet and Websites! I adore the Internet and my Website. I see the Academy Website as my Sistine Chapel. It is the never-ending book and architectural Taj Mahal in cyberspace! I think computers and the Internet are one of the greatest inventions in the history of man! For almost no money, I have a store that people from all over the world can visit. I don't even have to hire employees! It is incredible! Three quarters of my business comes through the Internet! I could literally stay home and never leave if I wanted to! What a freedom this can provide people!

I love being married and spending time with my wife Wistancia! I love going to the movies with her on our date night! Movies are really something I will miss when I no longer have a physical body! We get special videos as well, and there is nothing like getting into the comfort of one's own bed or a comfortable couch and watching a good video! We also have a few favorite TV shows. We would watch "Touched By An Angel," the "X files" if it isn't a violent one, and "Roswell." I also occasionally watch some of the news magazine shows like "60 Minutes." I use a lot of the things to raise consciousness in my books, articles, and teaching! I love learning on all levels.

One of my favorite things is working in the garden! I love watering the garden! It is like the most glorious meditation. Sometimes I can get so tuned in I can just feel the pulsation of GOD running through everything! I love communing with the plants themselves and the nature Spirits and plant devas!

I really even enjoy and love doing errands. I don't do a lot of them, for I send my employees to do most of them, but when I do do them I really enjoy it. I do a lot of writing and working at my desk, so getting out sometimes is really a nice break! I love buying flowers and little gifts and snacks for Wistancia at my favorite stores.

I love communicating and talking to people! Every person is such a precious incarnation of GOD and we are all so similar, in truth! I love answering emails, letters, and faxes from people. I love to help people, and I find it quite enjoyable to commune with fellow Brothers and Sisters around the world! It is always so interesting what the e-mails, fax machine and post office bring in each day!

I even enjoy doing chores. I am blessed to be able to afford to have employees that help me do almost everything; however, I do not see anything as separate from GOD. Whatever needs doing, if they are not around, I am happy to do. I look at it like an opportunity to get some physical exercise. I call the Angels and Masters in to help me! They run Spiritual current through my body!

I love writing books! This is one of my great joys! I usually try and spend at least five hours a day writing chapters; some days even more. Writing books is such a high! It is really an art form to me! I always use the metaphor of being an artist or a musician, for every word is like a brushstroke or musical note. A great chapter is a like an exquisite painting, fresco, or musical concert!

I love counseling, teaching, chanting the names of GOD, and meditating! I love talking and communicating with my friends. I love Spiritual leadership and planetary world service. It is a big responsibility; however, I love all the work!

I love sleeping after a long day of work! Usually my head hits the pillow and I am out in two seconds! I really love to sleep! However, I love Earth life so much and I love all the projects and everything I am doing so much I literally can't wait to get up in the morning! I honestly can't wait! I find working energizing! It is almost like the more I work, the more energized I feel. For everything I do, I do with 100% personal power, 100% unconditional love, and 100% active intelligence! I love experiencing life through all seven Rays! I even enjoy the business end of life! I love doing Huna prayers, every day calling in GOD and the Godforce for help! I love making my lists of everything I have to do and everything my employees need to do. I love the feeling of crossing things off my lists and getting things done. I love to accomplish things and create! I love to bring things into form. There is such a feeling of accomplishment when a new book is published. I love to receive letters from people to see how they have been helped. This is the greatest feeling of all! Helping people in truly a selfless and egoless manner to the best of my ability! To truly see everything as GOD! There is no better feeling then to turn people onto GOD, the Masters, how to achieve inner peace, prosperity, and God Realization!

The other thing I love is the enormous creativity that pulses through me. I know this is the creative energy of God that is in everyone! I have so many incredible ideas! Spirit and the Masters give me so many ideas! I love the third Ray action of actively taking my full 100% personal love, and love putting this into action and physical form! I am not a procrastinator and I am not lazy! I know how to take care of business and get things accomplished!

I also love a good sports event! I love for example watching the Olympics. I love watching the track and field. I love watching the gymnastics. I love the swimming. I love seeing incarnations of GOD manifest their highest potentials. I even wrote a chapter in my book *How to Release Fear-Based Thinking and Feeling*, on Spirituality and Sports! I love watching a championship basketball game, the Super Bowl, the Rose Bowl, the World Series, or Pete Sampras playing tennis. It is truly an art form and can be quite inspiring! To watch Magic Johnson or Michael Jordan play basketball! To watch Michael Johnson run! To watch Mark McGuire hit 70 home runs in a season. I really appreciate what professional athletes must go through to achieve success at that level, for I used to play sports myself! I truly see it as a Spiritual Art Form!

I love to listen to music. I often listen to Sai Baba Bhajans, or Santana's *Supernatural* album while I drive. Music is truly a doorway to GOD! I love burning Sai Baba incense, the Nag Champa!

I love talking to Wistancia at the end of the day and just catching up on things! I love having the car washed and watching it go through the car wash and get cleaned. I love the feeling of getting a haircut! It is like after I take a shower every morning! I love wearing my beautiful, colorful clothes! I love wearing my tuxedos at Wesak I now have seven different kinds of tuxedos. My newest one is all white and floor length. I like to dress as the Masters dress on the inner plane!

What I love most is practicing the Presence of GOD on Earth! I love to be God on Earth in action! I am very much into grounding GOD! This is why I wrote an entire chapter showing lightworkers and people how to ground into Earth life! The whole purpose of life is to be God and demonstrate God on the physical/earthly plane!

I love the feeling that I am actually doing something to help people and to help change this physical world! I love the feeling of fulfilling my Spiritual mission and fulfilling my puzzle piece on Earth! I love taking on Spiritual assignments and perfectly fulfilling them on Earth! I love the feeling of really making a Spiritual impact in this earthly world! I love the feeling of seeing myself as a light bearer for the New Age and being one of the Spiritual leaders that is really able to make a difference in this earthly world. Someone has to do this! GOD in Heaven is not going to do this. The Masters and Angels are not going to do this, for they don't have physical bodies! I love being the hands and feet for GOD, Christ, the Holy Spirit, and the Masters! The Masters told me once that I was like their point man on Earth! I like being a point man! It is a tough job, for a point man can take a lot of fire on the front lines; however, it is quite fulfilling to be relied upon by Spirit and the Masters to demonstrate mastery and competence and love in doing such assignments! I humbly suggest that not everyone has what it takes to do this, and I am trying to suggest to each one of you reading this book to take on the "Mantle of the Christ" and step forward in Spiritual leadership and planetary world service. If you step forward from the consciousness I am describing in this book, you will succeed and you will experience great love and joy in doing so! My books will provide you with all the "Psychic Self-Defense" tools you need to deal with being on the front lines! I love Spiritual leadership! I love planetary world service! I also have learned how to take care of myself, protect myself, and set boundaries. This is part of self-love!

I love to work hard but I also love to laugh and have fun when I work! I love to put all my 100% Spiritual passion into everything I do! My main goal is to be consistent and integrated on all levels! I am not just satisfied to realize God on the Spiritual plane, or the mental plane, or the emotional plane, or energetically and etherically. I want to demonstrate God on the earthly plane as well. I want to be the Mighty I Am Presence on Earth! I want to be God on Earth! I want to be a fully realized God on Earth! I am not just satisfied with ascension. I want to also fully realize my physical ascension and turn my physical body into light!

Once I do this, I am not going to leave! I am going to remain on Earth and continue serving! Someone has to turn this world around, "As for me and my house, I will serve the Lord!" I ask you, my Brothers and Sisters, to stand with me! GOD is not going to change the Earth and neither are the Masters. GOD and the Masters are counting on us! I ask you now to stand with me and all the other courageous souls around the planet who are doing the same, and let's change this world. We will change it with our 100% power, love, and wisdom! We will change it with the power of our Three-Fold Flame and all our other God qualities! When all you see is GOD, and all you see is love, it is not hard! It is really pleasure! The Power of GOD and the entire Godforce will come to your aid, for they know what a difficult assignment it is to be a light bearer for the New Age! I personally have great confidence in my fellow earthlings! We are made of the substance of GOD and I will proudly stand with any Brother and Sister earthling who will stand with me to completely reorganize and restructure our society! With our 100% personal power, unconditional love, and wisdom; and the 100% personal power, unconditional love and wisdom of GOD and the Godforce, we cannot be stopped! Let us show the Infinite Universe the "Strong, Loving and Wise Spiritual Stock" us earthlings are made of! It is time to change this earthly world and the time is now! Let us roll up our sleeves and be about The Father's business! Let us roll up our sleeves and be about the Divine Mother's business as well! Let us roll up our sleeves and be about the Earth Mother's business as well! Let us roll up our sleeves, completely transform, and change our earthly civilization and society into the utopian fifth dimensional civilization it is meant to become!

I always try and get the most difficult jobs done first so then everything else is easy! I love manifesting all my incredible ideas into Earthly existence. This is why I have written 27 books! I really would humbly and Spiritually like to leave a legacy in this world that can continue to help people. Books are a great way of doing this. I have also set up almost 15 branches of the Academy around the world as of the year 2000, and I am sure that within the next five years we will have over 200 branches. I just started opening them and I have been opening almost two a week! I receive almost 400,000 hits a month on my Website, and many people have read the flyer I have posted on this!

I love working on the Wesak celebrations in Mt. Shasta for 2000 people. The experience each year of starting from scratch and being in charge of every aspect of the event on a Spiritual, psychological, and physical/earthly level, seeing it grow over a year's time, and then to pull off a successful event, is one of the most amazing experiences I have ever felt. To manifest something this size that is so incredibly complex with the help of Spirit and the Masters and others in the Academy is incredible! By the grace of GOD and the Masters we have, as of the year 2000, had six perfect Wesaks! By the grace of GOD and the Masters, all six events have worked out perfectly! It is such a high Spiritual experience to have put so much work into a project each year and to see it come into manifestation on the Earth and help so many people! I am a firm believer in grounding everything I do! This is the energy of the third Ray. I also incredibly enjoy making everything I do beautiful and harmonious, this is the Fourth Ray energy! I love, for example, always decorating our home. Bringing new little statues of angels for our home and the garden. We do the same thing for the Wesaks!

I also love understanding the science of all things and explaining to people how the science of all things works. I love the feeling of making an impact and Spiritual contribution in the world. This is a tough school and a lot of people have a hard time on many levels. By the grace of GOD and the Masters, I am in a position to help people and I feel a little bit like I have taken kind of a partial vow of the Bodhisattva to be of service any way I can! Something that Jesus said in *A Course in Miracles* always touched me and corresponded to how I feel and I have stated this many times in my books. Jesus said, "True pleasure is serving GOD"! This is truly how I feel! I cannot honestly say I ever feel like I am working! From other people's lens and eyes they would say I am a very hard worker. That is not the way I experience it! I really don't! I absolutely love what I am doing! Working energizes me! I feel electrified with energy most of the time, for everything that I am doing is done in the context of serving GOD! If I am washing the dishes, I am washing GOD. If I am watering the garden, I am watering GOD! If I am typing, I am typing the ideas of GOD and expressing the feelings of GOD. If I am meditating or praying, I am tuning into the essence of GOD! When I meet people on the street, all I see are incarnations of GOD and/or Christs or Buddhas! Every specific thought I think, feeling I feel, word I speak, action I take, is in the context of serving my Spiritual path and GOD! I see and sanctify GOD in all Four Faces! I love GOD equally on all four levels. I have worked out my book series so I have 10 books written on the Spiritual level, 10 books on the psychological level, and 10 books on the physical/earthly level! This, my Beloved Readers, is the kind of thing that excites me the most! I love mastering GOD on all three levels! I love experiencing GOD on all three levels. I love sanctifying GOD on all three levels! I love loving GOD on all three levels!

I think one of the things I enjoy and love most about earthly life is co-creating with GOD and the Masters on Earth! I love the sparking of ideas! I love how GOD and the Masters really rely on us to fulfill our Spiritual missions on Earth! They cannot complete their Spiritual assignments unless we complete ours! We are their channels! God is using God to manifest a God world and New Jerusalem on Earth! I don't think earthlings have fully realized how much Spirit and the Masters rely on us to fulfill the Divine Plan on Earth! Spirit and the Masters don't want us to just be their channels. They want us to be God Realized beings and Masters in our own right as well! That is when they can really rely on us! I love co-creating with the Masters! This is why my enthusiasm and passion is so strong! It is a combination of my 100% personal power, unconditional love, and wisdom in combination with absolute total faith, trust, and patience that GOD, Christ, the Holy Spirit, and the Masters, Angels, Elohim, and Christed Extraterrestrials will help me with my every need if I pray and ask! I pray and ask constantly! The reason I enjoy and love Earth life so much is I know how to be a Master on a Spiritual level, a psychological level, and a physical/earthly level. Once you learn how to do this, life is not nearly as hard! The hard part of life is not really Earth life! It is not having mastery over your thoughts, feelings, emotions, energy, negative ego mind, lower-self desire, inner child, and subconscious mind. One you learn to master these things then life is really a piece of cake! Our thoughts create our reality; our thoughts create our feelings and emotions! Life is not that hard once you learn to truly cause your own reality! When you learn to transcend negative ego thinking and feeling and only see life from your Spiritual/Christ/Buddha thought and feeling system, all you see is God and unconditional love in everything! You are no longer a victim, and you become emotionally invulnerable for you cause your own reality by how you think! Then when you learn to live life as a co-creator with GOD, Christ, the Holy Spirit, and all the Masters; you have the full love, wisdom, and power of God utilizing the full love, wisdom, and power of GOD and the entire Godforce! So how can you not succeed in everything you do? Can GOD not succeed? It is almost comical! Can GOD not win this Spiritual battle against nothing more than illusion? Do you realize that is all you are battling! In truth, there is nothing but GOD, and separation does not exist! Once you get all your energies aligned, Earth life really becomes extremely enjoyable even if you really do have a big Spiritual assignment! The key is to practice God realization on all levels. Whatever you do, do it 100% decisively and do it Spiritually, mentally, emotionally, energetically, physically, and in an earthly sense! This is the great problem with lightworkers. Very few are doing it on all levels. Some do it Spiritually. Some do it mentally. Some do it emotionally. Some are doing it on the Earth, but don't have the full Spiritual. Some do it psychologically and in the Earth, but don't have the full Spiritual. Some do it Spiritually and Psychologically, but not physically and in the Earth! The great lesson of the New Millennium and Seventh Golden Age is that lightworkers must "Be God" on all levels at all times! I have used the term "fragmented ascension." This is where lightworkers are ascended in a Spiritual sense but not on other levels. This is rampant in the Spiritual movement! This book and my book *How To Release Fear-Based Thinking: An In-depth Study of Spiritual Psychology,* have been written to heal and correct this, and if you will read these books I humbly suggest you'll see that it does just that! Please turn all your friends, family, and students on to them, for there is no message lightworkers need to hear more!

So in conclusion, my Beloved Readers, I have shared with you the full Spiritual passion of my heart and soul, the wondrous nature of the material/physical/earthly face of GOD! It is my sincere hope and prayer that my sharing has opened your consciousness and eyes to the wondrous nature of GOD on this level! I can honestly say that I really, totally love and enjoy Earth life! This is not an affirmation or positive thinking, I really mean it! I go from one thing to another all day long: from my shower to my computer, to having something to eat and watching the news, back to writing, reading e-mails, having fun with my employees, visiting with Wistancia, entertaining millions of creative ideas, talking to people, co-creating with the Masters, praying, meditating, being in the garden, making money, watching the birds, playing "bally" with our dog Brianna, watching favorite TV shows, talking with friends, being with family, running errands, practicing being and demonstrating God, seeing God in everything, making love, being of service all day wherever I can, counseling, teaching, doing workshops, sharing, growing, and evolving into greater and greater God Realization! What is not to love! Sure there are challenges. However, I see them as Spiritual tests and as ways to be even more God-like! Each time I overcome them I am even more God-like, because of what I have learned and what I have mastered. Each lesson makes me stronger as I overcome it and learn from it! When you co-create with GOD, Christ, the Holy Spirit, and the Masters, and constantly pray for their help, you will become absolutely filled with Spiritual current. I am running so much Spiritual current through my 12-body system, I do not know what do with myself! I constantly feel filled with God Energy, for I am always claiming it, affirming it, seeing it, praying for it, and demonstrating it! Everything in life becomes one continual flow of God! With so much Spiritual current, Spiritual power, Spiritual love, Spiritual wisdom, Spiritual beauty and harmony, Spiritual science, Spiritual devotion, Spiritual freedom, order, structure and magic running through me and living a consciousness and life as I describe, what is not to love? I literally love everything about Earth life! I am sure I will love heavenly life just as much! However, as long as I am here I will love and enjoy it completely, and fulfill my Spiritual mission with 100% self-mastery and personal power as well! Don't you see, my Beloved Readers, you can have it all! You can have your cake and eat it too! You can have the best of the Spiritual world, the best of the psychological world, and the best of the earthly world! You can have total 100% self-mastery and get all your work done! You can have total 100% unconditional love of everything including Earth life in every facet! You can have 100% total wisdom on a Spiritual, psychological and earthly/physical level! You can have total 100% Spiritual ecstasy, bliss and joy, on a Spiritual, psychological, and physical/earthly level. You can have total 100% self-discipline, emotional invulnerability, and protection, and be a total cause of your reality! You can have total, 100% God and Goddess energies! You can have the best of your own co-creator consciousness and the best of GOD, Christ, the Holy Spirit, and the Masters! In truth, my Beloved Readers, you are God! You have and are everything! All that exists is God! So whatever happens in life just say, "Not my will but thine oh Lord, thank you for the lesson and Spiritual test!" Welcome adversity! It is all just stepping stones for Soul Growth! The key, my Beloved Readers, is to approach life from the proper perspective! As Sai Baba has said, "Your mind creates bondage or your mind creates liberation!" Once you learn to see life from your Spiritual/Christ/Buddha Consciousness and not from your negative ego/fear-based/separative mind, life becomes a trillion times easier! All you see is God and unconditional love in whatever place you look!

My Beloved Readers, it is my sincere hope and prayer that this chapter has helped you to open your eyes a little more to the importance and profundity of fully "unconditionally loving and enjoying the Earth and Earth life!"

So let it be Written! So let it be Done!

25

Multidimensional Realities and Communication

We all know and understand that, in truth, we are all multidimensional beings. This is true because we are Sons and Daughters of GOD and we are made in His image and likeness. GOD is multidimensional and we are multi-dimensional. The microcosm is like the macrocosm. In this chapter I would like to give you, my Beloved Readers, an overview of all the different multidimensional aspects and forms of communication we are connected to. This chapter, in essence, is a full spectrum prism presentation of our multidimensional beingness and forms of communication. When read in overview, it is quite astounding and amazing to review all these aspects and modes of communication in one sitting. It is my great pleasure to have the opportunity to share this all with you.

A discussion of multidimensional beingness and communication begins with the understanding that we are constantly receiving hundreds of different forms of communication on a Subconscious and Spiritual level. To begin with, we are receiving thoughts, feelings, emotions, impulses, desires, sensations, energy, appetites, instincts, imagery, from our subconscious and Higher Self and/or Mighty I Am

Presence. Each of these is a different level, form, and mode of multidimensional communication.

Our basic forms of multidimensional communication with people begin, of course, with verbal communication in a giving and receiving mode. We also communicate reciprocally in a nonverbal manner by our gestures, expressions, and body language. We also communicate mentally or telepathically with others all the time, over short and long distances. An example of this might be thinking of someone and then they call on the phone. We also communicate through our feelings and emotions. We communicate through physical touch. We also communicate back and forth through just basic energy, hence the expression "I will send you some good energy." We also communicate through imagery and/or imagination.

We also communicate with our world through the five physical senses, seeing, hearing, taste, touch, and smell. Each of these five physical senses has a corresponding subconscious inner counterpart sense which allows us to inwardly see, inwardly hear, inwardly taste, inwardly touch, and inwardly smell. This is why when we dream at night everything seems so real. The outer senses are asleep and instead we are using our inner senses to see, hear, taste, touch, and smell. This also explains why some people are clairvoyant (inner sight), clairaudient (inner hearing), clairsentient (inner touch), inner smell, and inner taste. This also explains as well why people can still see, hear, taste, touch, and smell while astral traveling, soul traveling, and when they physically die and translate to another dimension. These are all subconscious inner senses that can be developed and it is what we call being psychic. It also explains the process of channeling in a clairaudient or telepathic regard. So as we see now, my Beloved Readers, our modes of communication from within and from without are beginning to become quite complex, however, in truth, I have touched the tip of the iceberg as to our true multidimensional nature and communication methods.

At any given moment, we are also receiving communication from our inner child, various subpersonalities, good and bad habits, our negative ego and its illusionary thought system, as well as the Christ/Buddha thought system. We also receive communication from past life subpersonalities and/or aspects. Then we receive enormous creative impulses from subconscious and spiritual levels. We also receive dreams every night as another means of communication and feedback on a subconscious and spiritual level. We also receive communication from the outside world or life itself in the form of synchronicity and signs. I will never forget the experience I had as a college student in Northern California. I was trying to decide if I should leave the job I was in. I was walking for a couple hours around the Embarcadero, a section of San Francisco, trying to decide what to do. I was crossing the street and all of a sudden something made me turn my head and look at the license plate of the car in front of me. It said, "It's finished." That was all the synchronicity that I needed. I was leaning that way anyway; however, that ended my conflict. We all experience synchronicities and receive signs from life all the time.

Every time we go to sleep at night, our different bodies travel to their different planes of existence. I am speaking here of our astral body, mental body, etheric body, soul body, and spiritual body. Some people have a recollection of some of the experiences of these bodies when they wakeup in the morning. Some people can consciously travel in these bodies and see everything that is going on. I personally only recommend that you do this in your soul body and/or spiritual body. This is called the Science of Soul Travel or Spiritual Travel. Then there is another form of multidimensional communication called lucid dreaming where one can consciously awake in their dreams and with the use of their will change the outcome of dreams.

Then, on a Spiritual level, we not only communicate with our Higher Self and Mighty I Am Presence, but we also communicate with the inner plane Ascended Masters, the Archangels and Angels, Elohim

Masters, and Christed Extraterrestrial races. We also communicate with
our Spirit Guides, and Guardian Angels. If our psychology and spiritual
attunement and frequency is not of a totally Christ/Buddha nature we
can also communicate with entities on the mental and/or astral plane,
which I do not recommend. This also explains why some people have to
deal with abduction and negative implants, which are another form of
communication that is trying to limit our full Spiritual Realization. It is
for this reason that it is of the highest importance to keep one's
thoughts, feelings, and spiritual attunement at the highest
Melchizedek/Christ/Buddha attunement at all times. Then we also
receive direct communication from GOD, Christ, and the Holy Spirit if
we are open to hearing and receiving it.

From this Spiritual Guidance on all levels we can receive through our
higher senses, intuition, inspiration, guidance, direction, knowingness,
psychometry, comprehension, healing, divine vision, idealism, beatitude, response to group vibration, realization, light, love, and power, to
name a few. Adding to this it must be understood that we are multidimensional beings and are co-creators with GOD. Our true identity is
the Eternal Self which we share with all other Sons and Daughters of
GOD in the infinite universe. Given this fact, there are aspects of ourselves that exist in higher dimensions of GOD that are already functioning there which we may or may not be in communication with. We even
have an aspect of self that is functioning at the 352nd level of Divinity,
even though we may be operating at this time only in the first twelve
levels of GOD's infinite reality. Adding to this we each come from an
Oversoul that has eleven other Soul extensions or Souls that incarnate
in different inner or outer plane regions of GOD as we do. So, we each
have an Oversoul family of twelve that make up our true Soul reality.
We also have in our Monad, or Mighty I Am Presence, a total of 144
Soul extensions that make up our true monadic identity that we are also
connected with and communicate with on the inner plane. In truth, our
12 and 144 Soul extensions are all working for our Oversoul and our

Monad. Each Monad has 12 Oversouls, so we are also in touch with our 12 Oversouls. In truth, we are not all working for ourselves in our group spiritual family, but are working for the Monad. Once we realize the Monad and our own Mighty I Am Presence, then, in truth, we are working for GOD.

Now, my Beloved Readers, taking this all one step further. We also have not only past lives, we also have future lives, for in GOD's reality there is no time and space. Linear time is a product of third dimensional thinking for the purpose of spiritual growth. In the ultimate reality of GOD, all that exists is the Eternal Now. This is why prophecy is possible and why it is even possible to communicate with future selves as well as past life selves.

Taking this one step further still, we also have parallel lives. These aspects of self are living realities just as we are. I remember in Sanat Kumara's training to become a Planetary Logos for this planet 18.5 million years ago, part of his training was to split himself into nine thousand parts and bring them back into the oneness through the incarnation process. Sanat Kumara also said that in his service as a Planetary Logos he could be a thou-sand places at once simultaneously and have total conscious awareness of all of them. My Beloved Readers now consider GOD's reality. Sanat Kumara can do this for one planet. Melchizedek; the Universe. GOD can do this for the infinite Omniverse in all dimensions of reality, in all forms and kingdoms of Creation. Our eventual destiny is to not only be full-fledged and integrated Planetary Ascended Masters, but to become full-fledged integrated Cosmic Ascended Masters as well. Our ultimate destiny is to share a good portion of this Ultimate GOD Consciousness! We are in training now to do this within ourselves and on this planet. Once we master this multidimensional process on this level, we will do it on a Solar level, Galactic level, Universal level, Multiuniversal level, and then GOD level. So, my Beloved Readers, if you think this is complicated now, add infinite numbers of universes and 352 levels of reality into the equation and you have a glimpse of GOD's multidimensional reality, and a picture of our future destiny and process of eventual God Realization in the capacity of Sons and Daughters of GOD. The full unfathomableness of GOD can not be fully realized even as a Cosmic Ascended Master, for there will always be one difference between GOD and ourselves and that is that GOD created us, we did not create GOD. In saying this I do not mean that there is any separation, I just mean that there is a certain unfathomableness of GOD that is good for Sons and Daughters of GOD to understand and to maintain the proper grandeur, but also humbleness and humility. Many go around our world saying they are GOD Realized. In thinking that they are GOD Realized and not God Realized is really saying they are ego realized, without trying to be judgmental in the slightest here. All souls on this plane, except maybe Sai Baba, are not more than an inch or two at most up the ten-inch ladder of true GOD Realization. Any thought to the contrary is the height of egotism, and again without trying to be judgmental, is based on complete lack of understanding of the true infiniteness of GOD. We on this plane are working on Planetary Ascension and have not even begun Galactic Ascension, in the truest sense of the full totality of what this means. This is not to say that we cannot begin to realize some of those initiations; however, our full training will not begin until we leave this world. It is not enough to think that we are there, we must demonstrate our abilities at each level before we are allowed to fully realize the next one.

Now continuing this discussion, at this level it is possible to practice bi-location and tri-location. Bi-location in a spiritual sense is quite easy. You can send your Spiritual body to an Ascension seat, for example, while reading this chapter. Now Sai Baba, who is a Universal Avatar, has developed the ability to be in two physical places and in two different physical bodies at one time. Djwhal Khul from his inner plane Ashram can do fifty channeled readings at the same time around the world and have total conscious awareness of all of them. The higher we go Spiritually in our training and demonstration, the more conscious we can be of our multidimensionality. Each of us at this level also does all kinds of training and service work on the inner place while we sleep. We attend classes, we give classes, we visit the inner plane Ashrams, Ascension seats, Soul and Spiritual travel, and so on. Often we have recollections of these travels upon waking and in our dreams.

We also have very strong multidimensional communication with our Spiritual Teachers and/or Gurus. We also have inner plane communication at times with past life friends and family, as well as future life friends and family. We meet and know many of these people in this life.

Another aspect of our multidimensional selves and communication is with the Earth and Earth energies. We each have a unique relationship with the Earth Mother whose planet we live on. We each communicate multidimensionally with nature. We communicate subtly and sometimes not so subtly with nature spirits, the Devas or Angels of plants, with tree spirits and the elementals. The elementals I speak of here are the Gnomes, Sylphs, Salamanders, and Undines. We also have the ability to communicate directly with the four elements: fire, air, earth, and water. This is how high level initiates and Masters have been able to control the weather. Every aspect of nature, in truth, contains a spiritual essence or being that embodies that particular form. We also have the ability to multidimensionally communicate with crystals and gemstones, and the elemental beings that create the form and physical substance itself. We also each can communicate multidimensionally with animals. There are many on this plane that can talk to animals and they will telepathically talk back in words and images. Many of us have multidimensional communication with pets that have passed over to the other side and are functioning as spirit guides and helpers. There are also spirit animals such as the eagle, jaguar, owl, bear, lion, and tiger, which come as guides and helpers as well on a physical and/or etheric level.

On an Earthly/physical level, we also have the ability to multidimensionally communicate with the subatomic particles of matter and our bodies. We can communicate and work with our electrons, protons, neutrons, molecules, DNA, and even subatomic particles known as quarks. We can also work with subatomic particles coming from outer space in the form of light particles known as photons. This explains how we each have the multidimensional abilities to materialize and dematerialize and/or create substance or physical things right out of the ethers. Sai Baba has demonstrated this ability on a daily basis physically on this planet for almost seventy years. He was able to materialize things right out of the air even as a five-year-old. This happens only in the descent of a true Avatar. An Avatar in its true sense is God Realized at birth. Those claiming to be Avatars are not, except in the case of Sai Baba. Even Lord Maitreya/Jesus and Buddha were not Avatars for they were not God Realized at birth. They were extraordinarily high level initiates and were the most advanced Spiritual Beings in our planetary system, however in the true definition of an Avatar, they still needed spiritual training. So when people claim to be Avatars, they are either run by their negative ego or to give them the benefit of the doubt, have a misunderstanding of the term. To be God Realized at birth and not need any spiritual training is quite a profound concept. Sai Baba is a Universal Master living in a planetary world. This explains why he is able to perform the miracles he does on a daily basis with such ease and effortlessness. These are not psychic tricks and/or psychic powers as some may have who have not fully realized God, they are a true manifestation of the Divine walking the Earth at a Universal level of God Realization.

We also have direct communication on the inner plane with inner plane healers who work with us in many ways and often install, with the help of the Ascended Masters and Angels, various "light technologies" which are the opposite of negative extraterrestrial implants. They are Spiritual Technologies that the inner plane Masters have developed to accelerate spiritual growth and to increase and accelerate healing in our 12-body system. Our multidimensionality is also seen in the fact that we have hundreds of subtle Spiritual Bodies which are too numerous to mention here. Just a few of these are our: Buddhic body, Atmic body, Monadic body, Logoic body, Anointed Christ Overself body, Zohar body of Light, Elohistic Lord's body, Paradise Son's body, Lord's Mystical body, Light body, Love/Wisdom/Power bodies, Causal body, Soul body, Gematrian body, Epi-kenetic body, Electromagnetic body, Aka body, Merkabah body, Higher Admon Kadmon body, to name a few. All of these bodies have special abilities and functions in a multidimensional sense, and can and do communicate with us and we with them on a conscious or unconscious level.

Adding to this, we do not have just seven chakras or twelve chakras, we have in truth, 330 chakras taking us back to the 352nd level of Divinity. It is possible to anchor, activate, and actualize a great many of these chakras and chakra grids through the process of spiritual evolution. I teach much of this work in my Ascension book series. Each chakra and chakra grid being a different level and function of multidimensional communication.

We also have the ability to multidimensionally communicate with the Goddess energy in the form of the Cosmic Divine Mother and the many embodiments of the Divine Mother on a planetary, solar, galactic, and universal level. This can also be done with working with the Lady Masters of the Spiritual Hierarchy.

We each also have very strong multidimensional communication with all the people of the Earth. This is often done through the collective unconscious which Carl Jung, the famous Swiss psychologist, spoke about. We also have much stronger inner plane chords and connections with children, family, and spouses from this life, past lives, and future lives. Then there are the friends and families of our 144 Soul extensions of our Monad that make up our extended Monadic family. Add to this all their past lives. Most beings on the Earth who are considered old Souls have had as many as two hundred past lives. Also, consider that you may have had hundreds of spouses, hundreds of parents, and even as many as a thousand children. Also, consider that each person you have been sexually intimate with in this life has created a chord of energy. This chord of energy, which the Hawaiians called Aka chords, is another form of communication. By being Spiritual Masters and causes of our reality we can use these chords to uplift all that we have touched in our lives in a friends, family, and romantic relationship sense.

On a Spiritual level, we have multidimensional communication with GOD and the Cosmic inner plane Masters through the "Language of Light." This often manifests through the anchoring of multidimensional communication using Fire Letters, Key Codes, and Sacred Geometries. One of our highest senses is that of the ability to comprehend "All Knowledge"! There is one last multidimensional form of communication that is extremely rare but does happen on occasion and that is the experience of true "Revelation with GOD"! This is such an unfathomable and indescribable experience I will not even attempt to describe it here.

In final conclusion, I have attempted here in this chapter to share with you from a more full spectrum prism perspective a glimpse into our full multidimensional beingness and modes of communication that many do not realize are going on and/or just take for granted, in the integrated process of living one's life.

My Beloved Readers, I think you would agree that our true multidimensional nature and communication seen from the full spectrum prism perspective makes *Alice in Wonderland* look boring!

26

The Three Lines of Evolution

It is every person's path on Earth to become a Self-Realized Being. Not very many people realize that there are actually three lines of evolution in GOD's infinite universe. What this means is that there are actually three different kinds of beings that GOD created. GOD created Archangels and Angels, GOD created the Elohim, and GOD created the Ascended Master race. These are each three unique and separate lines of evolution, which ultimately integrate and function as one at the highest level of GOD's reality.

Most of the people of the Earth make up the Ascended Master line of evolution. Our Planetary Hierarchy is mostly made up of this line of evolution.

The Archangels and Angels span all the way from the Angels and Devas that embody our plants, flowers, and vegetables; all the way up the evolutionary ladder to the great Archangels such as Archangel Michael and Archangel Metatron, to name a few. There are, at times, Angels who embody in the form of people, and many of us know such people. On occasion, there is even the crossing of lines of evolution. The Angelic line of evolution relates more to the feeling tones of GOD.

When we pray to GOD for help, He sends His Archangels and Angels. When we pray for help in the garden, it is the plant Angels and Devas who help.

The Elohim line of evolution refers to the Creator Gods who helped GOD create the infinite physical universe. On the lower ladder of evolution the Elohim are the Elemental Beings who's job it is to create all physical substance in GOD's infinite physical universe. The Elemental Beings work closely with the Devas and Angels; however, they are from a completely separate line of evolution. The Elohim create planets, solar systems, galaxies, and universes. The Elementals create rocks, gemstones, plants, vegetables, flowers, and even our physical bodies. It is a good idea to talk to the Elementals and talk to the Devas, and thank them for all their wonderful help. This is something on Earth that the majority of the world takes for granted. Where the Angels are the feeling tones of GOD, the Elohim are more the thought side of GOD. The Ascended Master line of evolution is somewhere in the middle. I think you can see here what an exquisite beautiful plan of creation GOD has built.

So just as each person in GOD's creation is made of a different Ray or Rays of GOD which explains why people are so different, there are also these three totally unique lines of evolution, which explain the differences in all the diverse beings in GOD's infinite universe. Pan, the head of the Animal Kingdom, is of the Elohim line of evolution.

Everything in GOD's infinite universe is in a state of evolution. The tiny Elementals are evolving ultimately into Elohim. The Plant Devas are evolving into Overlighting Devas that have spiritual responsibility over much larger areas of land. Angels are evolving into Archangels. No matter what level you are at, evolution continues and refines itself.

Another interesting fact that most people don't realize is that our Monads have had incarnations of aspects of itself in the Mineral, Plant, and Animal Kingdoms. Now this is not to say we as souls have had incarnations as rocks, plants and animals. Some think this, but it is illusion. There is no such thing as transmigration of a soul; this means you as a soul have not been a rock, plant, or animal. What is true, however, is that our Monad, or Mighty I Am Presence, have incarnated aspects of itself in their evolutionary process in distant ages past.

What is also a fact is that on occasion, but not very often, animals have been allowed to evolve from the Animal Kingdom into the Kingdom of a real person of an Adam Kadmon type, which is the name of our type of bodies. This is a rare exception, but it can happen.

Even gemstones are in a state of evolution. The most evolved gemstone being the diamond. Most women know this, I know my wife does.

As these three lines of evolution move up the evolutionary ladder they work more closely together, functioning as an integrated team and unit much as your three minds will function as one unit once they are mastered and integrated. I am speaking here of the Conscious, Subconscious, and Superconscious minds.

My Beloved Readers, I hope this brief explanation of the three lines of evolution and how they function has enriched your understanding of the profundity of GOD in all His infinite manifestations!

27

How to Develop an Integrated Christ/Buddha Living Space

An aspect of integrating the Goddess deals with the issue of developing a Christ/Buddha Living Space. To begin this discussion it must be understood that "beauty is in the eye of the beholder" and "in matters of taste, there is no dispute." So, I am not going to write a chapter telling people how to decorate their home for that would be impossible. I would, however, like to share my own personal experience for this most important issue and share some under-lying principals in regard to this issue that I think you, my Beloved Readers, might find of value.

There is an ancient Spiritual Science in China, which I am sure you all are familiar with, called Feng Shui. This spiritual science deals with the art of physical placement of things in your home and environment for greatest spiritual benefit to all. I had a lady come to my home who was a Master of Feng Shui, and she had some wonderful ideas. Certain rooms were for business, some for romantic relationship, one for prosperity. It was very important that certain closet doors be blocked. It was important that beds be pointed in a certain direction. She recommended that we get a fountain for our living room, which we did. I can't remember all the different ideas she had, but we implemented most of them and it really did add an enormous amount to the spiritual atmosphere and energetic radiation of our home.

In my other books, I have spoken about the importance of cleansing the etheric and/or energetic atmosphere of one's home by the practice of burning pots, sage, and incense. The walls become embedded with energy, thought forms, and feelings as well as the psycho/spiritual atmosphere of the house. Clairvoyantly this can sometimes be seen as gray or dark clouds in the house. Just as is it is extremely important to clean your house well, it is also important to cleanse the psychic atmosphere on a regular basis. The best method I have found is the use of a burning pot, which is a pot with a hot plate under it where you add 1/4 of an inch of Epson salt with 1/2 an inch of rubbing alcohol. Light a match to it and it will cleanse the psychic atmosphere of that room in about five minutes. I recommend doing this once a week or once every other week in each room of your house. When people walk into your home, they can sense the psycho/spiritual atmosphere. In my experience, sage or incense alone is not enough. The other helpful method is to ask the inner plane Ascended Masters and Angels to help.

The next aspect of maintaining a Christ/Buddha Living Space is the importance of creating harmony, beauty, and aesthetics. This, again, is individual to each person; however; here are some ideas from my own personal experience. The first idea that comes to mind is the creation of spiritual altars in your home and if possible one room dedicated to your spiritual life and spiritual attunement. This could be a place to meditate and pray. I highly recommend buying some spiritual statues and spiritual pictures as well as your favorite incense and maybe some crystals or gem stones. Each time you go to this altar or even this room, a habit of spiritual attunement is created. The physical beauty of your Spiritual Altar will be an immediate attunement itself. It also must be understood that these statues and pictures hold energy and form conduits and lines of spiritual force from the inner plane. It may be interesting for some of you to know that Spiritual Statues even have chakras and can be seen spinning and vibrating with energy.

I myself take the approach of my home and property being a Temple as well as home and business. My entire home is filled with beautiful Spiritual Statues and pictures of the Masters and Saints of all religions. In a sense, every room is a Spiritual Sanctuary and Altar.

Quan Yin has advised me and my wife of the importance of having fresh flowers on our main Altars. This we do on a regular basis and it adds an enormous amount to the feeling in our home. We also have an enormous amount of plants, which we all know Spiritually and Physically cleanse the atmosphere.

I also recently have bought some beautiful silk flowers that are exquisite in color and beauty, which have added another dimension to the overall aesthetic nature of our home.

Being very much attuned to the principal of Synthesis, Integration, and Balance, we have attempted to honor all kingdoms of GOD. For this reason, we also have a great many crystals and gemstones of a small and large nature all over our home. We also have a beautiful female Golden Retriever by the name of Brianna and a wonderful male cat by the name of Mushroom, which adds to the family atmosphere. We also try to bring all the colors of the rainbow to our Spiritual Pictures, plants, silk plants, crystals, gemstones, and spiritual accoutrements. I have these beautiful glass pyramids each of a different color of the different rays. We also have beautiful stained glass spiritual pictures adorning our windows. We also have our favorite photographs that have the most sentimental meaning.

The Art of Decorating is also very important in how one creates a Christ/Buddha living space. There is a whole art to the placement of pictures, furniture, plants, and objects to form Divine Order and symmetry. The importance of being surrounded by spiritual beauty, nature, beautiful colors, the smell of beautiful flowers and incense, beautiful sounds of nature, a fountain and/or beautiful music cannot be underestimated.

In addition, the importance of having nice beautiful furniture that is all so comfortable. All of these aspects when put together create an enormous radiation of Spiritual energy. These physical aspects uplift the Spirit and all 12 bodies. In one of the Universal Mind Channelings of Edgar Cayce, the Universal Mind said that one should make their Earthly home where Angels would choose to come. Creating a Spiritually beautiful home draws higher spiritual forces to you and to your home.

Part of the purpose of life is to create Heaven on Earth. Creating a beautiful spiritual home is physically grounding one's spiritual life and energy into the Earth. Ideally, one should try to integrate all seven rays into one's home. Not just in color, but in principle. For example, the fourth ray is the ray of beauty, which we have been speaking of. The sixth ray deals with devotion and that could be grounded in your home by having spiritual altars. The seventh ray deals with ceremonial order and magic; and this could be manifested by keeping your house and office very orderly and clean in the same way that you would keep a church or temple orderly or clean. Your home and environment is the physical body of GOD, just as your physical body is the physical temple you live in. By creating our home also into a Temple or Spiritual Sanctuary, we are honoring and sanctifying the material face of GOD. When I look at our home and gardens, it honestly looks like an inner plane Ashram. Isn't that the purpose; to create Heaven on Earth? The Divine Plan is not to escape Earth or even leave Earth once Ascended, but rather be God and/or the Mighty I AM Presence on Earth and create a utopian civilization on Earth.

The fifth ray of New Age Science is integrated in the home by the Spiritually Scientific approach you bring to creating the Divine Order, Divine Symmetry, and Divine Geometry in how you decorate it and create it. The second ray is integrated through the love and wisdom that is manifested in how you decorate, and the love and wisdom that emanates from the objects you choose to place in your home. The first ray is integrated through the Spiritual Power that emanates through the spiritual statues, spiritual pictures, spiritual paintings, flowers, crystals, and gemstones, as well as Divine Order. The third ray is integrating in the form of active intelligence by making your home not only spiritually beautiful, but also spiritually functional so enormous amounts of spiritual service work and personal, social and family activity can take place.

Another important aspect of maintaining a Christ/Buddha living space is the importance of putting things away after using them and not letting one's house become too cluttered. On the other side of the coin, one does not want to become neurotic or overly orderly to the point of losing one's inner peace if a physical object is out of place. A proper balance must be found that honors both the feminine and masculine.

This brings me to the first aspect of creating a Christ/Buddha living space which honors the Goddess as well, which is the outside environment and gar-dens of your apartment or home. My wife and I have spent an enormous amount of time creating a beautiful garden around the entire perimeter of our home. In this garden, we have planted beautiful plants and flowers of all colors and varieties. We've also decorated our back yard with beautiful spiritual statues of Mother Mary, Quan Yin, Lord Buddha, Sananda, St. Francis, and a great many different kinds of Angels. We also have little statues of Gnomes and Fairies. We also have beautiful little statues of all kinds of different animals honoring the animal kingdom. In our beautiful garden we have statues big and small of deer, swan, ducks, owls, pigs, frogs, raccoons, fox, birds, to name a few. Each Spiritual Statue and animal statue are spiritually, aesthetically and scientifically placed to create the perfect Feng Shui in the garden. In the flowerbeds, there are even little statues of colorful butterflies, ladybugs, bumblebees, and birds. Our garden is filled with the colors of all the seven rays and even the higher rays. It is a Synthesis Blending of all the Kingdoms. The Rocks on the property are spiritually and scientifically placed around the flowerbeds to honor the mineral kingdom. When we moved into this place, there was a shed that we painted and turned into a Spiritual Chapel. The outside of this chapel is now violet and white; the inside is all white. We have carpeted it in a beautiful green carpet and placed some beautiful white flowers on the altar, with a white chair for meditation.

We have also placed in our garden beautiful bird feeders, which have attracted an enormous number of birds. My office where I work all day long looks out to the entire garden and those bird feeders. As I sit in my office, the garden is not only filled with birds but also many other kinds of wonderful animal life. There are chipmunks, butterflies, hummingbirds, blue birds, bumblebees, and squirrels to name a few. This does not even mention all the plant spirits and nature spirits that the garden is filled with and that we have invoked.

Now I must say that taking care of this property and garden and maintaining a Christ/Buddha Living Space takes a certain amount of work and time. The enjoyment that my wife and I, Academy, Ashram, friends, family, and others experience being here is greatly worth the effort to maintain it. Besides the enjoyment factor, an even more important principle is that it is each of our spiritual responsibility as integrated Ascended Masters and as caretakers for the Goddess energy to take care of our homes, gardens, and environment in a spiritually responsible manner. As I have mentioned many times in my writing, all four faces of GOD; spiritual, mental, emotional and physical, must be mastered and integrated to become a full-fledged Ascended Master and to fully integrate one's Goddess energies in the proper manner. I thank you for this opportunity to share some of my personal thoughts and feelings on this most important issue of creating a Divine Goddess/Christ/Buddha Living Space!

28

Inner Plane Spiritual Activism

This is a chapter I have really been looking forward to writing, because it is something that is very dear to my heart. It has revolutionary implications if lightworkers will respond to this Clarion Call. Regarding the Divine Plan for the Seventh Golden Age for this planet, it has been divided into seven main departments. These Seven Departments have to do with the seven major Planetary Rays and the Seven Ashrams of the Christ, whose job it is to implement this Divine Plan on Earth.

The First Ray Department is headed by the Ascended Master El Morya and deals with the political transformation of this planet. The Second Ray Department is a combined effort of Lord Maitreya, Kuthumi, and the Ascended Master Djwhal Khul, and deals with the spiritual education of this planet. The Third Ray Department is headed by Saint Germain, the Mahachohan, and Serapis Bey, and deals with the economic transformation of this planet! The Fourth Ray Department is headed by Paul the Venetian, and deals with the Spiritual transformation of this planet through the Arts. The Fifth Ray Department is headed by Master Hilarion, and deals with the spiritual transformation of this planet through New Age sciences. The Sixth Ray Department is headed by Sananda, and deals with the spiritual transformation of the major religions of the world into an individualized but cooperative force. The Seventh Ray Department is headed by Lady Portia and Saint Germain, and deals with the transformation of civilization and business aspects of our society.

There are a great many lightworkers on this planet, as they move through their initiation process, that feel the need to move into Spiritual Leadership and Planetary World Service, and rightly so. The only problem is that most lightworkers are not inclined to, for example, enter politics or get involved in political movements. This is quite understandable, for politics is quite an ugly business the way it is practiced on our planet. Most politicians are stuck in their personality, are run by the negative ego, and cannot see beyond partisan politics.

In conjunction with the inner plane Ascended Masters, I have come up with a way to solve this problem. I call this "Inner Plane Spiritual Activism." Since most lightworkers don't like to get involved with politics or the great social issues of our time in an outer sense, there is an opportunity for enormous spiritual service on a global scale in an inner sense that is equally as valuable. This has to do with dedicating a small part of every day, or every other day, to doing inner work to politically and socially transform our planet.

For example, pray to GOD and the inner plane Ascended Masters of your choice to help the candidates of your choice. Visualize them winning. Create affirmations and thought forms of success that you can verbally or inwardly put out into the ethers.

Pray to GOD, the Ascended Masters, the Archangels, and the Elohim Masters, for the awakening of the people of the Earth. Pray to these Masters for the saving of the rain forests, to stop gang violence, to save the whales. Pray for the economic systems of the Earth to become more responsive to cooperation and the dictates of the Soul and Mighty I Am

Presence. Pray to GOD and these Masters for a renaissance of the arts and music in a spiritual manner. Pray that scientists around the world be infused with New Age technologies, understandings and insights, so diseases such as AIDS, the Ebola virus, and cancer can be cured. Pray to GOD and these Masters for a complete transformation of the religions of the Earth, so the contamination of negative ego concepts is cleared from their doctrine, as well as judgmentalness, self-righteousness, and intolerance. Pray to GOD and the Masters for the complete transformation of every aspect of our civilization, to reflect the ideals and values of the Divine Plan of GOD and the Planetary Hierarchy!

Pray for the stopping of all Earth changes and natural catastrophes. Pray for the undoing of all thoughts of Armageddon and the ending of the world. Pray for a negative implant and elemental removal for the entire Earth and all her inhabitants, including our pets. Pray for the ending of animal cruelty, spousal abuse, and child abuse.

Do you, see my friends; the list is endless. At the end of this chapter, I will give you an even larger comprehensive list of all the things that can be prayed for and creatively visualized about.

My beloved readers, I do not need to share with you how incredibly powerful prayer is, especially when you call on GOD, all the Ascended Masters, the Archangels, and the Elohim Masters. You are literally calling on GOD, Christ, and the Holy Spirit, as well as the entire GOD Force of Creation, which nothing can stop.

On other occasions, I have prayed to GOD and the Masters to help heal physical health problems of world leaders if their higher-self was open to it and I was not infringing on their free choice and free will. Other times I have prayed for implant and negative elemental removals with the same qualifications that were made above.

On another occasion, when a nanny was accused of killing a child and there was a big uproar in England, when she was about to be sentenced, I prayed to GOD and the Lady Masters for forgiveness, compassion, and leniency. Lo and behold, to my amazement, the next day the judge completely let her go although she had been convicted. I intuitively know, with no ego investment here, that my prayers played a part in this. How much does not really matter. What does matter was that I was fulfilling my puzzle piece and being active and not passive about the things I believed in.

Most people do not take advantage of the power of prayer to GOD and the Masters, even for themselves, let alone for all the things going on in the world. Do not underestimate the combined spiritual power of GOD and all these spiritual Masters, as well as your own spiritual and mental powers.

On one occasion I was doing some personal world service work in regard to resolving a certain issue with another major spiritual leader who is a friend of mine. I needed to send this person an extremely important package and it was essential to get it to them immediately. I was rummaging through my desk trying to find an express mail form. I knew I had some, but I could not find them in the normal place I kept them. I looked through this draw three different times in a twenty minute period. During this whole process, I had been conversing with the inner plane Ascended Masters for four or five hours. I all of a sudden felt the inner guidance to look through that same drawer for the fourth time. To my absolute amazement the fourth time, right on top of the drawer lay 20 express mail forms. I had a world service personal need, and by the grace of Sai Baba, Saint Germain, Kuthumi, Djwhal Khul, and El Morya, they even saved me a trip to the post office because of the urgent need that this package had to go out.

These kinds of experiences are fun but I don't mean to focus on personal glamour experiences. I only share this with you to demonstrate to you the power of GOD and the Ascended Masters if you will call on them. They will help you personally with all your desires and needs, and will help you spiritually in your initiation and ascension process, and they will help you with all your world service prayers.

My beloved readers, can you imagine if all the lightworkers on this planet would become "Inner Plane Spiritual Activists"! Can you imagine if millions and millions of lightworkers around the globe, and eventually billions, would call in GOD and all these Masters for all the things going wrong in our world. Instead of getting depressed, upset, judgmental, or angry, isn't this a better way to use our energies as the sons and daughters of GOD. Isn't this a better way than just tuning out politics, social issues, the news and newspapers. With this method, watching the news and reading a newspaper would be for the direct purpose of finding things to pray for and finding ways to be of service.

What I am suggesting here to you, my beloved friends, is to pray to GOD and the Masters every time you see something in the world that is not right. Every time this takes place, call in GOD and the Masters to undo it and to fix it. In this way, the world will be changed and your own consciousness will be elevated a thousand-fold. By doing this you keep your own consciousness held steady in the light and in a perfected state. Instead of leaving it in a state of imperfection, your prayer and/or creative visualization creates perfection in your own consciousness and in that situation. Be not concerned with the results of your prayers or creative visualization. That is not important! As Krishna said in the Bhagavad-Gita, "Be not concerned with the fruits of your action." What is important is that you are doing your spiritual practice. You are fulfilling your service puzzle piece in GOD's Divine Plan. Do you sense, my beloved readers, the incredible spiritual leadership and planetary service work you can do without ever leaving the comfort of your own bedroom or office? Your television and newspaper can be the Divine service vehicles for showing you where your prayer and inner work needs to be focused that day.

Lightworkers need to be less focused on passing initiations and their own personal growth, and more focused on how they can be of service. This especially holds true once you've passed your sixth and seventh initiations. Focusing too much on initiations after this point can become selfish. What I am presenting here is a literal gold mine of ways to be of Planetary World Service.

I put forth the Clarion Call to Light, Love, and Powerworkers around the globe to spend at least half of your meditations each day on Spiritual Leadership and Planetary World Service Work. Archangel Gabriel's Trumpet has sounded forth! This is a call to prayer and creative visualization and thinking, to anchor GOD's Divine Plan on Earth, to bring in the New Millennium and the Seventh Golden Age!

I dedicate the rest of this chapter to sharing with you other ideas and issues to pray about and to do inner plane work in relationship to:

- Call on the Christed Extraterrestrial Races to openly reveal themselves to the governments and people of the Earth and to reveal and unfold to our planet their advanced technologies and wisdom to transform it both spiritually and materially as GOD would have it be.

- Call forth a Planetary axiatonal alignment.

- Call for a Platinum Net for our planet and all the people of the Earth and all the animals, if this prayer be in harmony with GOD's Will.

- Pray for the complete healing of the conflicts in the Middle East.

- Pray for the healing of the conflicts in Bosnia and Yugoslavia.

- Pray for the removal of all the Earth-bound entities trapped on Earth, to help them to be released.

- Pray for the Integration and Harmony between the Human, Elemental, and Angelic Kingdoms.

- Call for the Core Fear Matrix Removal Program for all the people of the world and for the Earth Herself and all animals, if this prayer be in harmony with GOD's Will.

- Pray for the removal of all physical pollution from the atmosphere of our planet with help from the Arcturians and the Ashtar Command.

- Pray for all the endangered species, to prevent their extinction.

- Pray for a mass clearing of all unwanted astral entities interfering with humanity's free will.

- Pray for the healing of any auric holes, spots, irritations, and leaks in the physical, etheric, astral, and mental body of the planet.

- Pray for a Cosmic Vacuum for clearing up all planetary glamour, maya, and illusion.

- Pray for a Cosmic Vacuum to clean up all planetary astral smog, mental smog, and etheric smog surrounding our planet.

- Pray to the Christed Extraterrestrial Races to repair the ozone layer.

- Pray to GOD and the Masters for the anchoring of the Monadic Blueprint Body for the Earth.

- Pray for the Specialized Meditation for a Shower of core love and core light for the Earth.

- Support for those who want to stop smoking. Cigarette manufacturers and companies being honest in regard to the deleterious effects of secondhand smoke.

- End to political corruption, partisan politics, gridlocks, and political selfishness.

- Total revamping of the tax system so that it is spiritual and fair.

- Proper money management in the governments of the world. The removal of the power and control of the power elite and trilateral commission. An end to the greed, selfishness and injustice of having only a small, select group which comprises the wealthiest families of the world, running the global economy.

- Return of all POW's.

- The establishment of true political spiritual party representatives.

- The importance of spiritual education and spiritual values being integrated into the school system in a non-fundamentalist way.

- Health insurance for every single person, which includes coverage for alternative medical treatment as well.

- The transformation of the criminal justice system from one of punishment to one of spiritual rehabilitation.

- An end to the predominance of violence on television and in movies.

- An end to the world's preoccupation with glamour and gossip.

- Better care and respect for the elderly.

- An end to unfair treatment and disregard for Veterans.

- Free and high quality treatment to all Veterans who are ill due to germ warfare used in Vietnam and the Gulf War.

- The resumption of peace talks between the PLO and Israelis.

- The establishment of comprehensive peace in the Middle East with all countries involved.

- An end to all illusory negative belief systems in religion and the New Age Movement involving the ending of the world and Armageddon.

- Enough jobs for everyone who seeks work. Provisions for those who have been kicked out of welfare to be helped to get back on their feet financially and on all levels.

- The ending of all wars.

- Greater power and influence of the U.N.

- An influx of the more highly evolved initiates into politics in order to revamp the system. An awareness on the part of all initiates whose puzzle piece this is to get in touch with it and to have the courage and fortitude to pursue their divine mission.

- Greater world focus on service work and on volunteering.

- More compassion for those who are suffering on all levels.

- The stopping of Drug Cartels and the psychic and physical poisoning of our children through drugs.

- The necessary insight to put spirituality before materialism, technology, and money.

- An end to pornography and the over-identification and over-glorification of the physical vehicle.

- An end to sexual harassment for both women and men.

- An end to sport hunting, rodeos, bull fighting, wearing of furs, and overall animal cruelty.

- An end to all Cults.

- A movement and integration of the more traditional medicine with holistic health and naturopathy.

- An end to crime.

- The admittance by the governments of the world as to the existence of UFO's.

- The destruction of all nuclear weapons, biological weapons, and all weapons of mass destruction.

- The ending of terrorism.

- Pray to GOD and the Masters to bring forth the Violet Transmuting Flame into all issues listed above and you yourself visualize the Violet Flame emanating from your heart and breath it into these situations as well. You are also invited to do any other creative visualizations you are intuitively guided to do to make this a co-creative partnership with GOD and the Masters.

- Anything that touches your heart that you choose to pray and meditate about.

Be creative!

Namaste!

29

Changing and Integrating Higher Rays

In my first book *The Complete Ascension Manual,* I spoke a great deal about Esoteric Psychology and the Science of the Rays. For those of you who have not read this book and would like a deeper understanding of the Twelve Rays I would highly recommend reading this book, for this and many other reasons.

One of the basic understandings of Esoteric Psychology is that our Monad, Soul, personality, mental body, emotional body and physical body all embody a certain Planetary Ray of GOD. The effect of these Rays is astounding. One of the very interesting advanced understandings of this process, which I did not get into in that particular book, is that it is possible to integrate and change your original Ray structure that you came in with as a child, to one of the more advanced higher Rays that came into this planet in the early 1970's. Of course, what I am speaking of here is not only these seven Rays that we are all familiar with, but also the five newer higher Rays. For your edification, enjoyment and convenience I have listed the Twelve Rays and their functions again, in the following chart:

Ray One (Red)
Personal power, GOD's Will, faith, protection, political training

Ray Two (Blue)
Love/Wisdom, spiritual education, spiritual teacher training

Ray Three (Yellow)
Active intelligence, business

Ray Four (Green)
Harmony, the arts, the art of healing

Ray Five (Orange)
Concrete mind, healing, the science of anchoring the New Age

Ray Six (Indigo)
Idealism, devotion, ministration, the oneness of all religions

Ray Seven (Violet)
Transformation, alchemy, freedom, the Violet Transmuting Flame, ceremonial order and magic

Ray Eight (Seafoam Green and Violet)
The Higher Cleansing Ray

Ray Nine (Blue-Green)
Joy, attraction of the Body of Light

Ray Ten (Pearlescent)
Anchoring of the Body of Light, invites the Soul Merge

Ray Eleven (Pink-Orange)
Bridge to the New Age

Ray Twelve (Gold)

Anchoring of the New Age and Christ Consciousness

The best way to explain this process would be to give some examples. Let us say you have a Second Ray Monad. Through your spiritual work and spiritual path, you may evolve yourself to becoming a Twelfth Ray Monad. Let's say you had a Fifth Ray emotional body; you may evolve yourself to developing a Eleventh Ray emotional body. Let's say you were a Fifth Ray mental body, this could evolve to become an Eighth Ray mental body. Let's say you were a Third Ray Soul; this might evolve to become a Tenth Ray Soul. Let's say you had a Sixth Ray personality; this might evolve to become a Ninth Ray personality. Let's say you had a First Ray body; this might transform to a Tenth Ray body. The possibilities are endless. This is not something that has to happen or even needs to happen. What I am saying is that it does happen at times and this is something lightworkers should be aware of in understanding the Science of the Rays.

It is also important to understand that even though your Ray structure and/or configuration can transform into ones utilizing the five Higher Rays, Djwhal Khul has told me that the original pattern and configuration is still there; however, it has been, in a sense, overlighted, or merged and integrated with this higher aspect. So the original Ray pattern is not lost, it has, in a sense, been integrated and merged with. I hope this new understanding of Esoteric Psychology and the five Higher Rays has enhanced your understanding and training in this most important Spiritual Science!

30

The Importance of Removing the "Earth Crystals" From Your Subtle Bodies

Another extremely important esoteric secret of GOD's infinite universe that very few lightworkers are aware of is the understanding of the fact that when all souls incarnate onto this planet, there are certain "Earth Crystals" that are placed within the etheric body for the purpose of helping incarnated souls adjust to the physical incarnation process. These Earth Crystals are placed there by the inner plane Ascended Masters and the Angelic Hierarchy.

It must be understood that these Earth Crystals serve a positive purpose in the beginning, and help to physically ground the individual in a mystical way that cannot be described here. We must all realize that we are visiting the Earth and it is not our true home. Our true home is in Heaven and/or the Celestial Realms. To take a physical body and come under the limitations of third dimensional reality takes some adjusting for the incarnating soul. These Earth Crystals that are placed in the etheric body serve to help in this adjustment process to functioning effectively on Earth.

Those persons who are most etherically ungrounded, heavenly, and sometimes Angelic in nature, tend to have more of these Earth Crystals. No matter how much Angelic clearing work you have done on yourself, these Earth Crystals will not be removed.

The problem is that once you move into adulthood and have embraced your spiritual path, initiation, and ascension process, you do not need these Earth Crystals anymore. What was once a positive thing, has now become a "limitation" and a slight block in the full understanding and realization of becoming an "Integrated Christ"!

By the grace of GOD and the inner plane Ascended Masters and Archangels, I have received permission to share this information with you, my beloved readers, and have secondly to share the good news that the Cosmic and Planetary Ascended Masters and Archangels will help you remove them!

Now, I must say here, that once in a while some of these Earth Crystals are very stuck or lodged in your four-body system, and in some cases it may be necessary to get help from a trained initiate to remove them. The first step, however, is to ask the Masters and Angels to help remove them. If you still feel that there are some left, then give me a call and I will put you in touch with a trained member of the Academy who can remove them. I consider the removal of these Earth Crystals not as important as removing your negative implants and elementals; however, they would be second in line to be removed!

Since I brought up the subject of negative implants and elementals, I would recommend all lightworkers to give me a call and set up a channeled phone session with the inner plane Ascended Masters for an "Ascension Clearing" and negative implant and elemental removal session. The meditation in this book called "The Mount Shasta 50 Point Cosmic Clearing Meditation," will clear an enormous amount of psychic debris and will probably clear a great deal of your negative implants and elementals. As was the case with the Earth Crystals, there are certain negative implants in your subtle bodies that remain stuck, and it really takes one channeled session with a trained initiate to remove them all for 100% sure. During this session, you can also request that all your Earth Crystals be removed as well. This session will 100% clean all your negative implants and elementals; however, in some cases a trained initiate healer in person must remove the Earth Crystals. There are people I can recommend who will travel to your area to do this service for yourself and your friends. We'll be honest with you here that the Cosmic and Planetary Ascended Masters removed most of my Earth Crystals that I came in with. The Masters have told me, however, that there are cases where a trained initiate may be needed to help remove some of them.

So, the process goes like this. First off, do the Mount Shasta 50 point Cleansing Meditation I have given you in this book. This will remove an astronomical amount of psychic debris from your auric field of an extreme subtle nature. We are polishing your diamond so to speak.

The second step is to ask in meditation, ideally right before bed, for the Ascended Masters and Archangels of your choice to remove your Earth Crystals. I would encourage you to include Melchizedek, the Mahatma, and Archangel Metatron in this prayer invocation! Also, call in the Ascended Master Djwhal Khul!

The third step is to set up an appointment with a trained initiate from the Melchizedek Synthesis Light Academy for an ascension clearing and negative implant and elemental removal, if you feel the need. I would highly recommend it; however, some of you may be able to do a complete clearing just using the first meditation.

The fourth step is, in this channeled session with the Ascended Masters, if you feel that some Earth Crystals still remain, ask the Masters to remove them in this channeled session if they can. You may not need this because the Masters may be able to remove them completely upon your own prayer request. This is a preventive measure to make 100% sure they were all cleared. Occasionally some are very stuck.

The fifth step is, if there are some Earth Crystals that are having a hard time coming out, it might be worth your while to set-up a session with a trained initiate healer who can remove them in person. The good news is that most of your Earth Crystals and all of your negative implants and elementals will be removed if you follow the aforementioned steps. For those who have a few stuck ones you might want to consider this final step; however, it is not essential, for the majority of them would have been removed. If you want this, however, this service is available from the Melchizedek Synthesis Light Academy.

Be not concerned about having negative implants and elementals, for they are not something to be fearful about. They are not debilitating in any way. Everyone on Earth has them, and they are very subtle in nature. You could go through your whole life and not have them removed and function quite effectively. I only bring up this information for those who really want to advance on their spiritual path in a very quick and decisive manner. If you are very dedicated to the spiritual path and want to become a fully Integrated Christ at your highest potential, it is a good idea to have both of these aspects removed. On a subtle level, they do create energy blocks and some limitations in your spiritual energy field. These blocks and limitations are of a subtle nature; however, the entire spiritual path is one really dealing with subtle energies, and working with the information and tools in this book will basically allow you to do this on your own. If there are a few stuck ones left after following the guidance given here then I offer you these other services, as a service and courtesy to you, my beloved readers. However, they are not necessary or required, and the majority of the clearing will take place from just reading this book and applying the instructions and tools given forth herein.

My beloved readers, I am happy to share this information and material with you for the purpose of accelerating your ascension and initiation process and helping you to become a fully Integrated Christ!

31

A New Species of Light and Higher Light Body Integration

It is very important to understand that we are all in the process of becoming a new Species of Light! This is achieved through the help of Spirit, the Masters, the Angels, and the Christed Extraterrestrials. It is also achieved through our own positive thinking, speaking, feeling, actions, and manifestation of our Spiritual mission and purpose on Earth!

One of the important things to understand, however, is that this transformation of our bodies into a new Species of Light is sometimes a Spiritual Mutation process that has a lot of physical symptoms. This is a normal part of the process! It has to do with four things. Some of it is just the higher frequencies of light becoming integrated into the etheric and physical vehicle. Another part is caused by specific Ascension Activation Work that is being done by the inner plane Masters on large numbers of initiates. Thirdly, it is also caused by, on some occasions but not always, certain blocks or genetic weak-nesses in certain areas of the body! I want to make it clear, however, that 99% of the time it has noth-ing to do with this. By this, I mean this will occur with a great many people even if they have no blockages or weaknesses. This is important to understand for many people think, or people lay trips on them, that they are doing something wrong because they have these symptoms and this is not the case. The symptoms are in truth just the opposite. It is a sign that just the opposite is true. The symptoms are a sign that you are in a highly accelerated Ascension Process. On the other side of the coin, if you don't have these symptoms you can also be in just as accelerated ascension process; however, because of your particular Spiritual Structure you do not need to go through these exact same symptoms. GOD creates each person uniquely and there are no generalized hard and fast rules for anyone!

Some of the symptoms that can occur from this transformation into a new Species of Light and Higher Light Body Integration are: Headaches, spinning, dizziness, nausea, heating up of the body, pain in certain areas of the body, pressure in different areas of the body, extreme fatigue, eye problems, inability to concentrate, short-term memory loss, cramps, emotional imbalance, rashes, and bumping into third-dimensional objects. There are many more symptoms, however, I think you get the idea!

Part of the reason for this occurrence of symptoms is also how fast this spiritual mutation is occurring! There will be more spiritual growth on this planet, from approximately 1980 to 2025, than in the last 3.1 billion years! From the perspective of Spirit and the Masters, this is a grand experiment. Even they are not used to this experiment of doing this so quickly! Even fifty years ago, one initiation a lifetime was a lot. Now it is possible to go through all twelve in one lifetime! The Spiritual Body usually evolves much faster than the mental, emotional, etheric, and physical body. The physical body being of course the densest of all the bodies has the most physical resistance to over-come. The more blocks you have on all levels, the more severe the symptoms; however, it is essential to understand that even if you have no blocks or resistance it is very common for people to have many or all of these symptoms. Others may have none yet are going through the same or a similar process. I cannot emphasize the importance of not trying to make any hard and fast rules on this subject for the process is, in truth, very unique and specialized for each person given the unique complex make up of each person's Spiritual, Psychological, Physical/Earthly, and 12-Body System structure!

32

The Issue of Living on Light

There are a great number of people in the United States and around the world who are teaching the general public the benefits of living on Light rather than eating physical food. I am the first to say that this is possible, and I personally know many people who are very good friends of mine who are doing it. Although this is the case, I have consulted in-depth with the inner plane Ascended Masters and they have given me very clear, loving guidance that this is not something they like the public to do. There are a small number of people on the planet whom they said this is appropriate for. The people in the United States and around the world that, indeed, are doing this are very sincere, good people with a very high degree of integrity. They are practicing what they preach and should be commended for this.

The inner plane Ascended Masters, however, have asked me to write this chapter to correct a very slight misconception in this process. The misconception is that they do not want the masses trying to live on Light. They want the masses to live on a partial Light diet and not try to force themselves to live on a full Light diet. By this I mean the Masters want people to eat a good, healthy diet, and to invoke and see GOD's

Light and Love sustaining them. People in general are too attached to food. Many people think they need seven course meals. They feel that if they miss a meal, they will get weak. They find it hard to conceive of fasting. Fasting is one of the most effective ways to heal the body when you are not feeling well. This, of course, can be done by just drinking water, vegetable juice, or vegetable broth for a day. Other types of fasting can be what I call a semi-fast of, let's say, just eating vegetables or fruit for one day or more. A wonderful fast is just eating apples for three days, for apples absorb the toxins in the body. Another wonderful fast, which I recommend even more, is fasting on Bieler Broth. Bieler Broth is green beans, zucchini, celery, and parsley steamed in a large pot and then blended in a blender to create thick vegetable soup. This wonderful soup is an incredible liver cleanser and re-builder. Fast on this for one or two days and it will do wonders for your physical health. I call it "Nectar of the Gods." While you are fasting, call on GOD and the Inner Plane Ascended Masters, especially Melchizedek, the Mahatma, Archangel Metatron, and Dr. Lorphan to program your body with the Fire Letters, Key Codes, and Sacred Geometries to help you partially live on Light. This way you can occasionally fast without getting weak, and be sustained by the Bieler Broth and/or another form of fasting along with GOD and the Inner Plane Ascended Masters' Light and Love.

The Masters, however, only want people to fast occasionally; like once a week or once a month when you are not feeling well and need some rejuvenation and revitalization. The rest of the time, they are recommending that you eat a healthy balanced diet high in vegetables, making sure you get enough protein in your diet. Many people eat too much starch and/or carbohydrates, forgetting that protein is even more important. The Masters recommend drinking lots of pure water and getting a little fresh air, sunshine, and physical exercise every day.

They also highly recommend learning to work with a pendulum to ask your subconscious mind and body elemental what kinds of foods it really wants, rather than the cravings of the lower self and the desire body. The Masters also highly recommend practicing the science of proper food combining. For example, fruits and vegetables should not be eaten at the same meal. When you eat fruit, it should be eaten alone as a meal itself. This is because the sugar in the fruit causes fermentation in the digestive tract when combined with other foods. Fruit is also a cleanser where vegetables are builders. Another proper food combining is that proteins and starches should be mixed ideally. It is not that anything will happen if you do so or choose not to do it sometimes, but rather, as a general rule, your body will function much more effectively if you follow these simple food combining laws. If you would like to know more about food combining, any health food store will have inexpensive pamphlets explaining these principles. I personally, highly recommend you explore this even if you do it just some of the time.

I would now like to get back to our discussion on why the Masters do not want most people to try to live on Light. The common teaching in the United States and around the world is that people can go on a 21-day program to transition to living on Light. Again, this is a wonderful process for those that have done it, and for a handful of people on earth who have a specific mission/purpose for doing this. Again, these people should be commended for their example, and I emphasize that many of these people are dear friends of mine. The mistake that has been made, however, is that what is 100% right for some of these people have been marketed for the masses. The inner plane Ascended Masters do not support this. This process that has been taught does not take into consideration some extremely important factors:

1. A person's initiation level. Even if this was part of your true mission and purpose, the inner plane Ascended Masters do not recommend even considering it until you take your eleventh major initiation, and then most eleventh stage initiates are not supposed to do it.

2. The second point that has not been considered by these teachings is the person's physical health. Does the person have a health history that makes this unwise? Is the person too malnourished already from eating an improper diet?

3. The state of a person's psychological health has not been considered. As we all know the subconscious mind runs the body, and if a person is too run by the negative ego, lower-self, astral body, inner child, and subconscious mind, such a practice can have disastrous consequences.

4. Is it the person's true spiritual mission and purpose to do this, or is it glamour?

5. Often the inner plane Ascended Masters will recommend against it because the person it too ungrounded already. Living on Light would just exacerbate the problem.

6. Then there is the question, is the person doing this for ego or for the true demonstration of Godliness? Are they doing it to achieve fame or humility?

7. Not eating food also has a way of separating you from people since eating is such an integral part of the social fabric of our lives. The Masters prefer that people integrate with people, not separate.

8. These teachings recommend going on this program without any consultation from a medical doctor or qualified health practitioner.

9. Most people who try this program are unable to do it, not because there is anything wrong with them but, rather, because it is not the soul's or God's wish that they be on this program. They have mistakenly bought into a glamour of a teaching that is not right for them, and end up feeling bad and very confused about themselves emotionally and/or mentally for not being able to do what has been taught.

10. What is happening is most people are starving themselves and creating a malnourished condition. A program with the intent to help, in truth, could have the opposite effect if not guided properly.

11. A deep-seated guilt and/or lack of self-worth is often created at not being able to live on Light. Not enough psychological or spiritual support is given for those who don't, and, in truth, should not do this program.

Conclusion

In conclusion, the Masters want me to say that 99.99% of the time they want lightworkers to not attempt to live on Light alone, but rather to strive to live on a partial Light diet that is balanced with a healthy physical diet. The people who are teaching the masses to live on Light are good and sincere people and are practicing what they preach. The only mistake they are making is trying to market it to the masses instead of just demonstrating this for them-selves. The right path for one may not be the right path for everyone.

33

Integrating the Twelve Levels of Initiation into Your Spiritual, Mental, Emotional, and Physical Vehicles

My Beloved Readers, to become a fully realized Melchizedek, you must fully complete your 12 major initiations. As I explained in the chapter on Integrated Ascension, initiations have to do with the amount of light quotient you are holding in your auric field. A great many lightworkers who are achieving higher levels of initiation think that just because they have completed that higher level initiation that makes them fully realized Masters. The inner plane Ascended Masters have asked me to write this chapter to explain to Light/Love and Power workers that this is not necessarily the case. The completion of your initiations is more a sign of the development of your spiritual body, but not necessarily the development of your mental body, emotional body, etheric body, or physical body. The completion of one's initiations used to be a more integrated process; however, because of this very unique period of history at the end of the Piscean Age and the beginning of the Aquarian Age, the beginning of a new millennium, the end of the Mayan Calendar, and the period in Earth's history called mass ascension, lightworkers have been given a Divine Dispensation to spiritually complete their first seven initiations, even though their four lower bodies have not necessarily been integrated.

This is an extremely important understanding, for a great many lightworkers have been told that they have achieved ascension and passed their sixth or seventh initiation, and these people think they are complete Masters and they are not. On the taking of your sixth initiation, you could call yourself a spiritual Master, but you could not call yourself an integrated Master or a full-fledged Ascended Master, unless you have fulfilled the requirements. Initiations, which took whole lifetimes to do, people are now doing in six months to two years if the teachings in this book and my other books are practiced.

It is essential, however, to integrate your seven levels of initiation and 12 levels of initiation into your four lower bodies. Initiations one through nine deal with the completion of Planetary Ascension. The 10th initiation deals with your first Cosmic initiation at the Solar level. Initiation number 11 is your Cosmic initiation dealing with the Galactic level. Initiation number 12 deals with your third Cosmic initiation focusing upon a Universal level of integration. This is why I said that to become a fully realized Melchizedek on Earth, you must complete all 12 levels of initiation.

To achieve liberation from the wheel of rebirth on Earth you must at least achieve the beginning of your seventh initiation. You can achieve physical liberation from the wheel of rebirth; however, if you don't integrate these initiations into your four lower bodies properly you will have to reincarnate on the astral or mental plane. Most lightworkers also do not realize this. Most lightworkers also do not realize that if they do not do their psychological work, they will not be allowed to pass any more initiations no matter how much work they do. The seventh initiation is the "ring-pass-not" for avoiding accountability on a mental, emotional, etheric, and physical level.

My Beloved Readers, let us examine now what it means to integrate your initiations into your four lower bodies. First, it must be understood that there are three levels to the spiritual path. There is the spiritual level, the psychological level, and the physical/earthly level. All three must be mastered. Most lightworkers are way more developed in their spiritual body than their psychological body, or physical/earthly body. Let us examine now what this means. To be developed in your spiritual body may mean that you have a high level of light quotient, you may be a channel for the Masters, you may have enormous amounts of spiritual information in your information banks, and/or you may be very psychic and clairvoyant and clairaudient. You may be at a very high level of initiation. This is fine and wonderful, you may be a Master at this level, and this is good. To become a full-fledged Ascended Master, however, and to become an Integrated Melchizedek/Christ/Buddha, you must also be a Master of the psychological level and physical/earthly level.

A person may have a highly developed spiritual body, however, they may function in their life like a child. They may be run by their emotional body and lower-self desire. They may be run by the inner child. They may be run by their mental body. They may be run by their negative ego and filled with all kinds of emotions. They may be run by their subconscious mind. This again I call fragmented ascension or a fragmented Christ/Buddha. Only one third has been mastered.

Most lightworkers have not been trained in the difference between negative ego thinking and Christ/Buddha thinking. This is not a judgement, just a statement of fact. I know lightworkers who are seventh degree initiates, who are totally run by the negative ego, total victims, live completely out of the child, are extremely lacking in integrity, yet are high level lightworkers. In almost all cases, they have almost no idea that they aren't clear. If you ask them, they think they have it all together and are Masters on all levels. It is almost comical.

The most important level is not the spiritual level; it is the psychological level. If you do not do your psychological work as I have stated, this will completely corrupt your spiritual work. This point I have stated is one of the main reasons the Masters have asked me to write this book. The point cannot be emphasized more emphatically. "To become an Integrated Melchizedek, you must master all three levels: spiritual, psychological, and physical/earthly!"

Let us now examine the physical/earthly level that must be mastered. This means you must take care of your physical vehicle, feed it the proper food, and give it exercise, proper sleep, fresh air, and sunshine. This also means you must get your earthly life mastered and in order. You must first off, "physically" manifest your service mission. A great many lightworkers have all these wonderful ideas floating around in their heads and which they talk about, but they do not physically do it. They also very often do not ground their mission on Earth. The ideal of the spiritual path is to bring heaven on Earth. The Piscean Age and the Sixth Ray planetary influence we have been under have not seen this happen. The new Aquarian Age with the new Seventh Ray Planetary influence is directly focused to make this happen.

Another example of becoming a physical/earthly Master is having integrity and consistency between the superconscious, conscious mind, subconscious mind, and physical body. A great many lightworkers have what I call a split. They say they are going to physically do something but they don't do it. This demonstrates a lack of integrity and a lack of self-mastery, and consistency of mind and body. Do not say you are going to physically do something if you are not going to do it. If you say you are going to call someone, follow through or don't say it. If you make a commitment to someone to have a certain project done, get it done when you say you are going to do it, or don't make the commitment. If you say you're going to be some place at a certain time, don't make the commitment if you are not going to follow through. Your word is your integrity, and too many lightworkers just space out on their word. If you make an appointment with someone, then be at that appointment or don't make that appointment. If you need to change an appointment, have the courtesy to call in advance and not at the last moment. Other peoples' time is as important as yours. Other examples of physical/earthly mastery are keeping your house clean and organized, taking care of business and earthly errands and responsibilities, voting, filing your taxes, basically just staying completely on top of your Earth life. This is not separate from your spiritual path.

Another good example of physical/earthly mastery is the difference between prosperity consciousness and poverty consciousness. Making money and being able to support yourself and your family is part of becoming a full-fledged Ascended Master. Lots of lightworkers do not take responsibility on this level and expect others to take care of them. There is nothing wrong with asking people for help at times; however, this should not become a lifestyle. The ideal here is to make a lot of money so you are in position to help others and not always just be receiving.

Mastering your sexuality would be another aspect of becoming an Integrated Melchizedek/Christ/Buddha on a physical/earthly level. Another example would be bringing the same care and love that you give to the spiritual level to the physical/earthly level. Make everything you put out physically in your business reflect your pursuit of excellence.

Another example would be honoring and sanctifying the material face of GOD. A great many lightworkers think that Earth is some kind of prison, or that matter is not spiritual. This is illusion my friends. The material universe is one of GOD's heavens. Ascension is not leaving the Earth, but rather grounding your true identity as a Melchizedek/Christ/Buddha on Earth.

Another aspect of physical/earthly mastery is integrating physical beauty and aesthetics into your life and home; making your physical home a sanctuary and temple that is physically beautiful as well as spiritually beautiful.

Another aspect would be integrating nature into your life and honoring the Earth Mother, the nature spirits and devas, as well as ecology. GOD is as much in the physical as He is in the spiritual, mental, emotional or etheric. A true integrated Melchizedek/Christ and Buddha knows this and demonstrates this.

One last example would be taking responsibility for the political aspect of life as well as the great social and moral causes in our earthly civilization. A great many lightworkers think this has nothing to do with their spiritual life and mission, and this is not true. One of the reasons our earthly civilization doesn't change is that lightworkers do not take responsibility on this level or feel that the spiritual path is somehow separate or not focused on these issues. This again, with no judgement intended, is illusion. GOD's Divine Plan is to bring "Heaven to Earth."

True ascension is really decension. It is the anchoring of your Mighty I Am Presence, which is your true self, into earth life. Remember my friends, the Master Jesus lived and served in the market place. Lord Buddha in his incarnation on earth, gave up the path of asceticism and removal from the world and followed the path of moderation and balance in all things. The question all lightworkers should ask themselves is, how can I contribute to people and our beloved civilization?

One of the main lessons of the spiritual path is to enjoy earth life and appreciate earth life. Until you have done this, you have not really learned your lessons of the physical/earthly level. Part of knowing GOD is taking care of people's physical needs. You can not separate these levels for they are all part of GOD.

Integrating Your 12 Levels of Initiation into the Mental Body

To integrate your 12 levels of initiation into your mental body, this means that the mind must become a servant of the Godself. To integrate your initiations into your mental body, you must learn to master your mind, and not let it run you. You must learn to get rid of all negative ego thoughts and only think with your Melchizedek/Christ/Buddha mind!

You must learn to quiet your mind so you are not driven in life and always processing and thinking. You must learn to see that your thoughts cause your emotions, behavior, and what you attract and repel in your life.

One of the biggest areas of proper integration of the higher levels of initiation into the mental body is developing a balanced spiritual philosophy. An enormous number of people on the Earth follow philosophies of life that are completely fragmented and see life through only a sliver of the full spectrum prism that GOD would have you ultimately see from. There are an enormous number of false teachings and erroneous teachings in the field of psychology, religion, and the New Age Movement. We can all see this in religion, how the negative ego has contaminated a many religions. In psychology we can see how short sighted many forms of psychology are. The same is true in the New Age Movement. There is an enormous amount of corruption and false teachings floating around. There is an enormous amount of glamour and illusion. There is an enormous amount of people channeling who do not realize that their own subconscious mind and belief systems are filtering and affecting the channelings. This is the case even with people who are channeling the Ascended Masters. Lightworkers should be more discerning about the spiritual groups they get involved with, the people they spiritually work with, and books and channeled material they read. Lightworkers most often believe that if it's channeled it's true, and nothing could be farther from the truth!

The Emotional Level of Integrating Your 12 Levels of Initiation

On the emotional level, to integrate your 12 levels of initiation you must realize that your thinking causes your feelings and emotions. All negative feeling and emotions are caused by the negative ego philosophy of life. Thinking with your Melchizedek/Christ/Buddha philosophy of life causes all positive emotions. When you can live in a state of basic unconditional love, forgiveness, non-judgmentalness, compassion, joy, happiness, inner peace, and equanimity all the time no matter what is going on outside of self, you have integrated your higher levels of initiation into your emotional body. This book and *Soul Psychology* were in part specifically written to help you do this.

Integrating Your 12 Levels of Initiation into Your Etheric Body

Your 12 levels of initiation get integrated into your etheric body when you completely repair your etheric body from past life or present life damage that has occurred to it. Most lightworkers do not realize that the etheric body can be damaged. The good news is that it can be repaired even from past life trauma. This can be done by calling in the Ascended Master healing team and requesting for the repairing of the body, which is the blueprint body for the physical. If you do not repair the etheric body, it is very hard for the physical body to recover from illness because it is working from a damaged blueprint.

Part of integrating your 12 levels of initiation into your etheric body, which is your energy body, is to learn to run very high frequency spiritual currents through it at all times, and also to learn how to keep your energy body filled with Love/Light and Power. This book will teach you how to do this. This book will also teach your how to keep your etheric energy body clean and clear and how to quickly clear it when it becomes contaminated with some kind of negative energy!

The 12 Levels of Initiation and the Physical Body and Earthly Level

To integrate the 12 levels of initiation into the physical body and earthly level, you must apply the ideas and principals already spoken of on this subject from the beginning of this chapter. Part of this integration also deals with learning to live partially on the Light, Love and Power of GOD to sustain your physical vehicle. I am still recommending the eating of food in the form of a healthy diet, however, the more evolved you become spiritually, the more you want to raise the physical frequency and vibration of the physical vehicle itself. It is possible, after completing one's 12 levels of initiation, to consider the possibility of raising the physical vehicle to such a state of Melchizedek Light/Love and Power frequency, that upon leaving the world when your spiritual mission is complete, you can dematerialize the physical body and raise it into the Light.

Lightworkers should not even consider this until they complete their full 12 levels of initiation in an integrated manner. Even after doing so, which I have, it will take training to learn how to do this. This is not something that one has to do at death or needs to do. Some lightworkers would prefer to just leave the physical vehicle behind and ascend in their etheric, emotional, mental and spiritual vehicle. This is an option; however, some can train for this if you have a desire to do this.

One of the reasons lightworkers get physically sick a lot is that they are evolving very quickly in their spiritual body but are not evolving as quickly in their physical and other vehicles. This often results in sickness or physical illness, which comes in the form of a cleansing crisis. The cleaning is an attempt to raise the vibration of the physical vehicle to closely match the spiritual vehicle.

To raise the vibration and frequency of the actual physical vehicle, eating a very refined physical diet is important, as well as keeping the physical body fit. Breathing is very important as well. Demonstrating integration on these three major levels is also a major key to raising the frequency of the physical. Your thoughts and emotions greatly affect the frequency of your spiritual body. Lastly, learning to run the Cosmic Spiritual Current of the Ascended Masters at all times, and for the purpose of healing self and others, is also extremely helpful in this process. This book will teach you how to do this, and you will experience these profound cosmic and planetary energies and how to turn them off and on at your will and pleasure for the different purposes you require of them!

Conclusion

In conclusion, if you apply the concepts and ideals set forth in this chapter, you will not only integrate your higher levels of initiations into your four lower bodies, but you will also accelerate your spiritual evolution by doing so. By following the precepts in this most important chapter you will not only become a spiritual master, you will become a psychological master. It is when these three levels are mastered and your full 12 levels of initiation are complete, that you will become a full-fledged Ascended Master and full-fledged integrated Melchizedek/Christ/Buddha on Earth. It is for this noble ideal all Light, Love, and Powerworkers are striving, whether they consciously know it yet or not. This, my friends, is the full spectrum prism understanding of initiations that the inner plane Ascended Masters have asked me to share with you this day! Is not this spiritual path, as seen from this full spectrum prism perspective, a beautiful journey?

34

Spiritual Discernment and the Issue of Non-Integrated Spiritual Groups, Cults, and Twilight Masters

The issue of discussing nonintegrated spiritual groups, cults, and Twilight Masters is a fascinating one. Let us begin our discussion here, with defining what a Twilight Master is. We all know from reading this book that there are two philosophies of life. There is the Melchizedek/Christ/Buddha philosophy and way of thinking, and there is the negative ego, lower-self, fear-based way of thinking. Those beings who serve the Light are a part of the Cosmic and Planetary Hierarchy of Ascended Masters, Angels, and Elohim, as well as Christed Extraterrestrials. Those that serve the negative ego have their own hierarchy, serve Darkness, and might be called confused souls. They are still sons and daughters of GOD, but have fallen into the illusion of separation and lack of love and do not believe in GOD. It is best to not focus on such beings and to just keep your mind focused on the Light. They are sons and daughters of GOD who might be called confused souls, and exist en masse on the inner plane and try to manipulate those on Earth who are victims and susceptible. As long as you do not think about them and keep your mind focused on the Light they won't bother you, you won't bother them, and this is how it should be.

There is a category of persons on Earth who are in between those two polarities. This type of person is called a Twilight Master. They serve the Christ/Buddha purpose and the negative ego purposes simultaneously. I am not talking here about the average person who has not been trained in this under-standing and is run by their negative ego and emotional body. This type of person has a good heart and is a good person, but through lack of proper training and understanding is somewhat victimized. This is most people on planet Earth. This is not a Twilight Master.

A Twilight Master is a person who is usually a psychological or spiritual teacher of some kind, who usually has a following of some kind. The only problem is that they have very little or no understanding of what the negative ego is and hence are run by it. They go on stage and show great mastery, but their motivations and purposes are purely self-centered even though they are doing workshops for spiritual or psychological growth, and they demonstrate enormous skill and even magician type powers, but they are corrupt. They are Twilight Masters, for they serve the Light and the Darkness simultaneously. There are millions and millions of them in the world. Some are doing this unconsciously and some are a mixture of both. There are an enormous number of lightworkers who are being deceived and manipulated by these so-called spiritual and psychological teachers. Did not the Bible warn at the end times to beware of the false prophets and false teachers. These Twilight Masters are, in truth, not serving GOD and the Masters even though some light comes from their teachings. They are interested in power, money, fame, sex, control and various other negative ego attributes.

My Beloved Readers, the inner plane Ascended Masters in this moment are asking me to give this information to lightworkers and people around the globe, so you may be more spiritually discerning in relationship to such people.

Non-Integrated Spiritual Groups

Without meaning this to sound judgmental, most spiritual and psychological groups fall into this category. There is great teaching that comes out of all these various groups, however, very rarely do you get a full spiritual and psychological program of teaching that is balanced and integrated. This is not to say that you should not get involved with these spiritual groups. Some groups specialize in meditation and chanting. Others may specialize in the Kabbalah and Tarot. Others may specialize in one particular lineage of Masters. It only becomes detrimental if the nonintegrated spiritual group is run by the negative ego in its motivation and demonstration.

So, I am defining two kinds of nonintegrated spiritual groups. The first one is highly spiritual and wonderful, but may not have a full balanced program of teaching and maybe a certain lens of the spiritual path. The ideal is to see the spiritual path from a full spectrum prism consciousness that sees and recognizes all paths to GOD. If you study, let's say the teachings of Paramahansa Yogananda, this is wonderful, however, it is a certain "Eastern" lens. For example, his teachings are completely different from the Ascended Masters' Teachings of let's say Saint Germain, Djwhal Khul and Madame Blavatsky! They are both wonderful, but come from a different lens. It is by following the path of synthesis that you develop the full spectrum prism consciousness that sees the path to GOD through all lenses. Certain of these more positive spiritual groups will be more integrated than others. It is okay to study these different groups, just go in with open eyes and recognize the strengths and limitations of each group and recognize that each group is a lens within a much greater lens or prism of how GOD sees the whole process. So, the ideal would be to develop the full spectrum prism consciousness of GOD as your ideal. The path of synthesis and becoming an integrated Melchizedek/Christ/Buddha leads in this direction.

The second type of nonintegrated spiritual group is one that has negative ego in it and unclarity in the teachings. This type of group should be avoided. Do not waste time cluttering your mind learning about such groups or being included in them. Time and energy is too precious on Earth to do this.

Cults

When nonintegrated spiritual groups take on too much negative ego within the leader and the followers, they become cults. At all costs, stay away from cults. There are millions of them. Lightworkers and people need to be much more discerning. As the Bible says, "The antichrist will appear in sheep's clothing."

The typical cult has a charismatic leader who has much spiritual know-ledge but the spiritual leader and/or group of leaders are completely run by the negative ego in their core self. The negative ego is using spiritual knowledge for the purpose of power, fame, money, greed, sexuality, and control.

The leaders of all these cults may again be conscious or completely unconscious of what they are doing. There are cults in every religion and even in all kinds of groups in the New Age Movement. A cult begins whenever the negative ego is using the teachings in an extreme way for a self-centered manipulative purpose.

The cult leaders are usually megalomaniacs, and have some grandiose, self-aggrandized vision of who they are. They proclaim themselves the Christ or Messiah or some Ascended Master. They will tell their followers that they are Ascended Masters or apostles, to feed their egos; however, their identities will never surpass the power that they have.

They quote scripture to give credence to their negative ego agendas. They will tell their followers to completely reject the world and their families. They create a philosophy of them against the world. The followers are told to give the leaders and organization all their money and material possessions. There are often suicide pacts and prophecies of some ending in violent catastrophe. The spiritual leader is often militaristic and keeps tight control over everything. The leader tells people literally how to run every aspect of their life, even whom to marry. The cult leader often has sex with a lot of the followers and deludes people into actually thinking that this is some kind of Divine Providence instead of the truth which is lower self indulgence.

This type of group often stockpiles weapons and moves to an isolated place so the leader can have more control.

My beloved readers, it is essential to understand that the people who get involved with these groups are good people, and are spiritual seekers like you and I. The description that I have given in this chapter is a little more of an extreme example of a synthesis of the more disturbed cults. Be aware my friends, there are subtler versions of everything I have stated here. One could say there is a level three cult, level two cult, and level one cult. I was describing more of a level three cult. The New Age Movement is filled with level three, two, and one cults.

The people who get involved with these cults as I said, are good people who are seeking GOD. The leaders of these cults have vast amounts of spiritual knowledge and information. For new people coming onto the spiritual path it is often very hard to see the negative ego motivations behind the enormous amount of spiritual knowledge that is given forth. If one has ever been involved in a cult, or you know of people who have, you should be very forgiving of self and others, for this is a very easy trap to fall into. There are millions and mill-ions of them all over the world. Some very small, some of a moderate size, and some large. In each one, there is a varying degree of negative ego contamination.

In summation, be very spiritually discerning when you get involved in any new spiritual group or teaching and keep your antennas up for any of the negative ego signs and red flags I have mentioned in this chapter! In all aspects of Earth life have faith, trust, be positive, give people the benefit of doubt, be a love finder and not a fault finder, however, always carry with you your "Sword of Spiritual Discernment." Don't ignore the red flags that will surface, and never give your power to any spiritual leader or teacher. Your intuition and inner guidance will always warn you of Twilight Masters and cults if you keep your Melchizedek/Christ/Buddha spiritual discernment and discrimination always properly in place.

The level one type of cult is the easiest to fall into and the most difficult to see. In this type of cult, the leader could be a New Age person, who is a channel for the Ascended Masters and ascension teacher. I am not thinking of anyone in particular here. I am just giving an example, for I know many who fall into this category, which I say with no judgment intended.

This type of cult leader has vast amounts of Ascended Master knowledge and esoteric knowledge. They know all the right things to say to sound like a New Age spiritual leader and person. They are very polished and professional and often have a great stage presence and charisma. They are often channels and sometimes have psychic abilities. On the surface, the follower will be completely blown away by the spiritual abilities, wisdom, and knowledge of this cult leader. They may have authored books and have advertising in spiritual New Age newspapers. My Beloved Readers, be not deceived! They are wolves in sheep's clothing! Their motivations are selfish to the core. This in some ways is even a more dangerous cult in this day and age, for it is much harder to discern and see. The key to seeing through this charade is to very carefully examine the motivations of the cult leader to see if they are always serving self or truly serving GOD and the Masters! Be joyously vigilant for GOD and His Kingdom!

35

The Issue of Psychic Attack from a Spiritual and Psychological Perspective

As a spiritual leader and teacher, I receive an enormous amount of calls and letters from people who are under psychic attack of various kinds. A great many of these people have been calling hundreds of people in the New Age movement trying to get help and also calling on the Masters, but nothing seems to be working. The inner plane Ascended Masters have asked me to write this chapter to clarify this whole subject and to explain why this occurs and why this can sometimes be a difficult lesson to solve. This is a chapter I have been greatly looking forward to writing, so I am glad to have this opportunity now to share this information with you.

This is a very complicated subject, so let me begin at the beginning and build a foundation of understanding. The first level of psychic attack is when we are being attacked by our own negative ego. This is extremely common and a great many people in the world are suffering from this in the form of the critical parent, lack of self-love, negative ego thinking, and sabotage, to name a few.

The second level of psychic attack comes from people in the world who attack you either in your verbal conversations with them, or are doing this on the psychic plane without your awareness. They may do this either consciously or unconsciously.

The third level of psychic attack is from some lower astral entity on the inner plane. This could also be a group of entities.

The fourth kind or level of attack is from negative Extraterrestrials.

I will now go through each of these forms of attack and explain what is happening, and share with you how to defend against this.

Dealing with the Four Kinds of Psychic Attack

The key question in this chapter is, why are so many people suffering from this problem and why are they having such a hard time solving it? I am going to explain this right now. What I am going to explain to you here is of the highest importance to every single lightworker on this planet, for every lightworker deals with psychic attack in one form or another on a daily basis. It may not be as extreme as the people who call me, however it is still occurring. This chapter can help to refine your understanding, to make you invulnerable to such attacks on all levels from within and outside of self.

The key understanding here to become invulnerable to psychic attack on any level, is that you must create a protection on seven levels. These seven levels are the spiritual, mental, emotional, psychic, etheric, physical and earthly levels. The reason a great many lightworkers are suffering from psychic attack is they are requesting protection, but are not doing it on all seven levels.

If for example you just pray to Archangel Michael for help, yet don't do your part on the psychological level, you leave an opening to be victimized. In one of the chapters of this book, I spoke of the need to develop an extremely high-functioning spiritual, psychological and physical immune system. Calling on the Archangels and Ascended Masters for help is wonderful and is part of developing a spiritual immune system to this type of thing; however, if you don't develop your psychological immune system or physical/earthly immune system, you can pray to the Masters from here to kingdom come and you will still be attacked by entities from the astral plane. So let us now start from the beginning and lay the foundation of how to protect yourself on all seven levels!

The First and Most Important Level

The most important level to prevent psychic attacks from occurring on any level is to learn to master your own thoughts, emotions, desires, subconscious mind, inner child, physical body, energy and most of all negative ego mind and thinking. If you do not learn how to do this, all other forms of protection will be extremely limited in effectiveness. Most people in this world are under psychic or psychological attack from their own thoughts, emotions, inner child, and negative ego mind. When the negative ego is programming your thoughts and emotions instead of the Melchizedek/Christ/Buddha mind, this will not only make you miserable, it will also leave an opening for you to be attacked by other people, astral entities or negative Extraterrestrials. It is because so many lightworkers and people have not learned to master their own psychological energies that the openings for these other types of attack can come in. So my beloved readers, please read and study this book completely, and read and study my books *Soul Psychology, How To Clear The Negative Ego*, and *Integrated Ascension*. There are so many people suffering from not having self-mastery over their mind, emotions, physical body, inner child, and negative ego. Please share with them my books on this subject, for in my humble opinion, I feel I have supplied some of the most easy to understand, comprehensive, and practical books on this subject ever written. Without the proper understanding and tools, it is almost impossible for a person to learn these lessons. It is for this reason the Masters have guided me to write these books. Please take advantage of them and share them with your friends and clients.

If this first level could be mastered, in my opinion, almost all psychic attack would stop without doing anything else. Mastering this level takes a little time however, and does not happen in one day. It takes great focus, commitment and spiritual vigilance. It can come quickly and efficiently if you follow the guidance I have given in this book and in other books.

The Spiritual Level of Protection

Once you have focused your energies to try and completely master the psychological level, then it is time to call in the spiritual forces for protection. I have made this process incredibly easy for you, my beloved readers. Enclosed in this book is one of the most profound protection meditations ever channeled and created. It works on all seven levels. It enormously invokes the help of the Cosmic and Planetary Hierarchy and Archangel Kingdom led by Archangel Michael and Faith, since they are First Ray Archangels who's job it is to protect. The combination of doing your psychological work as I have outlined, and doing this meditation whenever you feel the need, will create a force field of protection that is so profound that nothing will be able to get through unless you choose to allow it. The name of this meditation is "The Cosmic and Spiritual Hierarchy Protection Meditation."

The Physical/Earthly Level of Protection

The third level of protection that is required to ensure complete invulnerability to psychic attack on all levels is the physical/earthly level. By this I mean, first off to strengthen your physical immune system through proper physical diet, physical exercises, sleep habits, rest, sunshine, fresh air, positive affirmation, positive visualization and calling on the inner plane Ascended Masters and Angels to keep your physical body and etheric body (energy body) in perfect radiant health.

The reason this is important is that the physical body can be attacked as well by bacteria, viruses, parasites, fungus and so on, and keeping a strong physical immune system will fight any potential diseases off.

Also keeping a healthy physical immune system and physical body will keep you filled with physical vitality and physical energy. This will strengthen your aura and give your etheric, emotional and mental bodies energy to work with to create Love/Wisdom and Power on each of their levels. It is through balancing of this Three-Fold Flame in the aura on all levels that complete invulnerability is achieved. Keeping the physical body strong also allows you to not be physically tired and it makes it easier to remain in your personal power, self-mastery, and joyous vigilance at all times.

It is much harder to keep your psychological immune system and protection in tiptop shape and your spiritual immune system and protection in tiptop shape if the physical body is sick, broken down or tired all the time. Even if this is the case, invulnerability can still be maintained, but it is much harder and takes much more of an effort. My beloved readers, as you all can see, keeping the physical body healthy and strong is another crucial ingredient necessary to maintain strong protection on all levels.

Earthly Level of Protection

Most people would not consider an Earthly level of protection, however, it is of great importance and adds to the other six levels when you do it. An example of this would be if you drive your car into a dangerous neighborhood and park it on the street, be sure to lock the doors.

With no judgment, if someone is silly enough to leave the doors unlocked and the windows open, you are inviting someone to steal from you, especially if you have valuable things in the car. There are some in the New Age Movement who go around thinking, oh, I am protected and so do not do their psychological or earthly part. It is not just GOD and the Masters job to protect you. It is also your job on a psychological and Earthly level to protect yourself. GOD helps those who help themselves. It is a team effort on all levels, working in an integrated manner together, that is the key.

Another example might be locking your house at night, or when you leave on a vacation cancel the newspaper. The physical action of locking your door has a psychological counterpart and symbolism of locking your psychological house as well from intruders. Make sense? There is a spiritual saying to "trust in Allah and be sure to tie up your camel." I think you know what I mean here, my Beloved Readers.

The Seven Levels in Review

On the spiritual level, the protection meditation I have provided will give you all the tools you need to invoke GOD, the Masters, and Archangels for help.

On the mental level, you are going to deny all negative ego thoughts from entering your mind and you are going to replace them with only Melchizedek/Christ/Buddha thoughts.

On an emotional level, you are going to only create Melchizedek/Christ/Buddha emotions for you are only going to think with your Melchizedek/Christ/Buddha mind. You realize that your thoughts create your reality and your thoughts create your feelings and emotions. You take responsibility that if you feel negatively or positively, you are creating it by how you are interpreting the situation.

On a physical/earthly level, we have already discussed how you are going to strengthen your physical immune system, health, and take practical, common sense earthly precautions.

On an energetic level, the calling in of GOD, the Masters, and the Angel energies, as well as your own ability to shift and change the energy in your auric field and body, will keep your etheric body clear, strong, and full of energy and vitality.

On a psychic level, the doing of the meditation and the other six levels of practice will automatically keep you protected on the psychic plane. I would add to this, however, to do a prayer of protection and to put on your mental armor, so to speak, every morning and every night. The prayer protection could also be put on an audiotape and be done in that way.

The short prayer of protection I would recommend would be to call on Archangel Michael and Faith to place around you all day long and all night a platinum dome of protection that is invulnerable to all negative energies.

Putting On Your Mental Armor

It is not enough just to ask GOD and Archangels Michael and Faith to protect you; for you must consciously do your part as well on the psychic plane. By this, I mean every morning put on your mental clothing armor. When you first get up, say your prayer of protection and then visualize in you minds eye claiming your sword of power, your golden bubble of protection that you create yourself with the power of your own mind and heart. Put on your self-love, maybe by putting a red rose in your heart. Visualize your attunement to GOD and the Masters by seeing your Antakarana or tube of light from your heart chakra back to GOD. Put on your Melchizedek/Christ/Buddha thinking and see yourself getting rid of all negative ego thinking. Visualize the Three-Fold Flame of Love/Wisdom and Power burning bright in your heart!

My beloved readers, if you will do this short meditation every morning, which will take no longer than 30 to 60 seconds, you will be completely protected on the psychic plane as well. My Beloved Readers, can you sense the incredible invulnerable field of protection that will come if you practice all of these seven levels of protection I have discussed in this chapter? Then, once a week, I would recommend doing the protection meditation; which is a completely balanced and integrated meditation of protection, utilizing the power of all three flames of Love/Wisdom and Power on all levels. This will ensure that you remain in tiptop shape!

A Final Review of the Four Types of Psychic Attack

My Beloved Readers, let us now review the four types of psychic attack and examine your preparation and readiness to deal with them.

The first type of psychic attack is that of being attacked by your own negative ego thoughts, emotions, and inner child. You now have the understanding on how to deal with this from reading this book and this chapter, and if you need more help, definitely read *Soul Psychology* and *How to Clear the Negative Ego*. This level is the key to preventing all psychic attack. You do not have to be perfect at this level to prevent psychic attack. Even a modicum of success will do it if you apply all my other suggestions and tools!

The second type of psychic attack being that of being attacked verbally by other people. My beloved readers, you are prepared for that as long as you put on your mental armor every morning, do your prayer of protection and do your homework on a psychological, spiritual, and physical/earthly level.

The reason that you are prepared is that if you fully own your personal power and have a bubble of protection around you, and you have your self-love and self-worth within you and your attunement to GOD and the Masters; then other people's negative verbal attacks will slide of your bubble like water off of a duck's back. Instead of reacting, you will respond. Their mental and emotional arrow will have bounced off your shield. You will not have allowed them to cause your emotions or hurt you in any way. You will respond in a calm, rational, unconditional loving way because you have not reacted as a victim, you have responded like a spiritual Master. You have kept up your psychological immune system and not caught their psychological disease. You have passed the spiritual test GOD has given you and you have remained in oneness and Love and set a better example. As the Master Jesus said, "Love your enemy!"

The third type of psychic attack being comes from a negative astral entity. My Beloved Readers, the only way an astral entity can remain connected with you is if you allow yourself to be run by your negative ego, negative thoughts, negative emotions, and you do not parent your inner child with firmness and love. If you do these things, it is impossible for an astral entity to remain in your aura. What attracts the astral entity to you is your own negative thoughts, negative emotions and negative ego. This is not a judgment, just a loving answer from GOD as to who is causing this lesson. GOD and the Masters have guided you to this book so you can now heal this lesson and pass this spiritual test. If you work with the ideas and tools in this book and in my other books, you will easily learn this lesson if you will make the effort.

Your ability to master the psychological level is enough to get rid of the problem without having to do anything else. However, to ensure that this process works, you are going to do your short prayer of protection and/or meditation each morning and night, and you are going to do the meditation in this book when needed. You are also going to keep your physical body strong and take care of the earthly level and strengthen all three levels of your immune system. The combination of doing all seven of these steps will increase the strength of your aura one thousand fold and nothing will be allowed to enter your light/love and power bodies ever again without your permission!

The last type of attack comes from negative Extraterrestrials in the form of negative implants and abductions. My Beloved Readers, listen very closely to what I have to say! No one in life is a victim! We are made in GOD's image and we are each co-creators with GOD! No Extraterrestrial can abduct you or place implants within you unless you let them. GOD did not place you on this Earth to be a victim or to be victimized! GOD placed you on this Earth to be a spiritual Master and the complete cause of your reality on every level. This is your birth right as a Melchizedek/Christ and Buddha, which is who and what you are, in truth. Said differently, you are a son or daughter of GOD! You are the eternal self and the Mighty I Am Presence incarnated on Earth! You are literally an incarnation of GOD on Earth. GOD is not victimized by negative ETs and neither are you, if you claim your birthright! My Beloved Readers, if you claim your 100% personal power, your 100% unconditional love, and your 100% spiritual and psychological wisdom and never let go of it, then you cannot be touched!

You cannot and will not ever be abducted, and negative ETs will be prevented from putting implants in your subtle bodies and/or physical body. Who is more powerful, GOD or negative ETs? GOD created ETs, and most of them who visit the Earth are highly spiritual and Christed. The Masters have told me that 95% of the ETs visiting the Earth are of a Melchizedek/Christ/Buddha nature. Only 5% are run by the negative ego, and as long as you follow the program I have outlined for you, this is a non-issue! As I mention in another chapter, if you want to have an implant and negative elemental removal session with one of the trained initiates in the Melchizedek Synthesis Light Academy, give me a call and

I will set you up with and appointment. We also have Ascension Clearing sessions, Initiation, Light Quotient, and Ray readings all in one session. These are not necessary for you who can do this work yourself, however, the inner plane Ascended Masters make this service available through myself and the Academy to those who feel inwardly guided to take advantage of this service. I have tried to provide everything you need in this book, for this is my job and joyous mission to share with you, my Beloved Readers!

Final Thoughts

The final thought I wish to add here is for all lightworkers to recognize the tremendous power of your thoughts and emotions. For example, when a person is angry, even if that person is not in your physical presence, a dart or an arrow will go shooting towards that person on the psychic plane and visa versa. If you have a strong aura, which you do or you will have after practicing this seven level protection program, those darts or arrows will bounce of your aura automatically. The 50 Point Mt. Shasta Cosmic Cleansing Meditation I have provided will help remove all darts and arrows that have been lodged in your field from this life and past lives. So, this is nothing to be concerned about. This is also why it is important to keep a strong physical, psychological, and spiritual immune system; otherwise, some of these darts and arrows can be lodged in your field from this life and past lives. For example, anger darts usually get lodged in the etheric liver. So I remind you, my beloved lightworkers, of these facts; not only for the purpose of protecting yourself, but also of the purpose of being joyously vigilant against your own negative ego and its negative thoughts and feelings against others. Other people's immune systems and protective fields may not be as strong as yours. Remember that every one of your brothers and sisters is GOD incarnated. When you attack mentally or emotionally a brother or a sister with your mind or emotions, in truth, you are attacking

GOD; because GOD and his sons and daughters are one, which includes you.

The more advanced you become in your initiation process, the stronger the effect and power of your thoughts and emotions on others. The inner plane Ascended Masters are asking me to give you this gentle reminder to ever be vigilant for GOD and his Kingdom in this matter.

Most of the time when people think of psychic attack they just think of an astral entity. I tell you my friends, most of the psychic attacks that occur in this world occurs between physically incarnated sons and daughters of GOD who are working out their relationship lessons of all types.

Many people are getting sick mentally, emotionally and physically, not just from viruses and bacteria, but from this kind of psychic attack from people that builds up and accumulates or gets in when they are in a weakened condition. I have given you tools in this book to cleanse this process within self. Now that you are more keenly aware of this, it is an extra incentive to keep your protection up and to guard against your own negative thoughts and emotions. This is nothing to be fearful about for none of this can get into your field if you follow this simple program I have outlined!

If you feel concerned about negative thoughts or emotions you have had in the past that may have affected other people I have the cure for this. 1) Forgive yourself. 2) Realize that most people come into this life with reasonably good immune systems on all levels and most of your negative thoughts and emotions did not get into their field. If, however, you are concerned about any that did, then pray to the Holy Spirit to undo the negative effects in this life and all your past lives from any negative thinking or negative emotions you have sent to other people consciously or unconsciously. The incredible power and love of the Holy Spirit with its Omnipotence, Omniscience, and Omnipresence as the third aspect of the Trinity of GOD, can undo all negative effects by GOD's Grace if this prayer be in Harmony with His Will! So let it be Written, So let it be Done!

36

How to Become an Integrated Christ and the
Importance of the Eight Spiritual Quotients

One day while eating some broccoli for lunch I literally had a
"Revelation from GOD." This revelation was so profound that right after
finishing my meal, I immediately called in all the Cosmic and Planetary
Masters I work with and told them about it. To my enormous surprise,
they all collectively bowed to me in an act of genuine respect, for I had
channeled from my Godself an idea that the Cosmic and Ascended
Masters agreed was truly a revelation for the next millennium.

I must share with you that this revelation I received stemmed out of
my discussion with the Masters about how fragmented and disintegrated a great many of the lightworkers are, even though many are taking higher levels of initiation. The revelation I had had to do with the
understanding of initiations and light quotients. In my work I was finding that lightworkers were incredibly privileged with passing their initiations and building their light quotient. There is nothing wrong with
this of course, however, this is only a slice of what true GOD Realization
and Ascended Master Realization really is. For example, if you just focus
on building light quotient, which results in passing initiations, aren't

you forgetting Love, Wisdom, Christ Consciousness, transcending negative ego consciousness, integration and balance, psychological wisdom and clarity, spiritual leadership and planetary world service, and the proper integration of the power aspect of GOD acting with Love and Wisdom, to name a few?

The revelation I had while eating my broccoli (and I must say here, some of my best channelings come while eating or showering) was to set up quotients for the aforementioned qualities, as has been done with light quotient and initiations. In other words, what came to me was to set up a new comprehensive system of quotients which lightworkers would work on and check themselves against to insure they were striving for the ideal of becoming an integrated Christ and achieve integrated ascension. The eight quotients I came up with, which would be the new ideal for the understanding of Ascension in this next millennium are as follows:

1. *Light Quotient*

2. *Love Quotient*

3. *Wisdom Quotient*

4. *Power Quotient*

5. *Christ/Buddha Quotient*

6. *Transcending of Negative Ego Quotient*

7. *Service and Spiritual Leadership Quotient*

8. *Integration and Balance Quotient*

My beloved readers, if you strive to score high marks on a percentage basis on these eight quotients, you will be well on your way to becoming an integrated Christ and achieving integrated Ascension. If you just focus on initiations and building light quotients and neglect these other areas your realization of the Christ will be fragmented and your

Ascension Realization will be fragmented no matter what level initiation you are and no matter how much light quotient you retain.

The Cosmic and Planetary Masters, contrary to popular opinion, are not "into" Ascension, they are into "Integrated Ascension." They are not just into Christ Consciousness, they are focused upon Integrated Christ Consciousness. As I have already mentioned, they are very disturbed about the growing trend of fragmentation in the New Age Movement. They have asked me to write this book with their overlighting presence, guidance, and direction to correct this growing imbalance.

As mentioned in another chapter, even the idea of calling people lightworkers is a fragmented concept. It would be much wiser to call people "Light, Love, and Power Workers," for this would precisely describe the Three- Fold Flame of GOD. To just focus on Light is to build one fitting and neglect the others. The path of true GOD Realization is the path of integration, balance, moderation, synthesis, and synergy in all aspects of self and in all things.

Later the same day that I had this revelation I had a second epiphany which was that there were eight major quotients that all Light, Love, and Power Workers needed to focus upon, and that there were approximately 30 to 40 subquotients that spiritual seekers needed to focus on as well, to polish their diamond, so to speak. For the rest of this chapter, I would like to give you a description of the eight major quotients.

Light Quotient

Light quotient can be defined as the amount of light that you are currently retaining in your aura or 12-body system. Some of this light is created by your own thinking, feeling, and demonstration of the Presence of GOD in your daily life. It is also built by the continuing ongoing spiritual practices that you do, including practice and meditation. It is also possible to build light quotient by calling to GOD and the

Cosmic and Planetary Masters to have them channel it, so to speak, into your aura. This book contains an enormous amount of information and ascension activations to help you do this. The building of your light quotient is one of the keys to accelerating the completion of your 12 levels of initiation!

Love Quotient

The second major spiritual quotient to become an "Integrated Christ" is building your love quotient. On a psychological level, your love quotient is built by demonstrating unconditional love in your daily life, in all your personal and impersonal relationships. A person cannot realize GOD or the Christ/Buddha Consciousness without this quotient, regardless of your level of initiation.

My beloved readers, it is also possible to increase your love quotient by calling on GOD and the Cosmic and Planetary Masters to infuse you with love quotient from the spiritual plane. You can do this by calling forth a love shower. I warn you my beloved friends, this is a type of spiritual source you might become addicted to. You can also ask for a light shower and/or a light and love shower. This combination of your demonstration of unconditional love at all times in your daily life, and calling upon GOD and the Masters to infuse you with love through your spiritual channel or crown chakra, increases your love quotient level.

The Masters and I especially recommend calling upon the following beings to build your love quotient: the Divine Mother, the Archangels, the Lord Sai Baba, Melchizedek, The Mahatma, Lord Maitreya, Sananda, Mother Mary, Quan Yin, Lord Buddha, Paul the Venetian, Isis and Vesta.

Wisdom Quotient

The third major spiritual quotient to become an "Integrated Christ" is the development of your Wisdom Quotient. This quotient is divided into two levels of wisdom. There is psychological wisdom and spiritual wisdom. There are a great many spiritual people who are libraries of esoteric information; however, they may not be unconditionally loving, and they may be run by their negative ego. They also may be emotional victims and very disintegrated and fragmented in their spiritual focus. This is not true wisdom. This type of wisdom will build your wisdom quotient, however, you will never truly realize GOD unless you develop psychological or psycho-spiritual wisdom. This is the highest and most advanced form of the wisdom quotient and when learned and mastered, will allow you to utilize the spiritual wisdom you have gathered in a much more efficient and useful manner. Without wisdom, you cannot maintain Unconditional Love. Without wisdom, you cannot use your power appropriately at all times. I also recommend reading my books *Soul Psychology, How To Clear the Negative Ego,* and this book, for the building of the psychological wisdom quotient. The second step of course, is the importance of demonstrating and practicing the information and tools provided for the building of your spiritual wisdom quotient. I highly recommend my entire "Easy-to-Read Encyclopedia of the Spiritual Path" to also help in this process. Building your spiritual wisdom quotient has built what I call your information banks in your subconscious mind. Many times, lightworkers' information banks are not really filled, and the process of channeling utilizes the information in your information banks from this life and past lives. You will be a better channel of information for the Masters if you do this. I humbly suggest that I have provided a worldly service to Light, Love and Power Workers, to have written this Easy-to-Read Encyclopedia that literally contains a synthesis and balanced understanding of all paths to GOD.

The second way to build your wisdom quotient, which is truly a "Revelation from GOD," is to call upon GOD and the Planetary Ascended Masters to anchor and activate from the Celestial Realms "Light Packets of Information" from some of the different Ashrams of GOD.

For example, call forth to Lord Buddha for the light packets of information from the esoteric libraries of Shamballa, while you sleep. Call forth from the Lord of Sirius to anchor and activate the light packets of information and secrets of wisdom from the esoteric libraries in the Great White Lodge of Sirius. Call to Melchizedek our Universal Logos, to anchor and activate the Melchizedek light packets of information from his Golden Chamber in the universal core. Call directly to GOD, Christ, and the Holy Spirit to anchor and activate the light packets of information from the treasury of Love, Wisdom, and Power at 352 level of Divinity. Especially call for the anchoring of the light packets of information of the Torahor, True Cosmic Book of Life, the Elohim Scriptures, the Archangel Scriptures, the Cosmic Ten Commandments, and the Mahatma Scriptures.

My beloved readers, if you want to build your wisdom quotient, try some of these activations. They will knock your socks off. The combination of building your psycho-spiritual and spiritual wisdom quotient will accelerate the building of this overall wisdom quotient a thousand fold!

Power Quotient

The fourth major spiritual quotient to become an "Integrated Christ," is the building of your power quotient. My beloved readers, I would like you to notice that the last three quotients I have listed in this chapter deal with Love, Wisdom, and Power! This, of course, my friends, is the Three-Fold Flame of GOD. It is essential that this Three-Fold Flame be built equally. I think you are beginning to see here the importance of these eight quotients, and why they must be all developed simultaneously to fully realize the Christ/Buddha ideal.

The Third Flame of GOD and fourth major Spiritual Quotient is that of Power. Now this quotient has two levels. There is the aspect of power focused upon what I call, owning your personal power, and there is the second aspect and understanding of power in dealing with surrendering to GOD's Will. You cannot retain unconditional love in life, or attain any true psychological wisdom if you do not learn to own personal power. If you do not own your personal power then by the laws of energy you automatically give it to other people, life situations and give it to your mind, emotions, physical body, subconscious mind, lower-self desire, inner child, subpersonalities, and negative ego thought system. The spiritual path is the path of self-mastery. You cannot be a master if you do not own your personal power, you cannot be a cause of your reality through your thoughts if you do not own your personal power. This is the first psychological level of understanding what your power quotient means.

The second level of building your power quotient on a psychological level is learning to let go of the negative ego's will and instead surrender to GOD's Will in all things. Do you work for GOD or for yourself only? It is okay in life to have preferences, but not attachments and addictions. Strive for your preference with all your heart and soul and mind and might, and then surrender to GOD's Will in all things. Following this ideal will build this power quotient on this second level. The third level of building your spiritual power quotient is to anchor and activate the power packets of information from the different Ashrams of GOD!

The Masters that I especially recommended calling on for help in doing this while you sleep are: Archangels Michael and Faith, The Elohim, Hercules and Amazonia, El Morya, Allah Gobi, Melchizedek, the Mahatma, Metatron, as well as GOD, Christ and the Holy Spirit.

My beloved readers, if you follow this three-fold recipe, you will build your spiritual power quotient at an unbelievable rate of speed! The last thing I wish to say on this subject of building your Power Quotient is to be sure and always own your spiritual power, however use it in service of unconditional love, egolessness, and surrender to GOD's Will in all things!

Transcending Negative Ego Thinking Quotient

The fifth major spiritual quotient to become an "Integrated Christ" is to transcend negative ego thinking. Again, I state, in my humble opinion, it is one of the most important aspects of the spiritual path to get a handle on. For all challenges, lessons, or problems are caused by negative ego thinking. Again, there are two ways of thinking in the world and only two. Every person thinks with his or her separative/fear-based/negative ego mind, or they think with their Christ/Buddha mind. This quotient focuses upon the joyous vigilance you keep on a moment to moment basis of denying negative ego/lower-self thoughts from entering your consciousness.

The Christ/Buddha Consciousness Quotient

The sixth major spiritual quotient to realize "The Integrated Christ" is the Christ/Buddha thinking quotient. As stated in the previous quotient, every person on Earth, every moment of their life, either thinks with their negative ego lower-self mind or their Christ/Buddha higher-self mind. As Sai Baba says, "GOD equals man minus ego." "There are no neutral thoughts," as *A Course in Miracles* states. One of the premiere purposes in life is to interpret every situation of life with your Christ/Buddha mind. The world is nothing more than a projection screen for our own thinking. We are seeing our own movie. Our thoughts cause our reality. Our thinking causes the way we feel and the way we behave as well as causing what we attract and magnetize into our lives. If you think with your Christ/Buddha mind you will have only unconditional love, forgiveness, non-judgmentalness, lessons, joy, happiness, inner peace, equanimity and evenmindedness. You will remain one with GOD and one with your brothers and sisters in every thought, word, and deed.

If you think with your negative ego/lower-self mind, you will have just the opposite. You will be filled with negative emotions, inappropriate behavior and the negative ego will corrupt your spiritual life, channeling, and even your relationship to GOD in terms of how you understand and/or realize it. The negative ego will create motives that are impure and negatively selfish in origin. The negative ego will create personal agendas that you are not even aware of that will contaminate the purity of your GOD consciousness. As Sai Baba has said, "GOD is hidden by the mountain range of negative ego!" One of the main reasons I have written *Soul Psychology*, *How to Clear the Negative Ego*, and this book, is to help Love, Light and Power Workers get a better handle on this most important issue!

Spiritual Leadership and Spiritual Service Quotient

The seventh major spiritual quotient to become an "Integrated Christ" is to develop your spiritual leadership and spiritual service quotient. It is a natural by-product of the spiritual path, as you spiritually evolve and move through your seven levels of initiation and ascension development process in becoming an integrated Christ/Buddha, to at some point become less focused on your own personal growth and to begin to fully claim your spiritual leadership and find your spiritual puzzle piece in the Divine Plan as to where you can best be of service to your brothers and sisters and the world.

Now I want to say here that your main spiritual service is practicing the presence of GOD every moment of your life in every thought, word, and deed. It is the demonstration of unconditional love to self, others, and the world. Wherever you find yourself, be it as a receptionist, a secretary, a gardener, a car mechanic, or a bricklayer, you can be of service if you will take the attitude of being so. Wherever you find yourself, you can bring love and light into that arena. It must be understood that every situation of life is a spiritual test to see if you will choose GOD or ego, your lower-self or your higher-self, unconditional love or fear and attack, forgiveness or holding grudges, non-judgmentalness or judgmentalness, to name a few. As you evolve through life, your service will change and, in truth may change many, many times. It is less important as to what you do, then it is to understand the importance of serving wherever you happen to find yourself. Service is not just a job, it is every moment of your life. It is helping your friends, family, or a stranger on the street. It is how you treat the bank teller and the grocery clerk. It is how you treat your fellow employees, some of who in you may not like personally.

Do not wait for GOD or the Masters to tell you how to serve. It is definitely worthwhile to pray for this; however, the spiritual path is a co-creative process and GOD and the Masters help those who help themselves. Use your own creativity and GOD-mind to come up with ways that you can be of service as well as calling on the infinite intelligence of GOD and the Cosmic and Planetary Ascended Masters.

As you evolve spiritually, at some point it is very necessary for you to fully claim your personal power, full love, and full wisdom, and to step forward in spiritual leadership. Do not wait to feel perfectly comfortable, for that may never occur. At some point you must take the leap, trust in your own abilities, and have faith and trust in GOD and the Masters.

One opportunity I might offer you is to teach ascension classes in your home utilizing my book, *How To Teach Ascension Classes*. I have set up an incredible program which has been channeled from the Cosmic and Planetary Hierarchy, that is one of the most profound class programs in spiritual growth ever put together, and is very easy to understand, practice and implement! This is one possibility of infinite possibilities that are available to you to make a difference in this world.

The first step of the spiritual path is to become right with self and right with GOD and to become whole and complete within self once this is achieved. The second step is to then claim your spiritual leadership and be of service to the world. How you serve is up to you. GOD created each person differently so each person has a different puzzle piece and function to fulfill. As we evolve spiritually, the main reason we are on this Earth is to serve. Did not the Master Jesus say, "The greatest among you is the servant to all"?

You can build this spiritual quotient by taking this attitude of service every moment of your life. Do not focus on fame or public recognition, for the greatest acts of serving are the little things that only you and GOD know about. A helpful hand, a kind smile, a friendly gesture, helping a friend in time of need. Be not concerned about the fruits of your service, for what is most important is that you are serving. Do not compare your service work to others, and not remember everyone is supposed to be well known for their service. GOD appreciates humbleness and humility more than fame and the glamours of service that all lightworkers must watch out for. Always examine your motives of service to make sure that they are stemming from a pure heart and an egoless attitude. Many lightworkers think they are serving GOD and the Masters, but, in truth, they are serving self. Often it is okay to strive for success, however, the motivations of the negative ego, even in the area of spiritual leadership and service, must be watched out for. The most important thing to strive for is a pure heart and egolessness in all things in the way you serve, for this is what is dear to GOD's own heart. Always monitor and check yourself at different stages of your spiritual leadership and service. You want to make sure that your motivations are remaining pure. Do not try to live out another person's puzzle piece. If you do so, this will bring much stress upon self and will not work. Find the puzzle piece and spiritual mission that is best suited for your unique abilities and gifts and become a team player, for when your team wins, everyone gets a championship ring, so to speak. For there is only one being in the universe and that is GOD, and we are all incarnations of this One Eternal Self!

The Integration and Balance Quotient

The eighth spiritual quotient to become an "Integrated Christ" is the integration and balance quotient. This may be the most difficult quotient of all, for this quotient requires the integration, balance, and synthesis of all you have learned in life about self and the world. It requires the balancing of your superconscious, conscious, and subconscious minds. It requires the balancing of your feminine and masculine, and heavenly and earthly selves. It requires the proper parenting of your inner child, and the integration of your seven rays and 12 major archetypes. It requires learning to think with your Christ/Buddha mind rather than the negative ego mind. It requires the integration of your eight major spiritual quotients, the fifty major spiritual quotients, and the fifty major spiritual subquotients, to name a few.

This may seem like a lot. However, my beloved readers, if you follow the easy-to-read instructions I have provided in this book and my other books, and you utilize the tools I have provided, what seems very complicated is, in a very paradoxical sense, easy, once all the information, tools, and insights are provided. GOD has already given you everything inside of self to do this. My books and others like it just provide reminders and tools of things you already know within self. Remembering is half the battle won.

37

The Development of a Flawless Character through the Proper Integration of the 72 Subquotients of GOD

My beloved readers, in the chapter on "How to Become an Integrated Christ and the Importance of the Eight Spiritual Quotients" you were introduced to one of the revelations for this new millennium, which is the importance of achieving a high level of realization in the eight major spiritual quotients. This chapter you are about to read continues this discussion but focuses on what I call the realization of the Integrated Melchizedek/Christ/Buddha subquotients for achieving GOD Realization.

To truly become an "Integrated Melchizedek/Christ/Buddha" it is essential to realize a flawless character, and this chapter will complete this discussion of the areas that lightworkers need to focus upon to achieve this goal. Again, each quotient could be scored on a 1-100 scale. Be honest with yourself, free from the negative ego, and intuitively evaluate your demonstration of these Melchizedek/Christ/Buddha consciousness qualities. Do not judge yourself if your scores of some of these are not as high as you would like. Just learn from this, forgive yourself, and make a firm intent to do better today. It takes 21 days to build a new habit into the subconscious mind. You will have to be joyously vigilant for your entire life; however, a new habit is cemented into the subconscious mind every 21 days! On this note, let us begin a comprehensive overview of all the main spiritual subquotients that make up a true integrated Melchizedek/Christ/Buddha-Realized Master.

The Physical/Earthly Quotients

1. Integrating Spiritual and Earthly Energies Subquotient

The first subquotient is very important for it speaks to the importance of integrating heaven and earth energies. Many lightworkers or spiritual people are way too heavenly in their orientation and hence are ungrounded and are not taking proper responsibility of mastering Earth life. On the other side of the coin, other people are too grounded and too focussed on Earth life and are sometimes too materialistic, which causes one to be cut-off somewhat from heavenly energies and/or one's spiritual life. Just as every person must balance the feminine/masculine within self, everyone must balance also the heavenly and earthly aspects with themselves. As you intuitively meditate upon this Melchizedek/Christ/Buddha subquotient, give yourself a score from 1—100 on how you are doing keeping this proper balance. With this subquotient and the rest that follow, I would recommend that you maybe even keep a log and write your scores on a piece of paper. Every week you can do a recheck to see if your scores have improved. I call this "spiritual accounting" and this systematic approach to refining and purifying your character is one of the best methods available to become a Melchizedek/Christ/Buddha on the psychological level. I would recommend doing this process for one or two months, or until you get stabilized on a relatively high level. We are not looking for perfection here where no mistakes are ever made, for that is impossible. We are looking for a consistency of high scores over all the major and minor quotients if possible after a two to three month period of focused concentration and intent on refining your character. In truth, this is a life long process; however, enormous progress can be made in the first two or three months if you are really focused, dedicated, and committed to your spiritual path!

2. Environmental Conscious Subquotient

This next spiritual subquotient deals with the understanding that the Earth and your physical environment is an aspect or face of GOD as well, and needs to be sanctified and honored in the same manner that spiritual, mental, and emotional energies are. It brings into play such concepts as ecology, cleaning your house, maintaining order in your house, maintaining aesthetics and beautifying your home, as well as taking care of your Earthly responsibilities. Again, intuitively give yourself a score on this subquotient.

3. Political and Social Consciousness Subquotient

This spiritual subquotient deals with the responsibility you are taking on a political and social level for what is going on in our world. I have dedicated a chapter in this book to inner plane spiritual activism which is one alternative for lightworkers to take responsibility in this area. Other considerations are: Do you vote? Do you watch the news or read the newspaper to stay abreast with what is going on in the world? Do you ever actively get involved in these issues? Do you try to raise consciousness with your family and friends? Do you ever pray or do creative visualization to help in these issues? Do you ever donate money to these causes? I am not saying here that you have to do all these things. What I am saying is that it is important that you do something to take responsibility for being part of the solution. How you do this is up to you.

4. Physical Rest and Sleep Subquotient

This spiritual subquotient is quite straightforward. Are you getting enough sleep at night or are you sleeping too much? Are you getting enough rest or are you working too hard? Are you resting too much and not taking care of business? This is a fine balance that only you can intuitively decide for your-self. Give yourself an intuitive score and move on.

5. Enjoyment, Fun, and Recreation Subquotient

This next subquotient deals with if you are taking enough time for enjoyment, fun, and recreation. Has the spiritual path become too serious a focus and too work focused? Intuitively score yourself and move on.

6. Spiritualizing Sexuality Subquotient

This subquotient deals with how you are utilizing your sexuality. Is your negative ego running the show or are you channeling your sexuality through a Melchizedek/Christ/Buddha understanding? Is your sexuality being channeled through your higher-self or lower-self? Is your sexuality underindulgent? Is your sexuality being channeled through lust or carnal pursuits? Does your sexuality put your partner first or is it totally selfishly oriented? Are you focussed on pleasure for both your partner and yourself or are you focussed only on self-pleasure? Is some of your sexual energy being raised for higher spiritual pursuits or is it all being channeled through your second chakra? Is sexuality a sacred ritual or a lower-self indulgence? Give yourself an intuitive score on all these questions and move on. If you would like more information on sexuality from a spiritual perspective, read my book *Soul Psychology*.

7. Business Integrity Subquotient

This subquotient deals with whether you are running your business through Melchizedek/Christ/Buddha consciousness and principals or through negative ego business practices. Are you in integrity behind dealings with money? Are you there to serve in your business as your top priority or just to make money? Are you kind, courteous, and friendly in your business dealings? Give yourself a score and move on.

8. Proper Vitamin and Mineral Supplementation Subquotient

This subquotient deals with the straightforward understanding of if you are taking enough vitamin and mineral supplements to adjunct your physical diet with what it needs to be chemically healthy and in balance. In this stressful technological world we live in, this is a good idea for many people. Much of the food we eat is often not of the highest quality, and filled with pesticides and not as filled with vitality because of the worlds' lack of proper relationship to the Earth Mother, Pan, the Nature Spirits and Deva Kingdom. Are you getting enough vitamin C and calcium? Are there certain homeopathic or herbal products you should be taking?

9. Healthy Diet Subquotient

This is a most important subquotient dealing with your physical diet. Do you eat to live or do you live to eat? Are you eating enough vegetables? Are you getting enough protein in your diet? Are you eating too much sugar and sweets? Are you drinking enough water? Are you overeating or undereating? Are you eating the proper balance of different food groups? Score yourself and move on.

10. Physical Fitness Subquotient

Are you getting enough physical exercise? Do you have a balanced physical exercise program that integrates flexibility, strength, and stamina? Score yourself and move on.

11. Personal Hygiene Subquotient

This is a very important subquotient that some people do not take enough responsibility for. Do you take enough showers and/or baths? Do you brush your teeth, comb your hair, and shave if necessary? Do you clean your clothes and dress appropriately. This may sound silly to some, however I think we have all met people who do not take care of personal hygiene and it is very unpleasant to be around them! Give yourself a score and move on.

12. Tithing or Seed Money Subquotient

This subquotient deals with the question of whether you ever give money to spiritual causes or people in need. The negative ego will be miserly with money and material possessions. The Melchizedek/Christ/Buddha consciousness will give love on all levels including the giving of money or material things where appropriate to help their fellow brothers and sisters in times of crisis. Give yourself a score and move on.

13. Financial Responsibility Subquotient

This subquotient deals with your spiritual relationship to money and the issue of supporting yourself on this level. How do you deal with money? Are you responsible behind how you use money? Do you waste money too much inappropriately? Do you save enough money? Do you have a prosperity consciousness or a poverty consciousness? Are you actualizing your potential around money? Is the negative ego or your spiritual consciousness running your relationship to money? Are you allowing lower-self desire to waste your money, or are you being too frugal or conservative with your money? Are you using and relating to money as GOD would have you use it? Give yourself a score and move on.

14. Your Ascension Mission Subquotient

This subquotient deals with the issue of whether you have found and are fulfilling your spiritual mission and purpose on this planet. Have you found your puzzle piece? Are you serving with a good attitude in your present puzzle piece? Are you trying to live out someone else's puzzle piece? Give yourself a score and move on.

15. Tender Handling of the Animal Kingdom Subquotient

This subquotient deals with your relationship to the animal kingdom. Do you treat animals like younger brothers and sisters? How do you treat your pets? Do you wear fur? Give yourself a score and move on.

16. Meditation Subquotient

This subquotient deal with the issue of whether you are spending enough time meditating as one of your spiritual practices. If you would like to meditate more, I might humbly suggest you work with my 12 Ascension Activation Meditation audiotapes. They are some of the most powerful ascension activation meditations on the planet and I guarantee you will get miraculous results. They will literally accelerate your spiritual evolution 1000 fold. You will get a taste of the meditations from the meditations I have provided in this book. Give yourself a score on this subquotient and move on.

17. Prayer Subquotient

This subquotient deals with the issue of whether you spend enough time praying to GOD, the Masters and the Angels for help. As the Bible says, "Ask and you shall receive," "Knock and the door shall be opened." GOD, the Masters, and the Angels are not allowed to help unless you ask. Why try to do everything yourself when the infinite power of GOD and the Godforce is here to help you at the slightest call? There are all kinds of ways to pray and the form does not matter. What does matter is that you do pray and do so abundantly! Give yourself a score and move on.

18. Ascension Activation Subquotient

This subquotient deals with the question of whether you are doing enough ascension activation invocations. GOD and the Masters are willing to accelerate your spiritual evolution 1000-fold, and even 10,000-fold, if you utilize the ascension activation I have provided for you in this book and in my other books. Give yourself a score and move on.

19. Chanting the Name of GOD Subquotient

This subquotient is a most wonderful spiritual practice that very few people utilize. You can do this in your meditation or you can do this in your mind, in song, poetry or out loud. The chanting of GOD's name or names draw Him closer to you. I might recommend here that you read my book *The Complete Ascension Manuel*, for I have written a wonderful chapter with all the different names of GOD, Mantra's and power words of GOD, that can be chanted or recited. If you have not done this, definitely try it.

20. Silence Subquotient

Do you take enough time to be silent and quiet? In our Western world we are taught to always be achieving and doing and not just be! The mind is always racing and thinking and most people do not know how to quiet the mind and just enjoy the stillness and the silence. Many people spend so much time praying that they never stop to be silent to hear GOD's answer. The Holy Spirit is the still, small voice within. It will not compete with the noise and racket that the negative ego makes. It will also not enter if the mind is always racing and the person is always pushing and driving. Take time to just be, and enjoy the stillness of God!

21. Devotion to GOD Subquotient

This subquotient deals with the level of your devotion to GOD. This subquotient could be summed up by the words of Master Jesus when he said, "Love the Lord thy GOD with all your heart and soul and mind and might, and love your neighbor as you love yourself"! Devotion entails not just a mental focus on GOD, but also an emotional, heart relationship to GOD! Give yourself a score on this subquotient and move on.

22. Constant GOD Attunement Subquotient

This subquotient focuses upon the question as to whether you keep your consciousness always attuned to GOD and your Melchizedek/Christ/Buddha ideal. Do you keep your mind and emotions and heart steady in the light? Do you give into temptation? Do you give up? Do you let your attention move to other things but your GOD attunement? Give yourself a score and move on.

23. Spiritual Affirmation and Visualization Subquotient

This subquotient deals with whether you are spending enough time in your day doing spiritual affirmation, creative visualization and cultivating posi-tive thinking. Never forget, "An idle mind is the devil's workshop." If your mind is always affirming, visualizing, thinking, and chanting the names or ideals of GOD, you will always be happy, successful, and at peace. Give yourself a score and move on.

24. Spiritual Book Reading Subquotient

This subquotient deals with the question of whether you are spending enough time reading spiritual books and doing your spiritual studying. There are so many things in this world that pull our attention away from GOD and the things that are really important in life. Are you utilizing your energies and time for the proper priorities? Are you focusing your time and energy on the permanent or impermanent? Are you focusing your time and energy on things that will help you achieve GOD Realization or are you getting too caught up in the Earth life, materialism, and earthly pleasure? Are you being about the Father's business? Are your priorities in order in terms of how GOD would have them be? Give yourself a score and move on.

25. Spiritual Journal Writing Subquotient

This subquotient deals with the question as to whether you are spending enough time with your spiritual journal. It is so easy to get drawn and pulled in this world into an extroverted focus. Really get clear on what's going on in your life. In this journal you can write down your dreams and interpret them. You can practice channeling GOD and the Masters. You can write letters to GOD and the Masters. You can work each day on what lessons you have learned and where negative emotions have arisen. You can do attitudinal healing to learn your lessons. You can write down your meditation experiences. You can keep logs of your character development. You can do free flow creative writing. You can write poetry. You can make lists and keep victory logs and gratitude lists. Do not underestimate the importance of keeping a spiritual journal. These are but a few of many potentialities keeping a spiritual journal holds for you. Examine this issue for yourself. Give yourself a score and move on.

26. Spiritual Interaction and Fellowship Subquotient

This spiritual subquotient deals with the issue of the social and interactive aspect of the spiritual path. Many lightworkers spend far too much time by themselves and remain isolated from others. This is okay for certain phases of one's life, but not for a whole lifetime. We are interdependent beings and the spiritual path is not one to hide in a cave except in very rare instances. Anyone can be spiritual hiding in a cave, reading spiritual books and meditating. The true test of one's spirituality comes in the demonstration of the presence of GOD in one's daily life. How can you be of service if you never interact with people. We are meant to live in the "market place" for the most part, and have rich, full lives and to fully embrace our fellow brothers and sisters. Some stay isolated out of self-aggrandizement. Some stay isolated out of fear and low self-esteem. Both need to be transcended. One of the most important practices of the spiritual path is "Practicing the Presence of GOD." This is done in Earth life in fellowship with your brothers and sisters. Take time to socialize, for this is the horizontal aspect of GOD and is just as important as the vertical aspect. Give yourself a score on this most important subquotient and move on.

27. Seeing GOD in Everything and Everyone Subquotient

This is a most important subquotient. As I have stated many times in this book, there is only one being in this infinite universe and this is GOD. GOD is incarnated on Earth in every person, every animal, and every tree, plant, mineral, rock, and stone. Every interaction with one of these incarnations of GOD is a "holy encounter." This subquotient deals with the issue of whether you look at life this way. Do you treat every person and animal as an incarnation of GOD meeting you? Do you treat the plant kingdom and the mineral kingdom as incarnations of GOD? Do you try to practice the holy encounter at all times and see each person you meet as a fellow Melchizedek/Christ and Buddha? Give your-self a score and move on.

28. Pursuit of Excellence Subquotient

This subquotient deals with whether you strive for excellence in every-thing you do on every level of GOD including the physical/earthly level. Do you also see mistakes as positive, as lessons and as part and parcel to the spiritual path? Give yourself a score and move on.

29. Earthly Family Responsibility Subquotient

This subquotient deals with the issue of whether you are taking proper responsibility and time to meet your Earthly family responsibilities. This can be on a practical or personal level. Are you meeting your obligation to them in terms of your spouse, relationship, children, parents, and extended family? Are you giving enough personal time to your romantic relationship? Are you giving enough personal time to your children, parents, and extended family? Every-thing in life is balance and maintaining proper priorities. Are you achieving the proper balance and priorities in this subquotient? Give yourself a score and move on.

30. Joy Subquotient

This subquotient deals with the issue of whether you are maintaining happiness and joy in an ongoing way in your life. Are you too serious? Are you too much of a workaholic? Give yourself a score and move on.

31. Self-Discipline Subquotient

This subquotient deals with whether you are demonstrating enough self-discipline in all the various aspects of your life. Are you procrastinating too much? Are you being lazy? Are you giving in to the line of least resistance? Are you being efficient with your time and energy? Give yourself a score and move on.

32. Patience Subquotient

This subquotient deals with the Melchizedek/Christ/Buddha quality of patience. Are you being patient in all aspects of your life? Do things easily get you irritable or angry? Give yourself a score and move on.

33. Gratitude Subquotient

This subquotient deals with the question of whether you are grateful to GOD every day for all he has given you, even if that day did not go completely according to your preferences. Do you talk to GOD even when things don't go right? Give yourself a score and move on.

34. Preferences Rather than Attachments Subquotient

This subquotient deals with whether you have let go of all your attachments and whether you have only preferences in your life. As Buddha said in his four noble truths, "All suffering comes from attachment." There is nothing wrong with having preferences, but a preference is an attitude that even if you don't get it you are happy. Is your happiness inside of yourself or outside of yourself? Is your happiness a state of mind or can it be controlled by outside forces? Give yourself a score.

35. Looking at Things as Spiritual Lessons Subquotient

This subquotient deals with looking at everything that happens in life as a teaching, lesson, challenge, and opportunity to grow and not as a bummer and problem. Do you look at everything that happens in life as a spiritual test or do you get angry and upset? Do your thoughts create your reality or do outside situations and people? Give yourself a score and move on.

36. Forgiveness Subquotient

This subquotient deals with the question of whether you forgive yourself and others for all mistakes, or whether you hold grudges. Give yourself a score and move on.

37. Releasing all Attack Thoughts Subquotient

This subquotient deals with the question of whether you have let go of all attack thoughts toward self and others and replaced them with thoughts of only unconditional love. Give yourself a score and move on.

38. Non-Judgmentalness Subquotient

This subquotient deals with the question of whether you have spiritual observations and spiritual discernments in life in a loving manner, or if you indulge in judgmentalness and criticalness to self and others Give yourself a score and move on.

39. Organization Subquotient

This subquotient deals with the question of whether you are organized in all aspects of your life. Are you organized in your Earthly life? Are you organized in your spiritual life and spiritual path? Are you organized in your mental and emotional life? Are you organized in all your relationships? Give yourself a score and move on.

40. Priority, Time, and Energy Subquotient

This subquotient deals with the question of whether you have all the priorities in your life in the proper order. Are you using your time properly? Are you wasting time? Are you using your energies in the proper directions? Are you wasting energy? Is every thought, word and deed serving GOD, your spiritual path, your service mission and the process of becoming a fully Realized Integrated Melchizedek/Christ/Buddha? Give yourself a score and move on.

41. Oneness Subquotient

This subquotient deals with whether, in every thought, word, and deed, you are remaining in oneness with GOD and your brothers and sisters, or in separation from GOD and your brothers and sisters. When you react out of your negative ego thoughts and emotions, you move into separation. When you respond out of your Melchizedek/Christ/Buddha consciousness, you remain in oneness in your thoughts, emotions, and behavior. Give yourself a score and move on.

42. Decisiveness Subquotient

This subquotient deals with the question of whether you are decisive at all times in every thought, word and deed. Do you sit on the fence? Do you remain in the twilight zone? Do you fish or cut bait in all situations? Give yourself a score and move on.

43. Letting Go of Anger Subquotient

This subquotient deals with the important lesson of letting go of anger in all situations. Do you have true personal power or do you live out of negative anger? Do you fight life or work with life and learn from life? Do you accept or do you resist? Do you surrender to GOD's Will or fight GOD's Will? Give yourself a score and move on.

44. Spiritual Warrior Subquotient

This subquotient deals with the lesson of whether you are a spiritual warrior or spiritual fighter and never give up in life, or whether you are weak-minded and give up and hence indulge in depression. Give yourself a score and move on.

45. Releasing Victim Consciousness Subquotient

This subquotient deals with the question of whether you are the master and cause of your reality by how you think, or if you are a victim and effect of life. Give yourself a score and move on.

46. Selfish/Selfless Balance Subquotient

Are you balanced in the selfish/selfless understanding, or are you too selfish and/or too selfless? Give yourself a score and move on.

47. Responsibility and Accountability Subquotient

Do you take responsibility and accountability for everything you create and that happens in life or do you blame GOD, others and/or life? Do you take responsibility that you cause your own thoughts, emotions, behavior, health, prosperity and what you attract and/or repel in your life, or do you place the cause elsewhere? Give yourself a score and move on.

48. Faith Subquotient

Do you maintain your faith and trust in GOD, GOD's laws and yourself, or do you give into doubt and/or fear? Give yourself a score and move on.

49. Humbleness and Humility Subquotient

Are you humble and do you demonstrate humility in all that you do, or do you allow false pride to enter your consciousness? Give yourself a score and move on.

50. Self-Love and Self-Worth Subquotient

Do you have unconditional self-love and self-worth, or do you have conditional self-love and self-worth? Do you give love and self-worth to your inner child and receive it from GOD, or do you allow the negative ego to abuse your inner child and block you from receiving GOD's unconditional love and worth for you? Give yourself a score and move on.

51. Cooperation Subquotient

Do you cooperate with stress or do you compete with stress? Are we all on GOD's team or are we out for ourselves only? Give yourself a score and move on.

52. Evenmindedness and Equanimity Quotient

Are you evenminded and do you have equanimity to everything that happens in life, or are you bounced around by your negative ego on an emotional roller coaster and manic depressive ride? Give yourself a score and move on.

53. Transcending Duality Subquotient

Do you keep your inner peace whether you have profit or loss, pleasure or pain, sickness or health, victory or defeat, whether people vilify you or praise you? Give yourself a score and move on.

54. Compassion Subquotient

Do you have compassion for the suffering of others or has the negative ego numbed you to anything but your own suffering? Give yourself a score and move on.

55. Optimism Subquotient

Are you optimistic in life or pessimistic in life? GOD is the eternal optimist and positive thinker. Give yourself a score and move on.

56. Invulnerability Subquotient

Do you claim invulnerability to the psychic attacks of others, or do you see yourself as vulnerable and a victim to the psychic attacks of others? Children affirm "Sticks and stones can break my bones, but names can never hurt me." Much can be learned from children. Give yourself a score and move on.

57. Maintaining Your Golden Bubble of Protection Subquotient

Do you maintain at all times your Golden Bubble of Protection around you so other people's negative energy slides off like water of a duck's back? Do you let other people's negative energy get through your bubble and cause negative emotions? Give yourself a score and move on.

58. Grace Subquotient

Do you learn the easy way in life, or do you learn by the school of hard knocks? Do you learn from your mistakes and the mistakes of others or do you make the same mistakes repeatedly? Give yourself a score and move on.

59. Integrity and Consistency Subquotient

Do you maintain integrity and consistency in the demonstration of your spiritual ideals at all times, or do you give into the negative ego rationalizations and excuses? Give yourself a score and move on.

60. Joyous Vigilance Subquotient

Do you maintain joyous vigilance for GOD and His Kingdom at all times or do you give into automatic pilot, temptation, fatigue and lower-self desire? Give yourself a score and move on.

61. Honesty Subquotient

Are you honest with self in evaluating your quotients, or are you letting the negative ego seduce and delude you? Give yourself a score and move on.

62. Moderation Subquotient

Are you moderate in all things, or are you prone to extremism? Give yourself a score and move on.

63. Focus and Concentrate on Subquotient

Are you focused and concentrated at all times on GOD and you spiritual path or do you let your mind wander into areas that are inappropriate? Give yourself a score and move on.

64. Purity Subquotient

Do you retain the purity of GOD/Christ and the Holy Spirit in your every thought, word and deed, or have you allowed the difficulties of Earth life and the negative ego to harden and remove this from you? Give yourself a score and move on.

65. Enthusiasm Subquotient

Have you been able to keep your enthusiasm in life for GOD, love and the things you believe in, or have you allowed Earth life to beat you down? Give yourself a score and move on.

66. Surrender to GOD's Will Subquotient

Are you able at all times to maintain your preferences but simultaneously surrender to GOD's Will, or are you holding on to ego's will and fighting GOD's Will? Give yourself a score and move on.

67. Defenselessness Subquotient

Do you take the Melchizedek/Christ/Buddha attitude for defenselessness or do you take the negative ego attitude of defensiveness? Give yourself a score and move on.

68. Personal Opinion Subquotient

Do you state everything you believe or hold true as your personal opinion, or are you self-righteous in your beliefs in relationship to others? Give yourself a score and move on.

69. Guiltless Subquotient

Do you see yourself as completely forgiven and guiltless in all things from past lives and this life, or are you allowing the negative ego to hold grudges against self and make you feel bad about self for past actions? Give yourself a score and move on.

70. Open-Mindedness Subquotient

Are you open minded in relationships to others, or close minded in relationship to others? Give yourself a score and move on.

71. Discussion Subquotient

Do you have loving discussions with people, or do you argue with people? Give yourself a score and move on.

72. Responding Subquotient

Do you respond in life to all situations, or do you react out of your emotional body and negative ego in all situations? Give yourself a score and move on.

Conclusion

My beloved readers, quite synchonistically the subquotients added up to the number 72. GOD and the Masters have reminded me intuitively that there are 72 names of GOD! These 72 subquotients might aptly be called the 72 sub-quotients of GOD to become an Integrated Melchizedek/Christ/Buddha Spiritual Master on Earth!

38

How to Celebrate Wesak

The ideal and easiest way to celebrate Wesak is to come to the actual Wesak celebration I host every year in Mt. Shasta, California for 2000 lightworkers and spiritual leaders from around the globe. I invite some of the finest spiritual teachers, New Age musicians, and channels from around the globe to perform. There are tables set up for some of these leaders to share and sell their latest works and wares; the event is almost like a "Whole Life Expo." The whole event is professionally run and I personally guarantee that if you do come it will be one of the most profound spiritual experiences of your life. If you are not able to attend, the Masters have given me a format and structure for how to celebrate Wesak in your home with your classmates, which I am going to share with you here.

The Wesak Festival takes place each year on the day of the full moon of Taurus. Usually, this occurs in May; however, occasionally it is in April.

How To Officially Do the Wesak Ceremony in Your Home

Burning Pot

Holding Hands Resonation

Establishment of Ascension Column and Pillar of Light

Platinum Net

Axiatonal Alignment

Invocation of the Ascension Flame

Invocation to the Spiritual and Cosmic Hierarchy

Invocation of the Soul and Monadic Mantrum

Establishment of Golden Dome of Protection of Archangel Michael

Reciting of the *long version* of the Great Invocation together

Reciting of the Affirmation of the Disciple

Reciting of three Oms out loud together

Leader should read or play audiotape of "The Actual Wesak Ceremony"

Take a break

Leader should read "Golden Chamber Ascension Activation Meditation"

Reciting of three Oms out loud together

Social time with refreshments

Burning Pot

I would recommend setting up the burning pot about five minutes before you are actually going to start the class officially. Everyone will be seated and in the center of the room will be a hot plate on the floor. On the hot plate will be a little metal pot. In the pot you will pour about a quarter of an inch of Epsom salt. As you are about to begin, pour not more than a half an inch of rubbing alcohol over the Epsom salt. When everyone is quiet, throw a match into the rubbing alcohol. It will burn for about five minutes and it will burn up all the etheric, astral and mental negative energy in the atmosphere. I call this the New Age campfire. I guarantee that everyone in your group will love it. Explain to everyone the effect that the burning pot has. I would also recommend at this time lighting some sage or incense.

Holding Hands Resonation

When the burning pot burns out, the entire room will be extremely clear in terms of the spiritual atmosphere. The guide the group to hold hands, be it two people or twelve or one hundred, and for one minute have everyone hold hands and connect with each other's heart chakras as they are doing this. This will serve to unify the entire group instantly into a group consciousness.

The Establishment of the Ascension Column and Pillar of Light

The next step in the class is to call forth to the Planetary and Cosmic Spiritual Hierarchy for the establishment and activation of a gigantic ascension column to be set up in the room in which you are holding the class. Ask that this ascension column be connected also to a gigantic pillar of light and be connected to your group's planetary and cosmic antakarana which is the tube of light that connects you with your Monad and GOD.

The Platinum Net

Call forth to Melchizedek, the Mahatma, and Metatron to bring forth the platinum net, down through the entire group and your home.

Platinum is the highest frequency color available to Earth. The only frequency higher is the clear light of GOD, which has no color. The platinum net will clear the entire group and your home of all negative and imbalanced energies on all levels.

Invoking an Axiatonal Alignment

The next step in the class is to call forth from the Planetary and Cosmic Hierarchy a planetary and cosmic axiatonal alignment. The axiatonal alignment will serve to balance all the meridians of each individual and the entire group, and serve to instantly align the group energy with GOD and the spiritual hierarchy's consciousness on all levels.

Invocation of the Ascension Flame

The next step in the class is to call forth to the Spiritual Hierarchy and inner plane Ascended Masters for the anchoring and activation of the golden white ascension flame. Upon invocation, you will instantly feel and even see this energy coming in.

Invocation to the Spiritual and Cosmic Hierarchy

The next step in the class is to call forth to the entire Spiritual and Cosmic Hierarchy to join your class. Ask that, within Divine order, the appropriate Masters to overlight this particular class step forward please. If there are particular Masters who you are connected with, this is also the time to call these Masters forward. If you like you can also suggest to the group members to call forth the Masters that they would like to be present to help with this class or discussion.

Invocation of the Soul and Monadic Mantrum

The soul mantrum was brought forth to the Earth through the channelings of Alice Bailey of the Ascended Master Djwhal Khul. In my personal opinion it is one of the most profound mantrums on the entire planet and should be recited every time spiritual work of some kind is about to be ignited. The original soul mantrum goes as follows:

I am the Soul,
I am the Light Divine.
I am Love,
I am Will,
I am Fixed Design.

Since most of you, my beloved readers, have already passed your fourth initiation, it is appropriate to change the Soul mantrum to the Monadic mantrum which is the updated version. It is the same as the Soul mantrum but instead of saying, "I am the Soul," you say, "I am the Monad."

What I would actually recommend is that you say both of them. First the Soul mantrum and then the Monadic mantrum. The saying of these mantrums will ignite your Higher Self and Mighty I Am Presence (Monad) into action. "Try it, you'll like it!"

Invocation of Golden Dome of Protection

The next step in the class is to call forth the golden dome of protection for this group by Archangel Michael and his legion of Angels. Archangel Michael serves on the First Ray and has a specific function in GOD's Divine Plan of providing protection. You also might request protection for each member of the group in their spiritual paths and service work.

Invocation of the Great Invocation

The next step of the class is to have printed out in advance, copies of the Great Invocation which is a prayer that was brought forth by Lord Maitreya, the Planetary Christ, around 1945 to 1950. It is one of the most powerful prayers that has ever been given forth to lightworkers and the New Group of World Servers. I am first going to give it to you in the short version, and then I am going to give you the longer version. I would recommend doing the short version for most of your classes, however on special holidays or Holy days I would recommend doing the longer version. This was transcribed from the Alice Bailey book *Ponder on This*.

Short Version of the Great Invocation

From the point of Light within the Mind of GOD
Let Light stream forth into the minds of men.
Let Light descend on Earth.

From the point of Love within the Heart of GOD
Let Love stream forth into the hearts of men.
May Christ return to Earth.

From the center where the Will of GOD is known
Let purpose guide the little wills of men—
The purpose which the Masters know and serve.

From the center which we call the race of men
Let the Plan of Love and Light work out.
And may it seal the door where evil dwells.

Let Light and Love and Power restore the Plan on Earth.

Long Version of the Great Invocation

Let the Forces of Light bring illumination to mankind
Let the Spirit of Peace be spread abroad
May men of goodwill everywhere meet in a spirit of cooperation
May forgiveness on the part of all men be the keynote at this time.

Let power attend the efforts of the Great Ones
So let it be, and help us to do our part.

Let the Lords of Liberation issue forth
Let Them bring succor to the sons of men
Let the Rider from the Secret Place come forth,
And coming, save
Come forth, O Mighty One.

Let the souls of men awaken to the Light,
And may they stand with massed intent
Let the fiat of the Lord go forth
The end of woe has come!
Come forth, O Mighty One
The hour of service of the Saving Force has now arrived
Let it be spread abroad, O Mighty One.

Let Light and Love and Power and Death
Fulfill the purpose of the Coming One
The will to save is here
The love to carry forth the work is widely spread abroad
The active aid of all who know the truth is also here
Come forth, O Mighty One and blend these three.

Construct a great defending wall
The rule of evil now must end.

From the point of Light within the Mind of GOD
Let Light stream forth into the minds of men.
Let Light descend on Earth.

From the point of Love within the Heart of GOD
Let Love stream forth into the hearts of men.
May Christ return to Earth.

From the center where the Will of GOD is known
Let purpose guide the little wills of men—
The purpose which the Masters know and serve.

From the center which we call the race of men
Let the Plan of Love and Light work out.
And may it seal the door where evil dwells.

Let Light and Love and Power restore the Plan on Earth.

The Affirmation of the Disciple

I am a point of light within a greater light
I am a strand of loving energy within the stream of love divine.
I am a point of sacrificial fire, focused within the fiery Will of GOD
and thus I stand.

I am a way by which men may achieve.
I am a source of strength enabling them to stand.
I am a beam of light, shining upon their way, and thus I stand.
And standing thus, revolve and tread this way, the ways of men,
And know the ways of GOD. And thus I stand.

I strive toward understanding.
Let wisdom take the place of knowledge in my life.
I strive towards cooperation.
Let the master of my life, the soul, and likewise the one I seek to serve,
throw light through me on others.
In the center of the Will of GOD I stand.
Naught shall deflect my will from His.
I implement that will by love.
I turn towards the field of service.
I, the triangle divine, work out that will within the square, and serve
my fellow men.

I am a messenger of Light.
I am a pilgrim on the way of Love.
I do not walk alone, but know myself as one with all great souls, and
one with them in service.

Their strength is mine. This strength I claim.
My strength is theirs and this I freely give.
A soul, I walk on earth, I represent the One.

I am one with my group of brothers, and all that I have is theirs.
May the love which is in my soul pour forth to them.
May the strength which is in me lift and aid them.
May the thoughts which my soul creates reach and encourage them.

I know the law, and towards the goal I strive.
Naught shall arrest my progress on the way.
Each tiny life within my form responds.
My soul has sounded forth that call, and clearer day by day it sounds.

The glamour holds me not.
The path of light streams clear ahead.
My plea goes forth to reach the hearts of men.
I seek, I try to serve your need. Give me your hand and tread the path
with me

The sons of men are one and I am one with them.
I seek to love not hate.
I seek to serve and not exact due service.
I seek to heal not hurt.

Let pain bring due reward of Light and Love.
Let the soul control the outer form and life, and all events, and bring
to light the Love which underlies the happenings of the time.
Let vision come and insight.
Let the future stand revealed.
Let inner union demonstrate and outer cleavages be gone.
Let Love prevail.
Let all men Love.

We know, oh Lord, of life and love, about the need.
Touch our hearts anew with Love, that we too may love and give.

The Actual Wesak Ceremony Meditation

Close eyes—Let us begin again by taking a deep breath—Exhale.

We call forth the entire Planetary and Cosmic Hierarchy to help in this meditation.

We call forth the full opening now, of all our chakras, including the ascension chakra, which sits at the back of the head where a ponytail begins.

The meditation experience we are now about to begin, in truth, is the highlight of the entire Wesak Celebration weekend.

We are now going to soul travel together to the actual Wesak Valley in the Himalayas, to experience the actual Wesak Ceremony conducted by the inner plane Ascended Masters, that has been going on every year at the Taurus full moon for eons of time.

Let us now prepare ourselves for this Holy and Sanctified experience with a moment of silence.

We now call forward our inner plane spiritual hosts, and ask for the re-creation of our group Merkabah like a gigantic boat, to take all in attendance both on the inner and outer plane, to the Wesak Valley in the Himalayas, to now experience the Wesak Ceremony.

Let us feel ourselves now descending into the actual Wesak Valley, joining all the other Ascended Masters, initiates and disciples already gathered there.

See and/or feel the Presence of Lord Maitreya, the Planetary Christ, St. Germain, the Chohan of the Seventh Ray and the new Mahachohan.

Also, see Allah Gobi, who holds the First Ray position in the Spiritual Hierarchy, known as the Manu.

See these three Masters standing in a triangular formation around a bowl of water that sits upon a very large crystal.

See, feel, and/or visualize all the rest of the Masters of the Spiritual Hierarchy, standing in a circular fashion around these three masters.

Just prior to the precise moment of the rising of the full moon, which is now upon us on the inner plane, the expectancy and excitement begins to build, as we all await the arrival of Lord Buddha.

As the moment of the rising moon now takes place, a stillness settles down upon the gathered crowd, and all look toward the northeast.

Certain ritualistic movements and mantras sound forth under the guidance of the Seven Chohans of the seven Rays.

In the far distant northeast, a tiny speck can be seen in the sky.

This speck gradually grows larger and larger, and the form of the Buddha seated in a cross-legged position appears.

He is clad in a saffron colored robe, and bathed in light and color, with his hands extended in blessing.

While hovering above the bowl of water, a great mantrum is sounded forth by Lord Maitreya, that is only used once a year at Wesak.

This invocation sets up an enormous vibration of spiritual current.

It marks the supreme moment of intensive spiritual effort of all initiates and Masters in attendance for the entire year.

In this moment let us watch Lord Buddha hovering over this bowl of water, transmitting his Divine and Cosmic energies into this water and through Lord Maitreya.

The energy is then sent forth by Lord Maitreya, to the entire Spiritual Hierarchy, and into all of us who form a part of this Hierarchy on Earth.

Feel this massive downpouring of Cosmic energies from the Planetary and Cosmic Hierarchy, flowing not only through us, but also flowing out into the world and into the very Earth Herself.

As these energies continue to pour in, see the bowl of water that sat on the large crystal, being passed around the gathered crowd.

See and feel yourself taking a sip of this most Holy, Blessed, and Sanctified water.

See yourself now walking towards Lord Buddha, Lord Maitreya, Sanat Kumara, our previous Planetary Logos, who now overlights Buddha in his new position in the spiritual government.

Stand now before these three glorious Masters, and share with them on the inner plane as to what you feel your service work, mission, and puzzle piece is in GOD's Divine Plan on Earth. Take this time also, to make any prayer requests to GOD and these three Masters, for help in manifesting your mission, and for the answering of any personal prayer requests for self or for others.

Let us now take 30 seconds of silence to allow you to make these prayer requests.

Feel and visualize these prayers being answered, and thank Lord Buddha, Lord Maitreya and Sanat Kumara, for their guidance and blessings.

Find yourself walking now in the Wesak Valley towards a less populated and very beautiful nature spot.

Have a seat and just allow yourself to "Be," and resonate with all that has taken place.

Take a moment now to feel the full joy and blessings of this moment and of the entire Wesak Ceremony, and allow this feeling to become fully imbued into the very core of your being.

Know that all of us, and the entire Hierarchy of inner plane Ascended Masters are One!!!

Find yourself now looking towards the ceremonial circle and gathering where the large crystal and bowl stand.

See, feel, and visualize Lord Buddha begin to rise and make his ascent in the Lotus posture, and begin to now float back to the northeast to the realm from which he came.

As Lord Buddha again becomes a small speck in the distance, see and feel the arrival of our inner plane spiritual hosts, with their gigantic group Merkabah.

Feel yourself now joining this Merkabah in total oneness, joy and love.

Feel the group Merkabah floating now, through space and time, and now returning back to Mt. Shasta and into this auditorium.

Before opening our eyes, let us take one last moment to send love to all our brothers and sisters in this auditorium, who have shared this journey with us and who have shared this entire Wesak Celebration with us this weekend.

Let us send and receive this love now!!!

I would now like to call forth from the inner plane, His Holiness the Lord Sai Baba, the Cosmic Christ, to now give forth his final blessing and benediction to close this Wesak Ceremony, by having him sprinkle his Sacred Virbhuti Ash etherically upon all gathered in this auditorium.

Let us receive this final Wesak Ceremony and Wesak Celebration blessing now!!!

When you feel complete you may open your eyes.

***

Take a break before beginning the "Golden Chamber Ascension Meditation."

The Ultimate Golden Chamber Ascension Activation Meditation

Close eyes—let us begin by taking a deep breath—Exhale.

We call all the Masters of the Planetary and Cosmic Hierarchy to help in this meditation.

We now call forth a Planetary and Cosmic Axiatonal Alignment.

This morning's meditation is a little longer then some of my other meditations, and is purposely created this way so as to set in place all the spiritual hook-ups needed to fully activate each person present, to their highest ascension potentiality.

So allow yourself now to just completely relax and soak in all the Cosmic energies and Ascension activations.

We now call forth to the Seven Chohans, Djwhal Khul, Lord Maitreya and Lord Buddha, to provide a gigantic group Merkabah for all in attendance in this auditorium, and we ask to be taken spiritually to the Golden Chamber of Melchizedek, in the Universal Core.

We call forth each person's 144 soul extensions, from their Monad and Mighty I Am Presence, to join us, if they choose, for this meditation.

We call to the Seven Chohans, for the opening of all Chakras, the Ascension Chakra, and all Petals and Facets of all Chakras.

We call to Archangel Metatron, for the permanent anchoring and activation of the Microtron.

We call to the Lord of Sirius, for the anchoring and activation of the Scrolls of Wisdom and Knowledge, from the Great White Lodge on Sirius that are appropriate for this group.

We also simultaneously ask to be connected to the Cosmic Initiation that Vywamus has just recently taken, for the purpose of accelerated ascension activation.

We call forth Sanat Kumara, Vywamus and Lenduce, for help in establishing each person's Planetary and Cosmic Antakarana, back to each person's Oversoul, Monad and to GOD.

We call Melchizedek, Mahatma, Metatron, the Elohim Councils, and the Archangels, for the permanent anchoring and activation of the Planetary and Cosmic Tree of Life.

We request the complete opening and activation of the Seven Cosmic Seals, and the Ten Sephiroth, as well as the Hidden Sephiroth of Daath.

We call forth from the Cosmic and Planetary Hierarchy, the anchoring and activation of all Fire Letters, Key Codes, and Sacred Geometries to help in this process.

We call to the Archangels for the full anchoring and activation of our 50 chakras which takes us through Planetary Ascension, and request as well, the anchoring and activation of our 330 chakras, taking us back to the GODHEAD.

We call for the permanent anchoring and activation of our Twelve Bodies, including the Solar, Galactic, and Universal bodies.

We call to Melchizedek, the Mahatma, Metatron, Archangel Michael and the Planetary Hierarchy, for the anchoring and activation of the Anointed Christ Overself Body, our Zohar Body, our Overself Body, our Electromagnetic Body, our Gematrian Body, our EKA Body, our

Epi-Kenetic Body, our Higher Adam Kadmon Body, and the Lord's Mystical Body, as described in *The Keys of Enoch*.

We call forth the permanent anchoring and activation of the 64 Keys of Enoch, in all five Sacred Languages.

We call forth the illumination of the 72 areas of the Mind, as described in *The Keys of Enoch*.

We call forth the Deca Delta Light Encodements and Emanations from the Ten Superscripts of the Divine Mind.

We call forth to Metatron, for the anchoring and activation of the 76 names of Metatron, to permanently flow through us.

We call forth the removal of all veils of Light and Time.

We call forth Djwhal Khul, Lord Maitreya, and Lord Buddha, for the permanent anchoring of the Greater Flame of the Monad and Mighty I Am Presence, into the Lesser Flame of the Personality and Soul incarnated on Earth.

We call to the Mighty Archangels, for permanent anchoring and activation of the Twelve Heavenly Houses, and Twelve Cosmic Stations.

We call to Lord Buddha, whose festival we celebrate this weekend, for the permanent anchoring and activation now, of the Planetary Sun and the Planetary Cosmic Heart, into the core of our being.

We call to Helios and Vesta, for the permanent anchoring and activation of the Solar Sun and the Solar Cosmic Heart, into the core of our being.

We call to Melchior, for the permanent anchoring and activation of the Galactic Sun and Galactic Cosmic Heart, into the core of our being.

We call to Melchizedek, for the permanent anchoring and activation of the Universal Sun and Universal Cosmic Heart, into the core of our being.

We call to the Mahatma and the Multi-Universal Logos, to now permanently anchor and activate the Multi-Universal Sun and Multi-Universal Cosmic Heart, into the core of our being.

We call to the GODHEAD, for the permanent anchoring and activation of the Ultimate Great Central Sun and GOD's Own Heart, into the core of our being.

We call forth to the Source of Our Cosmic Day and Melchizedek, for the anchoring of the 43 Christed Universes.

We call forth to Melchizedek, to initiate each person attending this celebration, into the Order of Melchizedek.

Melchizedek, we ask you to do this now with your Rod of Initiation, if it is each person's individual free choice to receive this blessing at this time.

We ask that each person who has inwardly given this permission, receive the Rod of Initiation directly from you Melchizedek, with no Earthly person needed as an intermediary in this process.

Melchizedek told me that this next activation might be the single most powerful activation and Blessing of this entire meditation.

We call forth the entire Planetary and Cosmic Hierarchy, and hereby collectively request a complete merger of the Light bodies of all the inner plane Masters in attendance with this Group Body in this auditorium, both individually and collectively.

We call forth GOD, the Mahatma, Melchizedek, Metatron, Elohim Councils, Archangel Michael and the Archangels, to now anchor from the Cosmic Treasury of Light, the Light Packets of Information from the Tablets of Creation, the Elohim Scriptures, the Torah Or, the Cosmic Ten Commandments, and the Cosmic Book of Life.

We now call forth from the entire Planetary and Cosmic Hierarchy, and all the inner plane Masters that each person has brought with them to this festival, for a combined Light Shower the likes of which this world has never known before.

Let us begin the closing process of this meditation by repeating out loud together the famous mantra from *The Keys of Enoch*:

Kodoish, Kodoish, Kodoish, Adonai, Tsebayoth

Holy, Holy, Holy is the Lord GOD of Hosts!!!

We now call forth our inner plane Spiritual Hosts, and request now to be taken together in our group Merkabah, back into our physical bodies and back into the room.

***

The Movement towards World Peace via the Wesak Celebration

From the Ascended Masters' perspective, the annual celebration of Wesak is the holiest day of the year. It occurs each year at the full moon of Taurus, and is the high point of incoming spiritual energies to the planet. It is the time when all the inner plane disciples, initiates and ascended Masters from the East and West gather in the Wesak Valley in the Himalayas to celebrate Lord Buddha's birthday, day of enlightenment and ascension. It is a time for all the Masters to come together and commune in fellowship and to regenerate and rejuvenate before another year of world service. This celebration has been going on for eons of time.

In 1995, a most amazing occurrence took place in the history and evolution of Planet Earth. Beloved Sanat Kumara, our Planetary Logos for over 18.5 million years, moved on to a higher rung of his cosmic evolution, and beloved Lord Buddha stepped in to take his place as Planetary Logos. The Planetary Logos could be likened to the president of the planet in a spiritual or hierarchical sense. My beloved readers, I think you can see that this historic event makes the celebration of Wesak even more significant than ever before. This is because Lord Buddha ensouls the entire Earth and all her inhabitants within his auric field and heart. In essence, Lord Buddha is the being who is now responsible for the evolution of all Kingdoms (mineral, plant, animal, and people) of the Earth.

So, this brings us now to the issue of world peace. Lord Buddha has always been the embodiment of peace and tranquillity. The entire Earth and all her inhabitants now live and move within this auric vibration and resonance. When the atomic structure of the twelve-body system of the Earth begins to rotate and spin within the resonance and quality of the Planetary Logos, it charges the entire electrical circuitry of the entire planet from within to without.

Thirdly, the aspect of all inner plane Masters, disciples, initiates and ascended beings from all paths, religions, traditions and spiritual affiliations gathering together in oneness and unity, is the ultimate demonstration of world peace at its core and very essence.

At the actual Wesak ceremony this Light, Love, and Peace is transmitted by Lord Buddha to beloved Lord Maitreya, our Planetary Christ, which is then disseminated to the Chohans of the Rays and to the entire Spiritual Hierarchy simultaneously. This Love, Light and Peace then rains down upon Earth and all her inhabitants. So we see the fourth way and manner that Wesak catalyzes world peace for the planet.

Fifthly, there are so many thousands of Masters at Wesak in the Himalayas. All the peace each Master individually receives is then taken by them and spread the entire year to all of the initiates and disciples under their care, and into their service work on Planet Earth. So we see, my beloved readers, the ramifications for Wesak bringing about world peace are astronomical.

By the grace of God and the Masters, I have taken on the spiritual assignment of holding an extremely large global event each year in Mt. Shasta for 1500 to 3000 disciples, initiates, and ascended beings on Earth, to celebrate Wesak in coordination with the simultaneous celebration in the Himalayas. This serves to seed and anchor the peaceful vibrations, gifts, and blessings of Wesak physically into the whole of Earth and into the Heart of Earth where true peace originates.

At last year's Wesak celebration in Mt. Shasta, there were not only 1200 high-level initiates, disciples, and ascended beings, there were also over 500,000 inner plane Cosmic and Planetary Masters, Archangels and Angels, Elohim Masters, and Christed Extraterrestrials in attendance, pouring their Love, Light, energy, gifts, and peaceful intent to all in attendance on the inner and outer planes. My beloved readers, I think you can see that the ramifications for world peace, as a result of this many inner and outer plane Masters convening for the sole purpose of celebrating Love, oneness, unity, the integration of the Christ/Buddhic vibration and world peace, is enormous.

If this were not enough, the Masters guided me last year to create a booklet and audiotape called "How to Celebrate Wesak." To my amazement these booklets sold like hotcakes and thousands of groups from all over the world who couldn't make it to the event in Mt. Shasta etherically linked up with the Mt. Shasta program and, of course, the actual celebration in the Himalayas. This formed a type of triangular effect and set in motion a linking of lines of Light around the planet like a gigantic electrical light grid and circuit. This Wesak peace grid is now permanently anchored over and within the mountain of Mt. Shasta and is emanating these peaceful light rays twenty-four hours a day, seven days a week, and three hundred sixty-five days a year, to the entire planet. So, my beloved friends, the celebration of Wesak and the movement towards world peace are eternally connected. Earth will achieve the full manifestation of peace, as we all now move, with Godspeed and the Masters' blessings, into the New Millennium and the Seventh Golden Age

39

The Ultimate Spiritual Secret of GOD's Infinite Universe

My beloved readers, there is a saying in *A Course in Miracles* that says, "To have all, give all to all!" This is a very profound statement in my humble opinion. What this means is that if you want to have GOD and everything in life on all levels, you must give everything on all levels.

My beloved readers, that which we hold back in giving to our brothers and sisters and the world, is in truth that which we are holding back in giving to ourselves. This is true, because we each are, in truth, an incarnation of GOD and the Eternal Self. We are not, in truth, our physical bodies, living separate, unconnected lives to other people. In our true identity, as incarnations of GOD and sons and daughters of GOD, every person and everything in GOD's infinite universe is a part of us. So when we hold back giving to another out of fear, competition, comparing, jealousy, envy, selfishness, or any other negative ego quality, we are in truth not giving to ourselves, for GOD and our brothers and sisters are literally part of ourselves. When we hold back giving, we think we are helping ourselves, when in truth we are not giving to our Self, in the larger context of who we really are.

A Course in Miracles states in one of the lessons, "My Salvation is up to me." This is confusing to some, for most feel that GOD gives Salvation. The truth is, GOD does not need to give Salvation because GOD never took Salvation away. As *A Course of Miracles* also says, "The fall never really happened, we just think it did." In other words, we have always been the Christ or the Buddha; always have been and always will be. No matter how much we indulge in negative ego thinking, which tells us we are separate from GOD and each other and are just physical bodies, this does not change the truth. As the introduction to *A Course in Miracles* says, "Nothing real can be threatened and nothing unreal exists. Herein lies the peace of GOD." Our true identity as the Eternal Christ has never changed or will change, no matter how much we indulge in negative thinking. So in this holy instant, wake up from the bad dream of the negative ego and realize you are the Christ, I am the Christ, and we are both one with GOD. This is how it has always been, and how it will always be. One of the main reasons you have entered this mystery school is to wake up to this fact.

My beloved readers, given that you have now reawakened to this first Ultimate Secret of GOD's Infinite Universe I am now going to share with you the second one. I share this with you in the vein that "to have all, you must give all to all!" In my life, my books, my Academy, and my Spiritual Mission, I have tried to live this principle and ideal, and by the grace of God and the Masters it has served me well. I have given all and I can honestly, humbly say, by the grace of GOD and the Masters; I received all in return. My beloved readers, in my books and teachings I have shared with you everything, and this has brought me enormous love, peace of mind, and abundance. The negative ego will tell you that giving is losing and I am here to tell you that "Giving is Gaining." The only way to receive GOD and maintain GOD Realization is to give GOD every moment of your life. The second you stop giving GOD you have not lost GOD in truth, however, you have lost GOD in your Realization of His Holy Presence. So, no one can lose GOD in truth, however, you can lose your Realization of GOD by indulging in negative ego thinking and emotions.

So, in this vein again, I say this entire book is a testament too, I give you my beloved brothers and sisters, the Ultimate Secret of GOD's Infinite Universe to accelerate your spiritual evolution path of ascension and process of becoming an "Integrated Christ."

The second ultimate secret of GOD's infinite universe is that if you ask, GOD and the Cosmic and Planetary Ascended Masters will run all of your favorite ascension activations of the types I have outlined in this book, in all my other books, and in all my ascension activation meditation tapes and ascension activations not listed here, on a 24 hour a day, 7 days a week, 365 days a year for your entire incarnation basis!

My beloved readers, I do not know if you truly realize how profound this last statement is. In my own spiritual work I have uncovered and discovered by the grace of GOD and the Masters, the Ultimate secret and short cut of Spiritual Evolution.

Instead of having to do billions of invocations and prayers in a given lifetime, to have to invoke every day all these spiritual activations, by the grace of GOD and the Cosmic and Planetary Hierarchy they will run all of these ascension activations on the inner plane perpetually, so you are in the ultimate ascension activation seat, so to speak, of the Cosmic and Planetary Ascended Masters all the time.

My beloved readers, I have been doing this by the grace of GOD and the Masters since 1997, and what this incredible grace of the Masters has allowed me to do is focus all of my energies on Spiritual Leadership and Planetary World Service. Since the spiritual activations are running all the time, I have by GOD and the Masters' grace moved through the completion of my 12 major levels of initiation with lightning speed, and by their grace I have focused my energies on Planetary World Service and maintaining a strong physical vehicle.

I know that this Ultimate Secret of GOD's Infinite Universe works because I see how fast I have moved through my cosmic initiations 10 through 12 without even having to really focus on them. This is the ultimate grace and Love, Wisdom, and Power of GOD and the Cosmic and Planetary Ascended Masters.

When I stated in a previous chapter that working with GOD and the Cosmic and Planetary Hierarchy was the "Rocketship to GOD," I spoke from experience, and this entire book is again a testament to this fact.

I would especially like to thank Melchizedek, the Mahatma, and Archangel Metatron for providing this grace.

I share this with you, my beloved readers, for the purpose of suggesting to you that you call upon these most noble and loving Cosmic Masters, so you may have this grace as well.

On a practical note in terms of how to do this, you can make your own list of ascension activations that you want Melchizedek, the Mahatma and Metatron to run, as one possibility. The second way this can be done, is that you go through this book and/or my other books and make a list of your favorite activations and ask the 3 M's as I like to call them (Melchizedek, the Mahatma, and Metatron) to run these activations continually.

The third and maybe the easiest way to do this is to just ask Melchizedek, the Mahatma, and Metatron to run my 13 ascension activation meditations as described in the Melchizedek Synthesis Light Academy information packet, continually! These 13 meditations contain every ascension activation in the universe you could ever come up with. The 3 M's are familiar with these meditations since they helped me to write them along with the other Cosmic and Planetary Masters, so they can easily put this program in place for you.

One other last point here on the issue of the importance of giving and not holding back anything to your brothers and sisters. This does not mean that there is not a time in life to be spiritually selfish, to take care of yourself, and to set proper boundaries where necessary. This is an essential lesson to learn in becoming an "Integrated Christ." What this does mean, however, is to not hold back giving on all levels for the reasons of selfishness, greed, narcissism, self-centeredness, competition, jealousy, envy, comparing, and any other negative ego motivation you can think of. You will only fully realize GOD and have everything when you are able to give GOD to everyone and everything. Let the words of Sai Baba, "GOD equals man minus ego," ever be a mantra in your consciousness. Be spiritually selfish where GOD, the Holy Spirit and your own Mighty I Am Presence guides you to be. Never, however, hold back giving on any level to your brothers and sisters because of negative ego selfishness, which is the opposite of spiritual selfishness, which is a good and needed thing at times. It takes a very pure heart and great spiritual discernment to know the difference. The negative ego is very tricky in this regard and will do everything in its power to convince you that its negative ego selfishness is spiritual selfish-ness. Be unbelievably vigilant on this point and vigilant against the negative ego's personal agendas, for your revelation of GOD and the Christ/Buddha consciousness depends on it. There is no deceiving GOD or tricking GOD. The truth is the truth, and if you do not face it now with devastating honesty and purity, you will have to face it when you physically die and go through your three-day Bardo (death experience). As the Master Jesus said, "Be vigilant for GOD and His Kingdom." In my humble opinion, the single most important Christed quality after unconditional love is "purity of heart." To truly examine your motives, as GOD would have you see them, takes incredible courage, dedication, and devotion to GOD, and "purity of heart." This last paragraph is a spiritual challenge in the most positive and uplifting way, to strive for this degree of GOD purity on your spiritual path. Strive for this degree of joyous, spiritual vigilance against the corruption of the negative ego and all the pitfalls and traps it will lay before you. The more spiritually advanced you become and the more spiritual leadership and responsibility for others you will eventually have, the more spiritual tests you will be given by the negative ego. Will you be able to pass the spiritual tests of power, fame, money, sexuality, lower-self desire, attachment, fear, selfishness, false pride, anger, greed, jealousy, vanity, transcending duality and negative ego motivations and agendas! The more spiritually advanced and successful you become, the more difficult and complicated the tests will become. Once you have tasted spiritual and material success and power over others, will you be able to retain the spiritual vigilance and purity of heart that got you there in the first place? An enormous number of lightworkers do not pass these tests. They do not pass them in the beginning and they do not pass them at the more advanced levels. As the Bible says, "The spiritual path the higher you go is a straight and narrow path." Very few retain the spiritual vigilance, purity of heart and control over negative ego motivations and agendas, and become corrupted. This last section of writing is a spiritual challenge and request from GOD and the Cosmic and Planetary Masters to remember these words and ideals, for your salvation depends on it. GOD has already given you everything. You will achieve Salvation and GOD Realization if you can maintain this level of Christ/Buddha Consciousness and Purity of Consciousness within self! Strive for these things above all else, for this is the true path to GOD, Christ/Buddha Consciousness, Joy, Happiness, Inner Peace and Unconditional love and Purity of Consciousness within self!

My beloved readers, I have now provided you with the two "Ultimate Secrets of GOD's Infinite Universe," to accelerate you initiation, ascension and realization of becoming an "Integrated Christ" at the highest possible level. If you apply the insights and tools I have provided in this book, and the two "Pearls of GOD" I have given you in this chapter, you will achieve your goal of becoming a "Full-Fledged Integrated Christ" in the shortest amount of time you would have ever dreamed possible! I share these "Platinum Keys of GOD" and "Pearls of GOD" with you in this book with enormous unconditional love and joy! I have dedicated my entire life in every thought, word, and deed, to sharing with you all I have learned and more. Let the pristine words of *A Course in Miracles* ever ring through your heart, mind, and soul! "To have all give all to all!"

I have attempted to do this for you, my Beloved Readers, in my past books and in this book. Go forward my beloved friends, with great joy and inner peace, for the insights, ideas and spiritual tools given in this book will give you all you have ever spiritually dreamed of and more. This, my beloved readers, is the incredible grace and love of GOD and the Cosmic and Planetary Ascended Masters!

Namaste!

40

My Spiritual Mission and Purpose by Dr. Joshua David Stone

My Spiritual mission and purpose is a multifaceted process. Spirit and the inner plane Ascended Masters have asked myself and Wistancia (married since 1998), to anchor onto the Earth an inner plane Ashram and Spiritual/Psychological/Physical/Earthly Teaching and Healing Academy! This Academy is called the Melchizedek Synthesis Light Academy! We are overlighted in this mission by Melchizedek, the Mahatma, Archangel Metatron, the inner plane Ascended Master Djwhal Khul, and a large group of Ascended Masters and Angels such as the Divine Mother, Archangel Michael, Archangel Gabriel, Sai Baba, Vywamus, the Lord of Arcturus, Lord Buddha, Lord Maitreya, Mother Mary, Quan Yin, El Morya, Kuthumi, Serapis Bey, Paul the Venetian, Master Hilarion, Sananda, Lady Portia and Saint Germain, and a great many others who we like to call the "Core Group"!

I have also been asked by the inner plane Ascended Master Djwhal Khul, who again wrote the Alice Bailey books, and was also involved in the Theosophical Movement, to take over his inner plane Ashram when he moves on to his next Cosmic Position, in the not too distant future.

Djwhal holds Spiritual Leadership over what is called the inner plane Second Ray Synthesis Ashram. On the inner plane the Second Ray Department is a gigantic three story building complex with vast gardens.

The Ascended Master Djwhal Khul runs the first floor of the Second Ray Department in the Spiritual Hierarchy. Master Kuthumi, the Chohan of the Second Ray, runs the second floor. Lord Maitreya the Planetary Christ runs the third floor! When Djwhal Khul leaves for his next Cosmic Position, I will be taking over this first floor Department. The Second Ray Department is focused on the "Spiritual Education," of all lightworkers on Earth, and is the Planetary Ray of the Love/Wisdom of God. What is unique, however, about the Synthesis Ashram, is that it has a unique mission and purpose which is to help lightworkers perfectly master and integrate all Twelve Planetary Rays which is one of the reasons I love this particular Spiritual leadership position and assignment so much! For this has been a great mission and focus of all my work!

Wistancia and my mission has been to anchor the Synthesis Ashram and Teaching Academy onto the physical Earth, which we have done and are continuing to do in an ever-increasing manner on a global level. Currently, there are over 15 branches of the Academy that have been set up around the world! The Academy actually first came into existence in 1996! This we have been guided to call the Melchizedek Synthesis Light Academy for the following reasons. It is called this because of the Overlighting Presence of Melchizedek (Our Universal Logos), the Mahatma (Avatar of Synthesis), and the Light which is the embodiment of Archangel Metatron, who created all outer light in our Universe and is the creator of the electron! These three beings, Djwhal Khul, and a very large Core Group of inner plane Planetary and Cosmic Masters help us in all this work.

I have also been asked by the inner plane Ascended Masters to be one of the main "High Priest Spokespersons for the Planetary Ascension Movement on Earth." I have been asked to do this because of the cutting edge, yet easy to understand nature of all my books and work, as well as certain Spiritual Leadership qualities I humbly possess. In this regard, I represent all the Masters, which works out perfectly given the Synthesis nature of my work. I function as kind of a "Point Man" for the Ascended Masters on Earth, as they have described it to me.

The Masters, under the guidance of Lord Buddha our Planetary Logos, have also guided us as part of our mission to bring Wesak to the West! So, for the last six years we have held a Global Festival and Conference at Mt Shasta, California for 2000 people. This, of course, honors the Wesak Festival, which is the holiest day of the year to the inner plane Ascended Masters, and the high point of incoming Spiritual energies to the Earth on the Taurus Full moon each year! We invite all lightworkers to join us each year from all over the world for this momentous celebration that is considered one of the premiere Spiritual Events in the New Age Movement!

The fourth part of my mission and purpose is the 30 Volume Easy to Read Encyclopedia of the Spiritual Path I have written. So far, I have completed 27 volumes in this Ascension Book Series. The Ascended Master Djwhal Khul prophesized in the 1940s that there would be a third dispensation of Ascended Master teachings what would appear at the turn of the century. The first dispensation of Ascended Master teachings was the "Theosophical Movement," channeled by Madam Blavatsky. The second dispensation of Ascended Master teachings was the Alice Bailey books, channeled by Djwhal Khul, and the *I AM Discourses*, channeled by Saint Germain. My 30 volume series of books is, by the grace of GOD and the Masters, the third dispensation of Ascended Master teachings as prophesized by Djwhal Khul. These books are co-creative channeled writings of myself and the inner plane

Ascended Masters. What is unique about my work is how easy to read and understand it is, how practical, comprehensive, cutting-edge it is, as well as integrated and synthesized. Wistancia has added to this work with her wonderful book *Invocations to the Light.*

The fifth aspect of our work and mission, which is extremely unique is the emphasis of "Synthesis." My books and all my work integrate in a very beautiful way all religions, all Spiritual paths, all mystery schools, all Spiritual teachings, and all forms of psychology! Everyone feels at home in this work because of its incredible inclusive nature! This synthesis ideal is also seen at the Wesak Celebrations, for people come from all religions, Spiritual paths, mystery schools, and teachings. The event is overlighted by over one million inner plane Ascended Masters, Archangels and Angels, Elohim Masters, and Christed Extraterrestrials. Wesak, the books, the Academy, and all our work embody this synthesis principle. This is part of why I and we have been given Spiritual Leadership of the Synthesis Ashram on Earth, and soon on the inner plane as well. This also explains our unique relationship to Melchizedek who holds responsibility for the "synthesis development," of all beings in our Universe. Our connection to the Mahatma is explained by the fact that the Mahatma is the Cosmic embodiment of "Synthesis" in the infinite Universe. This is why the Mahatma also goes by the name, "The Avatar of Synthesis." Archangel Metatron who holds the position in the Cosmic Tree of Life of Kether, or the Crown, hence has a "Synthesis Overview" of all of the Sephiroth or Centers of the Cosmic Tree of Life! Djwhal Khul holds Spiritual leadership of the "Synthesis Ashram" on a Planetary, Solar, and Galactic level for the Earth! The Core Group of Masters that overlight our mission are the embodiment of the synthesis understanding!

The unique thing about our work is that it teaches some of the most cutting-edge co-created channeled work on the planet, in the realm of Ascension and Ascended Master Teachings. This can be seen in my books *The Complete Ascension Manual, Beyond Ascension, Cosmic Ascension, Revelations of a Melchizedek Initiate,* and *How To Teach Ascension Classes.* Because of my background as a professional psychologist and licensed Marriage, Family, and Child Counselor, I also specialize in some of the most advanced cutting-edge work on the planet in the field of Spiritual psychology. In this regard, I would guide you to my books *Soul Psychology, Integrated Ascension, How To Clear The Negative Ego,* and *Ascension and Romantic Relationships!* Thirdly, I also have humbly brought forth some extremely cutting-edge work on the physical/earthly level in the field of healing, Spirituality and society, politics, social issues, Extraterrestrials, Spiritual leadership, Spirituality and business, Goddess work with Wistancia, and of course the annual Wesak Celebrations. This can be found in my books *The Golden Keys to Ascension and Healing, Hidden Mysteries, Manual for Planetary Leadership, Your Ascension Mission: Embracing Your Puzzle Piece, How to be Successful in your Business from a Spiritual and Financial Perspective,* and *Empowerment and Integration of the Goddess* written by Wistancia and myself, to name a few!

Adding to this, the eleven new books I have just completed and am completing: *The Golden Book of Melchizedek: How To Become an Integrated Christ/Buddha in This Lifetime, How to Release Fear-Based Thinking and Feeling: An In-depth Study of Spiritual Psychology, The Little Flame and Big Flame* (my first children's book), *Letters of Guidance to Students and Friends, Ascension Names and Terms Glossary, Ascension Activation Meditations of The Spiritual Hierarchy, The Divine Blueprint for the Seventh Golden Age, How To Do Psychological and Spiritual Counseling For Self and Others, God and His Team of Super Heroes* (my second children's book), and *How To Achieve Perfect Radiant Health From The Soul's Perspective!*

Currently I have completed 27 Volumes in my Ascension Book Series. Fourteen of these books are published by Light Technology

Publishers. A new version of *Soul Psychology* has just been published by Ballantine Publishers which is owned by Random House, which I am quite excited about as well! The other books are in manuscript form and I am currently negotiating with various publishers for publishing rights! My books have also been translated and published in Germany, Brazil, Japan, Holland, Israel and this process continues to expand.

Spirit and the inner plane Ascended Masters have told me that because of this unique focus, that what I have actually done in a co-creative way and manner with them, is open a new Portal to God. This new portal opening stems out of all the cutting-edge Ascension Activations and Ascended Master Teachings, the totally cutting-edge Spiritual Psychology work because of my background as a psychologist and licensed Marriage, Family, and Child Counselor, and the unique ability to ground all the work into the physical/earthly world in a balanced and integrated manner. Spirit and the Masters have told me that this new Portal to God is on an inner and outer plane level, and continues to be built in a co-creative way with Spirit, the Masters, myself, and certain other Masters and High Level Initiates who are helping me on the inner and outer planes! I have Spiritual leadership, however, in spearheading this project, and it is one of the most exciting projects I am involved in.

In terms of my Spiritual initiation process as I have spoken of in my books, I have currently now taken my 14th major initiation. These are not the minor initiations that some groups work with, but are the major initiations that embody all the minor initiations within them. The Seventh Initiation is the achieving of Liberation and Ascension. The Tenth Initiation is the completion of Planetary Ascension and the beginning of Solar Initiation. The Eleventh Initiation, being the first Galactic Initiation. The Twelfth Initiation, being the first Universal Initiation from an Earthly perspective. Having taken my 14th initiation, what is most important to me is that these initiations have been taken in an "integrated manner," for, in truth, the Masters told me that they are not really into Ascension, which may surprise a great many light-workers. The Masters are into "Integrated Ascension"! There are many lightworkers taking initiations, but many are not doing so in an integrated and balanced manner! They are taking them on a Spiritual level, but they are not being properly integrated into the mental and emotional bodies or psychological level properly. They are also not transcending negative ego fear-based thinking and feeling and properly balancing their four-body system. They are also not integrating their initiations fully into the physical/earthly level addressing such things as: Healing, Grounding their Missions, Finding their Puzzle Piece Mission and Purpose, Prosperity Consciousness and Financial and Earthly Success, Integrating the God/Goddess, Embracing the Earth Mother and the Nature Kingdom, Properly Integrating into Third Dimensional Society and Civilization in terms of the focus of their Service Mission. This is just mentioned as a very loving reminder of the importance of an integrated and balanced approach to one's Spiritual Path. The grace to have been able to take these 14 major initiations and be able to have completed my Planetary Ascension process and to have moved deeply into my Cosmic Ascension process, I give to GOD, Christ, the Holy Spirit, Melchizedek, the Mahatma, Archangel Metatron, and the Core Group of Masters I work with. I have dedicated myself and my life to GOD and the Masters service, and I have humbly attempted to share everything I know, have used and have done in my Spiritual path and Ascension process with all of you, my beloved readers!

Melchizedek, the Universal Logos, has also inwardly told me, that because of the Cosmic work I am involved with, that I have taken on the Spiritual assignment of being one of the "Twelve Prophets of Melchizedek on Earth." I am very humbled to serve in this capacity, because Melchizedek is the Universal Logos, which is like the President of our entire Universe. In truth, all religions and Spiritual teachings have their source in Melchizedek and in the Great Ancient Order of

Melchizedek. It is my great honor and privilege to serve GOD and Melchizedek in this capacity. This is something I have never spoken of before, although I have known of this for many, many years. I have been guided after all this time to share a little more deeply about my Spiritual mission on Earth at this time.

The Academy website is one of the most profound Spiritual websites you will ever explore, because it embodies this "synthesis nature," and is an ever-expanding, living, easy-to-read Spiritual encyclopedia that fully integrates all 12 Rays in design and creation! This is also embodied in the free 140 page information packet that we send out to all who ask who wish to get involved and know more about our work! The information in the information packet is also available by just exploring the Academy website!

We have also set up a wonderful Ministers Ordination and Training Program, which we invite all interested to read about. I am also very excited about a relatively recent book I have written called *How to Teach Ascension Classes*. Because I have become so busy with my Spiritual leadership and global world service work, I really do not have the time to teach weekly classes, as I have in the past. I firmly believe in the motto "Why give a person a fish when you can teach them to fish?" In this vein, the Masters guided me to write a book on how to teach people to teach Ascension classes based on my work. I humbly suggest it is a most wonderful channeled book that can teach you in the easiest way and manner on every level to teach Ascension classes in your home or on a larger level if you choose. These classes are springing up now all over the globe and have been successful beyond my wildest dreams and expectations. When I wrote the book I was so involved with the process of writing it, I never fully envisioned the tremendous success it would have on a planetary and global level. Using this book and my other books, I have really done the initial homework for you, which can and will allow you to immediately begin teaching Ascension classes yourself.

I humbly suggest that you look into the possibility of doing this yourself if you are so guided!

One other very interesting aspect of our Spiritual mission is something the Masters have been speaking to us about for over ten years which is what they described as being "Ambassadors for the Christed Extraterrestrials"! We have always known this to be true! This was part of the reason I wrote the book *Hidden Mysteries*, which I humbly suggest is one of the best overviews and an easy-to-read and understand manner, of the entire Extraterrestrial Movement as it has affected our planet. If you have not read this book, I highly recommend that you do so. It is truly fascinating reading! My strongest personal connection to the Extraterrestrials is with the Arcturians! The Arcturians are the most advanced Christed Extraterrestrial race in our galaxy. They hold the future blueprint for the unfoldment of this planet. The Arcturians are like our future planet and future selves on a collective level. Part of my work, along with the Ascended Master Teachings, that I have been asked to bring through, is a more conscious and personal connection to the Arcturians, the Ashtar Command, and other such Christed Extraterrestrial races. This year's Platinum Wesak, because of being in the year 2001, will have a special connection to these Christed Extraterrestrials, and we invite you all to attend for this reason and many others! I also encourage you to read my book *Beyond Ascension*, where I explore some of my personal experiences with the Arcturians and how you may do so as well!

Currently, behind the scenes, we are working on some further expansions of this aspect of our mission, which we will share at a later time! Wistancia has also been involved with White Time Healing, which is another most wonderful Extraterrestrial healing modality that she offers to the public!

One other aspect of our mission deals with having developed with help from the inner plane Ascended Masters, some of the most advanced Ascension activation processes to accelerate Spiritual evolution that has ever been brought forth to this planet. In this co-creative process with the Masters, we have discovered the keys to how to accelerate Spiritual evolution at a rate of speed that in past years and centuries would have been unimaginable! This is why I call working with the Ascended Masters "The Rocketship to GOD Method of Spiritual Growth." There is no faster path to God Realization than working with the Ascended Masters, Archangels and Angels, Elohim Masters, and Christed Extraterrestrials! What is wonderful about this process is that you do not have to leave your current Spiritual practice, religion, or Spiritual path. Stay on the path you are and just integrate this work into what you are currently doing! All paths as you know, lead to GOD my friends! This is the profundity of following an eclectic path, and path of synthesis! I humbly suggest I have found some short cuts! I share this with all lightworkers on Earth, for I love GOD with all my heart and soul and mind and might, and I recognize that we are all incarnations of GOD,and Sons and Daughters of this same GOD regardless of what religion, Spiritual path, or mystery school we are on. We are all, in truth, the Eternal Self and are all God! There is, in truth, only GOD, so what I share with you, I share with you, GOD, and myself, for in the highest sense we are all one! What we each hold back from each other, we hold back from ourselves and from GOD. This is why I give freely all that I am, have learned and have, to you, my beloved readers, giving everything and holding back nothing! In my books and audiotapes, I have literally shared every single one of these ideas, tools, and Ascension activation methods for accelerating evolution that I have used and come to understand. My beloved readers, these tools and methods found in my books and on the audio tapes will "blow your mind as to their effectiveness," in terms of how profound, and easy-to-use they are! I would highly recommend that all lightworkers obtain the 13

Ascension Activation Meditation tapes I have put together for this purpose. Most of them were taped at the Wesak Celebrations with 1500 to 2000 people in attendance, with over one million inner plane Ascended Masters, Archangels and Angels, Elohim Masters, and Christed Extraterrestrials in attendance, under the Wesak full moon and the mountain of Mt Shasta. You can only imagine the power, love, and effectiveness of these Ascension activation audiotapes. I recommend getting all 13 tapes and working with one tape every day or every other day! I personally guarantee you that these tapes will accelerate your Spiritual evolution a thousand fold! You can find them in the information packets and on our Website. They are only available from the Academy! Trust me on this, the combination of reading my books, Wistancia's book, and working with these audio ascension activation tapes, will accelerate your Spiritual evolution beyond your wildest dreams and imagination!

One other extremely important part of my mission, which is a tremendous Spiritual passion of mine, is the training of lightworkers on Earth in the area of Spiritual/Christ/Buddha thinking and negative ego/separative/fear-based thinking! These are the only two ways of thinking in the world, and each person thinks with one, the other, or a combination of both. If a person does not learn how to transcend negative ego thinking and feeling, it will end up over time corrupting every aspect of their lives including all channeling work, Spiritual teaching, and even healing work! One cannot be wrong with self and right with GOD. This is because our thoughts create our reality, as we all know! I cannot recommend more highly that every person reading this read my books *Soul Psychology, The Golden Book of Melchizedek: How to Become an Integrated Christ/Buddha in this Lifetime,* and *How to Release Fear - Based Thinking and Feeling: An In-depth Study of Spiritual Psychology!* I humbly suggest that these three books will be three of the most extraordinary self-help books in the area of mastering this psychological area of life. They are extremely easy to read, very practical, and filled with tools that will help you in untold ways. The last two books I have mentioned are only available through the Academy. Being a channel for the Ascended Masters and being uniquely trained as a Spiritual Psychologist and Marriage, Family, and Child Counselor, as well as being raised in a family of psychologists, has given me an extraordinary ability to teach this material through my books in a most effective manner. The combination of my books on Ascension, and these books on Spiritual Psychology, along with Wistancia's book on the art of invocation, will literally revolutionize your consciousness in the comfort of your own home! The most extraordinary thing about all this work is how incredibly easy to read, and easy to understand it is. It is also incredibly comprehensive, completely cutting-edge, and totally integrated, balanced and synthesized. It contains the best of all schools of thought in the past, present, and channeled cutting-edge future understanding that is available now! I humbly ask you to trust me in this regard and just read one of these books and you will immediately want to buy the others!

One other aspect of our work and mission is our involvement with the "Water of Life" and the Perfect Science products for the healing of our own physical bodies and the physical body of Mother Earth of all pollution in the air, water, and earth. This is the miracle Mother Earth has been waiting for to bring her back to her "original edenic state" after so much abuse. This is not the time or the place to get into this subject in detail, however I invite you to check out the "Water of Life" and the Perfect Science information in the information packet and on the Academy website! It is truly the miracle we have all been waiting for to help heal the Earth!

One other aspect of our work and mission is a project that the Ascended Masters have asked us to put together on behalf of lightworkers and people around the globe. It is called the "Interdimensional

Prayer Altar Program"! The Masters have guided us to set it up in the Academy located in Agoura Hills, California on the property we live on. We have set up a "Physical Interdimensional Prayer Altar" where people can send in their prayers on any subject and we will place them on this Altar. In consultation with the Masters, Archangels and Angels, Elohim Masters, and Christed Extraterrestrials, we have set up an arrangement with them that all physical letters placed upon this Altar will be immediately worked upon by these Masters. We have been guided by the inner plane Ascended Masters to create 15 Prayer Altar Programs in different areas of life that people can sign up for. For example, there is one for health and another for financial help in your Spiritual mission. There are 15 total, and two-thirds of them are free. There are five or six that are more advanced Spiritual acceleration programs where written material is sent to you to work with in conjunction with these programs to accelerate Spiritual. All letters we receive by e-mail, fax, or letter are placed on the Altar by myself or my personal assistant. It is kept 100% confidential and is an extremely special service provided by the inner plane Ascended Masters and Angels to help all lightworkers and people on Earth with immediate help for whatever they need, should they desire assistance. Other examples of Prayer Altars are: Building your Higher Light Body, Extra Protection, Relationship Help, World Service Prayers, Help for your Animals, Prayer Altar for the Children, Integrating the Goddess, Integrating your Archetypes, Integrating the Seven Rays and working with the Seven Inner Plane Ashrams of the Christ, Integrating the Mantle of the Christ, Ascension Seat Integration, and Light, Love, and Power Body Building Program! These Prayer Altar Programs have been co-created with the inner plane Ascended Masters as another tool for not only helping all lightworkers with whatever they need help with, but also as another cutting-edge tool to accelerate Spiritual evolution!

In a similar regard, the Masters have guided us to set up a Melchizedek Synthesis Light Academy Membership Program which is based on three levels of involvement. Stage One, Stage Two, and Stage Three! Stage One and Stage Three are free. Stage Two costs only $20 for a Lifetime Membership with no other fees ever required. You also receive free large colored pictures of Melchizedek, the Mahatma, Archangel Metatron, and Djwhal Khul for joining. It is not necessary to join in order to get involved in the work; however, it has been set up by the inner plane Ascended Masters as another service and tool of the Academy to help lightworkers accelerate their Spiritual evolution! When joining the different Stages, the Masters take you under their wing so to speak, and accelerate your evolution by working with you much more closely on the inner plane while you sleep at night and during your conscious waking hours. The joining is nothing more than a process that gives them the permission to work with you in this more intensive fashion! Again, it is not necessary to join to get involved in the work, and it is really just another one of the many fantastic tools and services the Academy has made available to you to accelerate your Spiritual, psychological, and earthly/physical evolution in an integrated and balanced manner!

I had a dream shortly after just about completing my two new books, *The Golden Book of Melchizedek: How to Become an Integrated Christ/Buddha in this Lifetime* and *How to Release Fear-Based Thinking and Feeling: An In-depth Study of Spiritual Psychology*. In this dream, I was being shown the different Spiritual missions people had. My Spiritual mission was the embodiment of the Holy Spirit. I was clearly shown how other people within GOD, Christ, and the Holy Spirit, had missions of being more detached off-shoots of the Holy Spirit, and continuing outward from there with all kinds of different Spiritual missions; however, mine was the embodiment of the Holy Spirit on Earth.

My beloved readers, I want to be very clear here that in sharing this I am in no way, shape, or form claiming to be the Holy Spirit. There is enough glamour in the New Age Movement and I am not interested in adding any more to it. What I am sharing in this chapter to more clearly and precisely share my Spiritual mission and purpose, is that which I am here to strive to embody and demonstrate. The Holy Spirit is the third aspect of the Trinity of GOD. I have always greatly loved the Holy Spirit, for the Holy Spirit is like the "Voice of GOD"! It is the "Still, Small Voice Within"! When one prays to GOD, it is the Holy Spirit who answers for GOD. The Holy Spirit is the answer to all questions, challenges, and problems. The Holy Spirit speaks for the Atonement or the At-one-ment! It teaches the Sons and Daughters of GOD how to recognize their true identity as God, Christ, the Buddha, and the Eternal Self! In truth, there are only two voices in life! There is the voice of the negative ego and the voice of the Holy Spirit! There is the voice of the negative ego/fear-based/separative thinking and feeling, and there is the voice of God/Spiritual/Christ/Buddha thinking and feeling! There is the "Voice of Love" and the voice of fear! There is the "Voice of Oneness" and the voice of separation!

I was given this dream after completing these two books because, I humbly suggest, this is the energy I was embodying in writing them and that I am striving to embody at all times in my Spiritual mission and purpose on Earth. This is not surprising in the sense that this has always been my Spiritual ideal and the dream was just an inward confirmation in that moment that I was embodying and demonstrating that Spiritual Ideal in the energy flow I was in. This is what I strive to do in all my work, be it my Ascension Book Series, Wesak Celebrations, Teaching, Counseling, Video Tapes, Audio Tapes, and all my work, which is to strive to be the embodiment of a "Voice for God"! By the grace of GOD, Christ, the Holy Spirit, and the Masters, I provide a lot of the "answers" people and lightworkers are seeking! I teach people how to "undo" negative ego/fear-based/separative thinking and feeling and show then how to fully realize God/Christ/Buddha thinking and feeling! I show them how to release and undo glamour, illusion, and maya, and instead seek "Truth," as GOD, Christ, the Holy Spirit, and the Masters would have you seek it!

My real purpose, however, is not to just be the embodiment of the Holy Spirit on Earth, for I would not be embodying the Voice and Vision of the Holy Spirit if I just focused on this. The Voice and Vision of GOD, Christ, the Holy Spirit, and Melchizedek is that of synthesis! This is the other thing I feel in the deepest part of my heart and soul that I am here to embody! So my "truest and highest Spiritual ideal" that I am here to strive to embody is to try to embody GOD, Christ, the Holy Spirit, the inner plane Ascended Masters, he Archangels and Angels of the Light of GOD, the Elohim Councils of the Light of GOD, and the Christed Extraterrestrials of the Light of GOD. I feel in the deepest part of my heart and soul and what I try to embody every moment of my life is "All that is of GOD and the Godforce on Earth"! In this regard, it is my Spiritual mission and purpose to strive to be the embodiment of the "synthesis nature of God on Earth"! This is why I have been given Spiritual leadership of the Synthesis Ashram and Academy on Earth, and future leadership of the inner plane Synthesis Ashram that governs our Planet.

The other thing I strive to do in my Spiritual mission is to embody Spiritual mastery on a Spiritual, psychological, and physical/earthly level. What most people and lightworkers do not realize is that there are three distinct levels to God Realization. There is a Spiritual level, a Psychological level, and a Physical/Earthly level! To achieve true God Realization, all three levels must be equally mastered! Another way of saying this is that there are "Four Faces of GOD"! There is a Spiritual Face, a Mental Face, an Emotional Face, and a Material Face! To truly realize God, all four must be equally mastered, loved, honored, sanctified, integrated, and balanced! The "Mental and Emotional Faces of GOD" make up the psychological level of GOD. So, my Spiritual mission and purpose is to fully embody Spiritual mastery, unconditional love, and wisdom on all three of these levels and in all Four Faces of GOD! In a similar vein, my Spiritual mission and purpose is to embody self-mastery and proper integration of all "Seven Rays of GOD," not just one or a few. For the "Seven Rays of GOD" are, in truth, the true "Personality of GOD"! My Spiritual mission and purpose is to not only strive to embody all levels of GOD, but to also try and develop all my God-given abilities and Spiritual gifts; on a Spiritual, Psychological, and Physical/Earthly level, and in all Four Faces of GOD!

My beloved readers, all these things that I have written about in this chapter are what I strive to fully embody and demonstrate on the Earth every moment of my life, and is what I strive with all my heart and soul and mind and might to teach others to do as well!

As the Founder and Director of the Melchizedek Synthesis Light Academy along with Wistancia, with great humbleness and humility, it has been my great honor and privilege to share "my Spiritual mission and purpose in a deeper and more profound manner at this time." I do so in the hopes that all who feel a resonance and attunement with this work, and will get involved with the "Academy's Teachings" and all that it has to offer. I also share this so that all who choose to get involved might join this vast group of lightworkers around the globe, to help spread the teachings and work of the inner plane Ascended Master. The inner plane Ascended Masters and I, along with the Archangels and Angels, Elohim Councils and Christed Extraterrestrials, put forth the Clarion Call to lightworkers around the world to explore this work, integrate this work, and become Ambassadors of the Ascended Masters, so that we may at this time in Beloved Earth's history bring in fully now the Seventh Golden Age in all its Glory!

About the Author

Dr. Joshua David Stone has a Ph.D. in Transpersonal Psychology and is a Licensed Marriage, Family, and Child Counselor, in Agoura Hills, California. On a Spiritual level he anchors **The Melchizedek Synthesis Light Academy and Ashram**, which is an integrated inner and outer plane ashram that seeks to represent all paths to God! He serves as one of the leading spokespersons for the Planetary Ascension Movement. Through his books, tapes, workshops, lectures, and annual Wesak Celebrations, Dr. Stone is known as one of the leading Spiritual Teachers and Channels in the world on the teachings of the Ascended Masters, Spiritual Psychology, and Ascension! He has currently written over 27 volumes in his "Ascension Book Series," which he also likes to call "The Easy-to-Read Encyclopedia of the Spiritual Path!"

For a free information packet of all Dr. Stone's workshops, books, audiotapes, Academy membership program, and global outreach program, please call or write to the following address:

Dr. Joshua David Stone
Melchizedek Synthesis Light Academy
28951 Malibu Rancho Rd
Agoura Hills, CA 91301

Phone: 818-706-8458
Fax: 818-706-8540
e-mail: drstone@best.com

Please come visit my Website at:
http://www.drjoshuadavidstone.com

Printed in the United States
101188LV00001B/96/A